ULTIMATE CARS

ULTIMATE CARS

Published in 2010 by
World Publications Group, Inc.
140 Laurel Street,
East Bridgewater, MA 02333
www.wrldpub.com

10 9 8 7 6 5 4 3 2 1
ISBN 978-1-57215-663-0

Authors: Tim Slade, Adam Phillips, Mark Holmes, Ivan Berg

Pictures contributed by ActionLibrary.com, LAT Photo, National Motor Museum/MPL, SeriousWheels.com, Tim Slade, EVO magazine, Ford Motor Company Ltd, Bugatti Automobiles S.A.S, Aston Martin, Koenigsegg Automotive AB, Mitsubishi Motors Ltd, Ariel Motor Company Ltd, DaimlerChrysler, Ford, General Motors, Motoring Picture Library

Printed in Malaysia

CLASSIC CARS

Contents

SUPERCARS

MUSCLE CARS

Ultimate Cars offers a selection of what are undoubtedly the most desirable cars of the past five decades, by exploring three distinctive categories: Classic Cars, Supercars and Muscle Cars. Examining the history and thought that goes into each unique design, this book tackles the ultimate question; just what is it that draws us to them?

CLASSIC CARS

What is it that attracts people to classic cars? Why bother spending so much time and money on old motor cars when you could have a perfectly good modern one, and enjoy clean fingernails and a healthy bank balance? Perhaps we need to start with the question - what exactly is a classic car? The obvious answer that most of us would come up with, is that a classic car is an old car. In fact the word 'classic' seems to have been commandeered just lately and redefined as an alternative for old. Of course the term 'classic' means far more than simply aged. It implies that something is, 'of the first rank or authority'. Plainly there is more to this classic car thing than simply age. Does dodging the crusher for a few years really turn any car into a classic? Well, it's going to upset a few old car owners, but there is a bit more to it than that.

The cars that we've chosen for this book are pretty much all models that you are going to find it tough to argue against. It was no easy task to whittle down the tens of thousands of models built since Karl Benz took his three-wheeler onto the streets of Mannheim in 1885. There are many different ways to earn the moniker 'classic', and for every car here, there is a different combination of all these reasons.

Breaking new ground is perhaps the most sure-fire way to earn your 'classic' status. The Mini, the Model T, the Beetle, the Citroen DS and even the Reliant Scimitar GTE can claim their place on this count. Providing reliable and much loved transport for vast

numbers of people is another reason, claimed by the Model T and the Ford Cortina among other contenders.

Then there is the little matter of desire. There are cars that inspire the sin of covetousness in just about anyone who lays eyes on them. How do you avoid wanting a Mercedes 300SL or an Aston Martin DB4? Although, perhaps it was the designers of the '30s who best knew how to tap into those parts of our brain that make us want and desire; The Duesenberg S and Mercedes 'K' cars appear to have been styled with little other than automotive lust in mind. The Mercedes 540K Special Roadster did such a good job that even so many decades later it still has much to do with our perception of the Mercedes brand.

So what are the other factors that fail to convey classic status? Performance alone is not enough, and there have been some ugly Ferraris and Lamborghinis that are beaten to the classic finishing line by the humble Fiat 500. Huge production figures won't necessarily get you there either. Many cars sold well but failed entirely to generate affection in their owners. Generally these models have simply vanished, as no one felt motivated to make the effort necessary to keep them going. When did you last see an Austin Maxi or a Hillman Avenger? Even expensive cars went this way. What ever happened to all the Jaguar Mk Xs and Humber Super Snipes?

With cars having been around since 1885 it makes for an intriguing question to ask when the concept of the classic car might have first appeared delivered. And yet, at a time when the excitement and romance of the motor car was all about the new, there is evidence that some motorists were already becoming attached to the old.

In October 1910 an article appeared in the British magazine The Motor, concerning a journey made in the car belonging to a friend of the author. The author claimed to have owned five different motor cars by this date, but his friend stuck with his first; a Benz from 1901. Even in 1910 this vehicle was considered an archaic contraption, and yet its owner professed many excellent reasons for preferring it to a more modern motor car. The solid tyres almost never wore out and, of course, there were no punctures to deal with. Another is that it travelled for 24 hilly miles on five pints of petrol – that's 38.4 miles to the gallon!

We have to wait until a few years later for the formalisation of the 'things ain't what they used to be' ethos. It can be claimed with some authority that this came about in 1934, with the formation of the Vintage Sports Car Club, or VSCC. A group of enthusiasts met in a pub called the Phoenix at Hartley Wintney, a village about thirty miles west of London. They were there to discuss a proposition, in a now long-defunct magazine called The Light Car, that a club should be formed for the 'not so rich'. They were concerned that the heyday of historic motoring was coming to an end, and they felt that mass production was leading to quantity being considered more important than quality – arguments that are hard to quarrel with. And so they formed a club to encourage the use of cars built before 31 December 1930. Things were not all bad, and an approved list of modern cars was drawn up. The VSCC now welcomes cars from this list that were built up until 1941, as well as anything made before 1931.

The VSCC has endured and prospered, promoting racing and events for its members' cars, members will even get their cars out for the New Year's Day lunchtime gathering at the Phoenix, where you will see vintage Lagondas and Bentleys, whatever the weather and however much salt there is on the roads.

Speaking of 'vintage', it might be best to clarify the meaning of the word. All vintage cars are welcome to the VSCC fold; ie those made before 31 December 1930. Many people believe

The Humber Super Snipe may be an old car, but is it a classic car?

any car made before the Second World War to be vintage; in fact the correct, though rather pedantic term, for cars made between 1931 and the war is, 'post vintage thoroughbred', or PVT. Quite where this leaves the less than thoroughbred is difficult to say.

The very earliest motor cars are referred to as 'veteran'. All cars built before December 1904 are veterans. These are the cars that are eligible for the UK's famous London to Brighton run. Cars built between 1905 and 1918 are properly called 'Edwardians'.

There are many reasons to endure the rigours that are an unavoidable part of classic car ownership. The essential one is using the car. You could say that if a car isn't driven then it becomes something else – a work of art, a museum piece, a curio, a piece of junk, a waste of space or, perhaps, just forgotten. The essence of any motor car is in the driving – luckily this is a major motivation for most owners. A trip to the supermarket becomes a special event, and a sunny day is enough to provide an excuse for a drive. In London, for example, despite the traffic and terrible driving, it won't take long on a summer weekend before you see something special. It might be a Ferrari or a Morris 1000, but the enjoyment of using a classic is the same.

If you use your old car then it's very probable that you will want to use it for old-car events. If you are lucky enough to have a veteran, then the one event that can't be missed is the London to Brighton run. It is so popular that it can mean that a car made in 1904 will be worth many times the value of a similar 1905 car.

Held early in November every year often in typically miserable English autumnal weather, with breaks only for the two world wars, there is always a good selection of registration plates from as far afield as the US and Australia. Around five hundred cars take part. Some get little further than the gates of Hyde Park, London, where the run begins, but most make it to the seafront of Brighton. The event was first held in 1896 to celebrate that it had at last become legal for motor cars to be run upon English roads. The uniform 12mph speed limit, which seems very low, would not have been a major inconvenience at the time.

The oldest competitive event, the Brighton Speed Trials, is held along the same stretch of road as the veteran's destination: Madeira Drive on Brighton seafront. It was first held in 1905, though due to disputes over the cost of resurfacing with the 'modern' tarmac it didn't happen again until 1923. Since 1932, it has only taken a break for the Second World War, and is still held every September. It is a fabulous place to see classics of all eras, on both two and four wheels, being given a real pasting. It seems strange that anyone would want to risk their valuable, often tempremental and, quite possibly, irreplaceable classic by belting it around a race track.

And yet all over the world there is historic racing taking place just about every summer weekend. In the US there are the legendary Monterey Historic Automobile Races at the Laguna Seca circuit in California. These events have grown in stature every year since the races were first held in 1974 – it is unlikely that better classic racing will be seen anywhere in the US. Part of the same weekend is the Pebble Beach concours, where the finest and most fabulous classic cars compete for the honour of being the best and most beautiful in the world.

In the UK, it is the two events held at Goodwood that have captured everyone's imagination. A hill climb, or indeed a sprint, is an event where each car runs individually against the clock. First held in 1993, it instantly became a 'classic' in the old-car calendar. The combination of the country house location and the best competition cars from around the world being put through their paces is unmissable.

Later in the summer the Goodwood Revival meeting takes place, held at the historic Goodwood circuit nearby. The first event was only held in 1998, and yet it has come to be generally regarded as the finest historic automotive event in the world. Racing is for pre-1966 cars – the year that contemporary racing stopped at Goodwood. The attention to the pre-'66 detail is terrific, and it has become the biggest fancy dress party in the world, as most race-goers arrive in period costume. Many also arrive with period transport – the special pre-'66 visitors' car park is one of the largest classic car meetings all on its own.

There are shows and gatherings for classics all over the world and to suit all tastes. Everything from one-marque meetings to enormous shows where 1,000 cars might turn up, to a few old cars brought together for the village fête.

One feature connects all these events: whether you drive a Rolls Royce or an Aston Martin, a Beetle or a Cortina, the enthusiasm is the same. It's the love for old cars that's important, and not the cost of your ride. The classic car world is anything but exclusive. At any event you go to you're going to find a bunch of friendly people who, given half a chance, will chat to you for the whole afternoon. Whether you own a classic car, or simply enjoy them, membership of one of the biggest, friendliest clubs in the world comes as part of the deal.

BUGATTI

FORD GT

SUPERCARS

What makes someone want to buy a car that costs a small fortune? Or a very large one for that matter? Surely a nice little Japanese hatchback with a 1.4-litre engine will do the job. After all, you don't need 1,000bhp to pop down to the local shopping centre or to pick up the kids from school. But that's missing the point – us humans have a passion for pushing forward; for wanting to out do and challenge ourselves, and supercars are one of the ultimate expressions of this desire. And people will always want to buy into that.

And there has never been a better time than now for supercar aficionados to indulge in their passion for automobile excellence. However, it has taken over 50 years of cumulative development and hard work by the world's greatest designers and engineers to bring us up to the modern day.

Naturally, there are those that merely want a supercar as a trophy; to be driven once in awhile to impress their peers and to show the world that their bank balance is in fighting form. Equally, there are those who understand that only the best will do; who want to experience the sensation and thrill of cars designed for pure driver indulgence. And if we can't afford them, then we want to respect and admire the creativity and engineering that has made the supercar what it is today.

After all, the early days of supercar development were heady ones – bold but small steps into the future where one supercar would offer the greatest performance while the other would deliver the best driving experience. And now the fruits of all that blood, sweat and tears over the past five decades since the supercar's birth in the 1950s, are seemingly reaching their peak.

The supercars of the last 50 years show a culmination of what the best minds in the supercar business have to offer. From Britain and Italy through to America and Japan, the combined genius of designers and engineers has seen the supercars of today blend so many elements perfectly. From GTs through to roadsters, they all offer the true car-lover a wealth of treasures to indulge themselves in; looks that are intoxicating; performance that is G-force defying; and a driving experience that is truly unforgettable. Welcome to the state-of-the-supercar-art.

And they have to – we're a demanding bunch after all. We want those looks – the ones that linger in the mind well after glimpsing that exotic machinery for the first time. We want to know about the performance – the kind that defies belief when first scanning down a supercar's specifications. And we want the handling – the kind that offers huge grip, accessibility and feedback. Yes, we're a greedy bunch.

Modern supercars offer the best of all worlds (well, apart from the miles-per-gallon and luggage space that is) – and this book is a tribute to them. From supercars on a budget to exotica that can cost you a cool million, the automotive art featured in these pages show that we're all still as passionate about progress, and going fast, as we ever were.

It seems like we've hit perfection with the supercar. So where do you go from here? How do you top what seems insurmountable? Well, judging from the various developments and news (and a fair smattering of rumours too), the best is inevitability still to come. The supercar community's desire to outdo each other and seduce buyers will see the arrival of more potential supercar classics over the next few years.

For example, McLaren is all set to re-enter the scene aproper in 2008 with its supercar codenamed the P8. Featuring a Mercedes-sourced 6.3-litre V8, the P8 should be able to produce above 500bhp and over 440lb ft of torque, all for the estimated price of £150,000/US$200,000.

K8 MCL

PORSCHE

Then there are the left-of-the-middle entries such as Project 1221's MF1. Details are scant about this emerging supercar but the makers claim it will have unmatched handling and agility plus a large luggage capacity. Yes, you may have heard such hyperbole a dozen times before but the MF1 could actually deliver. After all, it's being engineered by the former technical director of Lamborghini and Bugatti, Mauro Forghieri.

As for the far future, there's that 300mph barrier to break, and it has been predicted that supercars will produce in excess of 2,000bhp, weigh 25 percent less than current crop and could even hit 350mph. Sounds like the ramblings of the mad but there is a supercar that's set to touch down later this year

which could potentially leave the outrageous performance of current supercars for dead, and offer an enticing and very real glimpse of what the future of the supercar has in store for us... enter the Bugatti Veyron.

Save winning the lottery, it's inevitable that the intoxicating delights of owning a Lamborghini or a Pagani are well out of the reach of most us; for now, at least. But there's no reason to despair (or seriously consider a career in armed robbery) because there are cars out there that can offer similar thrills to the supercar, but for a fraction of the price.

At the end of this section we feature four candidates for your deliberation here cover a lot of the 'supercar bases' such as great (or outlandish) looks, thrilling performances and handling that delights at every corner. And if none of these suit your budget, take solace in the fact that a quick flick through those local classifieds for secondhand cars will reveal some real driving gems. Think Mazda RX-7 or Subaru Impreza Turbo to name but two of the classics available that guarantee maximum fun for minimal money. After all, there's something for everybody to live out those driving dreams. We'll see you on the road...

S LR 2020

MUSCLE CARS

It's the sheer simplicty of the Muscle Car that makes it so universally appealing. The recipe is just so straightforward. Take a compact automobile and install an incredibly-powerful engine (preferably a V8) to deliver a tire-frying performance. No auto enthusiast can argue with that one. It's a formula for success that has been tried and tested for 50 years and has created some of the most exciting cars in history. Just mentioning the names Mustang, Charger, GTO, Corvette or Viper sends a shiver down the spine.

The Muscle Car story began in America's post-war boom of the 1950s as inter-brand rivalry in Detroit saw horsepower figures steadily rising through the decade. But these big engines were being fitted to big cars and they didn't have mass-market appeal.

That would all change in 1964 when Pontiac installed a full-size engine into a mid-size car and created the awesome GTO, the first true Muscle Car. And the rest of Detroit followed. Fast. The Ford Mustang, Plymouth Road Runner, Dodge Charger, Plymouth Barracuda and Chevrolet Camaro all appeared before the eager public could pause for breath. Horsepower went through the roof as the cars competed on the streets and on the track. Ford managed to wring 675bhp out of its Cammer V8, the highest power of any Detroit engine ever. Hertz bought up a whole series of Shelby GT350 Mustangs to rent out to weekend racers and Plymouth's Road Runner Superbird and its Dodge Daytona rival brought NASCAR to the streets. It was Muscle Car mania.

But dark clouds were looming. Tough emissions rules and the oil crisis forced automobile manufacturers to rethink. Power outputs fell through the floor during the 1970s and there were plenty of casualties. The Dodge Charger and Challenger, Plymouth Road Runner and Pontiac GTO all fell victim to the legislation and it looked like the Muscle Car was dead.

Only Pontiac's Firebird Trans Am, Chevrolet's Camaro and Corvette and Ford's Mustang kept the spirit alive. But the truth was that for many years these cars were anything but muscular, offering a lot more show than go.

It was only towards the very end of the 1980s that things were looking up. The survivors were beginning to pack more punch and at least one company was reminiscing about the good old days.

That company was Chrysler. In a bid to re-establish its Dodge and Plymouth brands the designers and engineers had been studying their

history. In 1989 the Detroit Auto Show ground to a halt as the wraps came off the Dodge Viper concept car. The Viper was never imagined to have had the life-span that it has been able to achieve. Chrysler were in need of a flash muscle car that could turn heads and revitalize the Chrysler name. With its epic V10 engine and muscular lines, the Viper accomplished this and much more and became the muscle car that fans had been dreaming about for two decades.

Dodge put the Viper into production and it was a phenomenal hit. Come 1997 the company was ready to do it again, this time with the Plymouth Prowler – a hot rod for the 21st Century. The Prowler was in the style of the 1930s, but redone in the mode of the '50s, and looked like no other modern car on the road. Motorcycle-type front fenders, for instance, moved along with the front wheels. Performance and style were hot again.

Today Muscle Cars are back with a vengeance and legendary names are reappearing in dealerships, drag strips and ovals. The 2005 C6 Corvette cut a tighter, more taut profile – with virtually no loss of usable space. Building on the foundation of the C5, it had increased performance and refinement all wrapped up in a new design, packing 500bhp in SO6 trim. Chrysler has brought back the 300 and the Dodge Charger. Ford has revived the Mustang Shelby GT500. It's like the glory days of the 1960s all over again.

The Muscle Cars of the new millennium are faster than ever before and not just able to rip up the quarter-mile, but relish twisty roads too with advanced suspension and the latest electronic driver aids. If that sounds too complicated for die hard Muscle Car fans don't worry, because none of the newcomers has forgotten that basic principle. Horsepower is still the number one priority as the Muscle Car legend lives on.

CLASSIC CARS

Like a phoenix from the flames, the Curved Dash Olds became the first mass-produced car

Ransom Eli Olds had been building experimental motor cars since 1887. By the 1890s, Olds had moved on to making gasoline-powered engines for use in factories and boats. It was in 1897 that he got serious about building motor cars, establishing the Olds Motor Vehicle Company. Then, in 1899, he moved the firm to the town that was to become known as 'Motor City' – Detroit. Now called the Olds Motor Works, it was here that several prototype cars were constructed.

Curved Dash Oldsmobile

Unfortunately, a catastrophic fire in March 1901 destroyed all but one of Old's creations. Heroically pulled from the flames, this one car was all that Olds had left to work with. He claimed that even the blueprints had been lost and that new ones had to be drawn up from the single survivor. Fortune appeared to have played a part, because this was to become the Curved Dash Oldsmobile – and a runaway success. The role of the fire took on almost mythical status, although it must be added that a reliable source stated that the blueprints did survive, and that there were 334 advance orders for the car before the fire, so production was already assured. Olds was plainly an excellent public relations man!

With its premises in ruins, it was essential to get the car into production quickly to keep the company afloat. Olds made the clever decision to contract out the manufacture of his car's component parts: engines, transmissions and the skimpy little bodies were all made by other companies, and then assembled by Olds. He can be credited with single-handedly inventing the production line, with the cars rolled along while different groups of workers assembled the various parts of the vehicle, although Henry Ford would later take the idea much further.

The car was simple and fairly typical of American cars of the time. It had a wooden frame with long leaf springs running the length of it and providing front and rear suspension. High ground clearance meant it could cope with the rough roads of the time. The engine was a single cylinder 1,565cc unit utilising a two-speed epicyclic to achieve a heady 500rpm at its top speed of 20mph, and was said to provide, in the parlance of the time, 'one chug per telegraph pole'.

By the time production ceased in 1905, nearly 19,000 had been built. This made Oldsmobile the largest motor manufacturer in the world from 1903 to 1905. Many survive, and around 30 regularly take part in the London to Brighton run.

Specifications

Production dates	1901-1905
Manufactured units	18,525
Engine type	Single-cylinder, rear mounted
Engine size	1,565cc
Maximum power	5bhp
Transmission	2-speed epicyclic
Top speed	20mph
0-60 mph time	N/A
Country of origin	USA

128
KM

15 million Tin Lizzies put America and the world on wheels

In 1904, Henry Ford became the fastest man on earth when he drove his crude 'Arrow' across the frozen Lake St Clair at 91.37mph. It provided invaluable publicity for his first production car, the 'A', which debuted soon after, although the experience was so terrifying that it robbed Ford of any further interest in speed. By 1908, Ford was running through the letters of alphabet in naming his cars, and got as far as the Model T – arguably the most important car in history.

Model T Ford

In 1902, Ford stated his intention to 'build a car for the great multitudes'. By 1906, he was already America's largest manufacturer, but the T was to revolutionize the industry.

The four-cylinder 2,884cc engine had a detachable cylinder head, which was a new idea, but otherwise the T was fairly typical of its day, with high ground clearance and a two-speed gearbox.

Introduced in October 1908, it carried the rather hefty price tag of $850. Henry was under pressure to bring the price down, but refused to compromise on quality, so another way to reduce costs had to be found – and the answer came in the form of the world's first moving production line. Assembly time fell from 12 hours and 28 minutes to a remarkable 1 hour and 33 minutes. As production soared, the price dropped to an all-time low in 1925 – an extraordinarily cheap $290.

Ford paid his workers well and they worked hard as a result. Production numbers were phenomenal, rising to nearly two million cars per year. The 'Tin Lizzie' lasted all the way through to 1927, by which time it had sold 15,007,033 units. It took until the 1970s for this number to be exceeded by the VW Beetle.

The Model T changed remarkably little during its 19-year run, although the brass radiator went in 1917 and its styling was modernized. The cars were lowered in 1923, no doubt as roads improved, and then again in 1926. This was the year that also saw the introduction of a choice of colours aside from the original black.

Model Ts were designed in a range of styles – from touring, runabout and coupé to two- and four-door sedans, not to mention delivery and commercial vehicles. Racing on banked board tracks was popular across the US in the 1920s, and cut-down Model Ts were a popular racer.

As the car of choice for everyone from the man on the street to Laurel and Hardy on the silver screen, The Tin Lizzie integrated itself into the American psyche like no other automobile.

Specifications

Production dates	1908-1927
Manufactured units	15,007,033
Engine type	4-cylinder side-valve front-mounted
Engine size	2884cc
Maximum power	20bhp at 1,800rpm
Transmission	2-speed epicyclic
Top speed	42mph
0-60 mph time	N/A
Country of origin	USA

'Available in any shade – as long as it's black. Henry Ford found that black paint dried faster, speeding up production'

VA.

Austin Seven

Generations of British motorists learned to drive in the charming little Seven

Although primarily an engineer, Herbert Austin was no less an entrepreneur. By 1906, he had formed the Austin Motor Company, and by 1917 his famous factory at Longbridge was Britain's biggest motor works, due in part to large-scale war contracts. Austin was knighted for his services to the nation and became a Lord in 1936.

Impressed by Henry Ford's methods with the Model T, Austin implemented a single-model policy and a production line. Unfortunately, the large 20hp model was not a success, and Austin escaped bankruptcy and a merger with General Motors by the skin of his teeth.

Deciding that cheaper cars were a safer bet, Austin introduced the Twelve in 1921, following it up in 1922 with the diminutive Seven.

The Seven was a simple little motor car. A small 747cc four-cylinder side-valve engine produced a modest 10bhp. This was set in a rather spindly A-shaped chassis. Its flexibility, combined with soft leaf springs front and rear, gave the Seven 'interesting' handling. It had four wheel brakes, but they were tiny and operated by stretchy cables. A top speed of only 42mph saved many an inexperienced driver from a grisly end. Untold numbers of Brits learned to drive in the Seven, and this, combined with its enormous charm, gives it a unique place in British motoring history.

The Seven appeared in numerous forms, including open tourers, two-seat convertibles, saloons and vans, with names like Chummy, Ruby and Pearl. There were also sporting models, the Ulster being the most sought after. Sevens were the first cars bodied by Swallow Sidecars, which became SS, in turn becoming Jaguar. A whole cottage industry emerged, transforming Sevens into little competition cars, and there are innumerable Sevens still racing. The factory even built a twin-cam supercharged racing car that circulated the Brooklands track at amazing speeds in the 1930s.

The Seven went international, being built under licence in France, Germany and the US. In Germany, it became the first ever BMW car, the Dixi. In the US it was built by American Austin, but Americans were suspicious of such a tiny car and bankruptcy became inevitable. A little later, the Seven re-emerged as the American Bantam, but even then it didn't sell well.

By the time it bowed out in 1939, over 375,000 Sevens had been built. The later models were more modern in their manners than the earlier ones, but any Seven remains a great car for spanner-happy enthusiasts who aren't in a hurry.

Specifications

Production dates	1922-1939
Manufactured units	375,000+
Engine type	4-cylinder side-valve front-mounted
Engine size	747cc
Maximum power	10-14bhp (more for racing versions)
Transmission	early cars 3-speed; later cars 4-speed
Top speed	42mph
0-60 mph time	N/A
Country of origin	UK

XO 6852

'Swallow Sidecars built bodies for Austin Sevens that most definitely had ideas above their station. Swallow sidecars became SS, and of course after WW2 they hanged their name to Jaguar'

Famous victories at Le Mans for the Bentley Boys made the 3.0 ltr a legend

Bentley 3.0 ltr

Ettore Bugatti, who created the Bugatti car, famously remarked that Bentleys were 'the world's fastest lorries'. He had a point. Walter Owen Bentley had trained as a locomotive engineer and a certain weight and solidity were common to all his designs.

During the Great War, he designed two rotary aero engines for the Admiralty, and by 1919 he had the prototype of his 3.0-litre car displayed at the Olympia show in London, not that far from his Cricklewood factory. It took another two years, however, before he could offer it for sale.

The Bentley was fairly conventional, even if its four-cylinder engine did have the modern configuration of four valves per cylinder operated by an overhead camshaft. This was mounted in a massively constructed chassis, and all of WO's four- and six-cylinder cars shared these features.

Sales were slow and racing success was needed to promote the car. An entry into the inaugural Le Mans 24 Hour in 1923 netted fourth place. Drivers Duff and Clement returned in 1924 with the new Speed Model, and they won.

Both 1925 and 1926 brought only retirements and so WO decided to develop a more powerful car – the 4.5-litre. Always strapped for cash, WO persuaded diamond millionaire and racing driver Woolf Barnato to take the chair of the company and finance the new model. Barnato was one of the 'Bentley Boys', extremely wealthy young men who raced Bentleys, the most famous of their set being 'Tim' Birkin.

1927 is perhaps the most famous of all Le Mans 24 hours, and it was the 3.0-litre's finest hour. Three 3.0-litres and one 4.5-litre car were entered, and were likely favourites. The big car took the lead, but three of the Bentleys became involved in a terrible six-car pile up at White Horse corner. Miraculously, nobody was killed, and Sammy Davis managed to limp his 3.0-litre back to the pits. It was very badly damaged, but after half an hour of repairs the mangled car was back on the track. Davis and his co-driver Benjafield took a victory worthy of the pages of 'Boys Own' magazine.

There were further victories in the French race in 1928, 1929 and 1930, but they couldn't save Bentley from bankruptcy, and in 1931 the company was bought by Rolls Royce.

The 'Cricklewood' Bentleys remain the most archetypal of vintage cars, and more British than fish and chips or Buckingham Palace.

Specifications

Production dates	1921-1927
Manufactured units	1,633
Engine type	4-cylinder 16-valve front-mounted
Engine size	2,996cc
Maximum power	80-90 bhp
Transmission	4-speed
Top speed	80mph
0-60 mph time	N/A
Country of origin	UK

KU 5702

3

'At the 1927 Le Mans 24 hour race there was a terrible pile up at White House corner. The Bentley of Davis and Benjafield was involved, but somehow it limped back to the pits. Although it took half an hour tostraighten out, it went on to score an heroic victory'

The exquisite little blue cars from Molsheim won literally hundreds of races, including the first Monaco Grand Prix

Bugatti Type 35/35B

Ettore Bugatti was an Italian who built the most celebrated cars ever to wear French racing blue. He was perhaps an artist first and an engineer second. Together with his son Jean, he produced what were quite simply some of the most fabulous automobiles ever made.

Ettore set up in the town of Molsheim in Alsace and began trading on 1st January, 1910. The town had been German, but after a war spent designing aero engines in Paris, Ettore returned to a French town. His successful Brescia model, based on the pre-war Type 13, became a respected racing car, with many victories to its name.

In 1922, Ettore designed the engine for the Type 30 – a 2.0-litre straight eight with one exhaust and two inlet valves per cylinder, driven by an overhead camshaft. In 1924, a development of this engine was used to power the new Type 35 competition car. It was a Grand Prix car, but had two seats so that it was capable of carrying a riding mechanic.

Every detail was meticulously conceived, designed and manufactured. The aim was to save weight, but the result was an exquisite automobile. At a time when many cars ran on wooden wheels and sports cars all had wire wheels, Ettore created beautiful eight-spoke cast aluminium wheels, with integral brake drums. The engine was also a work of art, with a simple unadorned design.

The Type 35 was a huge success, and as it developed it became faster and faster. The Type 35B was the ultimate version, with a 2.3-litre engine fed by a supercharger. In 1926 it was capable of reaching 125mph, and in that year it won the World Championship. By the end of the 1920s Bugattis had won more races – including the first Monaco Grand Prix – than any other manufacturer, and Type 35Bs were credited with winning an average of 14 races per week! The Type 35 was developed into the 51, with twin overhead cams and yet more power, but by that time German teams ruled the Grand Prix roost.

Today, the Type 35B is one of the world's most valuable cars – and if you've seen one racing, you'll know why. The music of the unsilenced straight eight, overlaid with the high-pitched scream of the supercharger, is never forgotten. In its day, it was described as 'tearing calico'. In reality, it's the sound of mechanical genius.

Specifications

Production dates	1926-1928
Manufactured units	45
Engine type	Straight 8 supercharged
Engine size	2,262cc
Maximum power	138bhp
Transmission	4-speed
Top speed	125mph
0-60 mph time	N/A
Country of origin	France

'The Type 35 and 35B Bugattis were phenomenally successful competition cars. In the late 1920s it was said that they averaged 14 race wins per week!'

BUGATTI

Duesenberg Model J/SJ

For Clarke Gable and Gary Cooper, only a Duesenberg would do

Fred and August Duesenberg were German born, but came to America in the 1880s. In 1913, they began manufacturing engines at the Duesenberg Motor Company, and in 1917 the first car bearing their names was released. Despite undertaking aero engine contracts during the Great War, the brothers' passion was for racing, and after the war they moved their business to Indianapolis. In 1920, one of their cars reached 156mph – a new world record that was never officially recognised.

Fred and Augie's first road car was the Model A of 1920. It was expensive, but this was America's first straight eight, and the first with hydraulic brakes. Another first occured in 1921, when a Model A won the French Grand Prix – the first victory for an American car in Europe.

Unfortunately, the brothers went bust, and in 1926 the company was bought by entrepreneur Errett Cord, who owned Auburn. He announced his intention to build the world's most expensive car, releasing the Model J in December 1928.

The engine was a 7.0-litre straight eight with four valves per cylinder and twin overhead camshafts. The chassis came in two lengths, and this alone cost $8,500. Once bodied, the whole thing would have cost around $17,000 – four times the price of the most expensive Cadillac!

Bodies were designed and built by the best coach builders, but Cord wanted a stronger, more individual identity, and so employed the gifted designer Gordon Buehrig, just 25 at the time. His fabulous designs were executed by coachbuilders such as Derham, Murphy, Brewster and Le Baron, and the results were some of the most opulent and extravagant automobiles ever seen.

This was not a great time to be selling expensive automobiles, as the Wall Street crash left few people able to afford them, but in 1932 the SJ was released. Built on a new shorter chassis, it had a supercharged engine reputed to make 320bhp, capable of pushing it up to 140mph. Only 36 people were rich enough to buy one. There was also a 400bph SSJ, bought only by movie stars.

The company staggered on, but in 1937 Cord was investigated by the Securities and Exchange Commission. He was put out of business, and the Duesenberg factory was eventually sold on to a truck company.

Duesenbergs are the most treasured of all American cars, and on the rare occasions they change hands, it's usually behind closed doors for undisclosed – and unbelievable – sums of money.

Specifications

Production dates	1928-1935
Manufactured units	470
Engine type	Straight 8 twin cam DOHC; SJ/SSJ supercharged
Engine size	6,882cc
Maximum power	J 265bhp; SJ 320bhp; SSJ 400bhp
Transmission	4-speed
Top speed	J 115mph; SJ 140mph
0-60 mph time	J 8.6 seconds
Country of origin	USA

'The Model J Duesenbergs were the most fabulous American cars ever made - and so they should have been, as they were the highest priced cars in the world'

'32 Ford

With his first V8 Henry Ford really did bring power to the people

After 15,000,000 Tin Lizzies came the Model A. Within 18 months of its 1928 launch, there were 2,000,000 of them on America's roads. It had a four cylinder engine, and although a little dearer, Chevrolet could give you six. Then came the Depression, during which sales fell so low that, in July 1931, Ford had to lay off 75,000 of his workers. Ford knew that something radical was needed to win back sales.

Since 1930, his best engineers had been working on a low cost V8 engine that was to be the Ford secret sales weapon. Cadillac had built a V8 as early as 1914, and other makes were also V8 powered. These engines were expensive to manufacture, being made up of several separate castings. Ford's plan was to cast it in one, with the crankshaft also a single casting. The technology didn't come cheap, and rebuilding the forge at the Rouge River plant cost $55,000,000. However, when production got underway, his factory was able to turn out 3,000 engines every day.

Released on April 2nd 1932, there were 14 V8 models to choose from. The styling was sleek, modern and very attractive. Priced from $460 to $650, with an 80mph top speed they were faster than most sports cars. Ford won back sales from the competition, but the Depression meant that only 232,125 cars were built in 1932.

With some developments, the 'flat head' V8 engine powered Fords up until the war, as well as Bren gun carriers, armoured cars and boats during the war, and French and British Fords well into the 1950s.

The 3,621cc side valve engine had huge tuning potential, and it was the 1932, or 'Deuce', which got hot rodding going all on its own. A few stripped-out, hopped-up '32s would make their way to the dry lake beds in California for illegal races. When GIs returned after WW2, the Deuce was a cheap way to go fast, and the whole hot rod and drag racing scene took off. Tuning the flat head and V8s that followed grew into a massive industry of its own.

Immortalised by the Beach Boys in 'Little Deuce Coupé', and by George Lucas as John Milner's car in 'American Graffiti', even now the '32 remains the world's favourite hot rod.

Specifications

Production dates	1932
Manufactured units	232,125
Engine type	side valve V8
Engine size	3,621cc
Maximum power	65bhp
Transmission	3-speed synchromesh
Top speed	80mph
0-50 mph time	12 seconds
Country of origin	USA

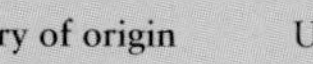

Radial T/A

Charismatic or caricature; the K cars were the ultimate embodiment of 1930s style

The Mercedes marque had become associated with supercharging in the late 1920s with the mighty SS and SSK sports cars. These were stripped down racers where form obeyed function – something that could never be said of the K cars.

On paper, their specification followed that of the Mercedes Grand Prix cars – straight eight supercharged engines and all independent suspension – but that's where the similarity ended.

Mercedes 500K/540K

The first of the line was the 380 in 1933. Although it was blown like its big brothers, it was felt to be underpowered. In 1934 came the 500K, and a legend that lives to this day was born.

The 500K was built to be magnificent. Its 5.0-litre engine was moved 7in back in the chassis to allow the radiator grill to be set right back behind the axle line. The bonnet was impossibly long, though this was partially excused by the length of that engine. There were many body styles, designed and built in-house at Sindlefingen, and all were breathtaking. Performance was good, but not quite up to expectations.

In 1936 came the 540K with 180bhp. This was produced only when the supercharger was engaged, which could be done only in short bursts. It was renowned for making a fearsome scream, although there are those who say that this had more to do with the perception of increased performance than any extra horse power involved. With that blower going, fuel consumption dropped to 8mpg!

Unusually for exclusive cars of the time, nearly all of the K cars were bodied at the factory. The four-seater cabriolet B and the two-seater cabriolet A are highly prized, but the Special Roadster is the supreme embodiment. It has more curves and chrome than almost any car in history; the epitome of 'erotic' aesthetics in car design.

The cars were bought by the world's richest men – an Indian Maharajah even used his to hunt tigers. Unfortunately, we can't pretend that the charisma of these cars did not appeal to the Nazi high command. There was even an order for 20 armoured versions of the 540K for the more jittery Third Reich officers.

The styling of the K cars may be overblown and even verge on caricature, but the Special Roadster is one of the most recognised cars ever. Seven decades later, its image is still selling Mercedes.

Specifications

Production dates	500K 1934-1936 540K 1936-1939
Manufactured units	500K 354; 540K 406
Engine type	straight eight OHV supercharged
Engine size	500K 5,018cc; 540K 54,01cc
Maximum power	(with supercharger) 500K 160bhp; 540K 180bhp
Transmission	3 speed + overdrive / 4 speed / 4 speed +
Top speed	105mph
0-50 mph time	16 seconds
Country of origin	Germany

'Even when clothed in coachwork that was relatively restrained, and wearing sombre black paintwork, the 'K' cars could manage a flamboyance that few could approach'

BXW 316

Genius Buehrig's makeover creates an all-time classic design

Auburn 851/ 852 Speedster

Auburn is the town in Indiana where brothers Frank and Morris Eckhart established their automobile business in 1903. Starting with simple single-cylinder devices, they had progressed to a six-cylinder car by 1912. In truth, their cars were undistinguished and pricey, and by 1924 they were failing, with 700 unsold cars on their hands.

Errett Lobban Cord had made and lost his fortune three times over by the age of 24, but by 1924, his genius for selling seemed to have cemented his wealth. Taken on to run the ailing Auburn company, he immediately spruced up the unsold cars with jazzy colours – and, sure enough, they sold. He soon bought the company, becoming its dynamic president in 1926 at the age of 32.

A new Auburn range was introduced, the most important being a straight eight. The engine was built by aero engine makers Lycoming, which Cord had also bought. In fact, by 1929 his Cord Corporation controlled over 150 companies!

In 1928 came the Speedster. Cord always believed that if a car looked good it would sell – and the Speedster looked great. By 1931, all Auburns were straight eight powered, and it became their best ever year. However, from there things began to slide. In 1934, the Speedster received a makeover, but it wasn't enough. What the Speedster needed was a complete redesign, but unfortunately there simply wasn't the money for an all-new car.

The young designer Gordon Buehrig had been doing amazing work for the Cord Corporation, including creating the 'Duesenberg look'. Given the job of sorting out the Speedster, but with 100 bodies in stock needing to be used up, his redesign could only be superficial. Taking the 1928 car he created a new rear end, hood, grill and fenders. With this he managed to fashion what appeared to be a completely new car, and one of the all time great automotive shapes. It was introduced in 1935 as the 851, and then again in 1936 as the 852, although little more than the badge had changed between the two.

The 851's simple side valve straight eight was supercharged to 150bhp, but it was essentially a cheap car in a fancy suit. At $2,245, it should have sold, but these were hard times in America, and in 1937 Auburn went under.

With their cut price underpinnings forgotten, the 851 and 852 Cords are now held up as the pinnacle of art deco automotive styling.

Specifications

Production dates	851 1935; 852 1936-1937
Manufactured units	851/852 all styles 6,850; Speedster approx 600
Engine type	straight eight supercharged
Engine size	4,585cc
Maximum power	150bhp
Transmission	3-speed + 2-speed (6-speed)
Top speed	103mph
0-50 mph time	15 seconds
Country of origin	USA

BXY 525

'Buehrig managed to fashion what appeared to be a completely new car, and one of the all-time great automotive shapes'

Islander

Rolls-Royce Phantom III

The last word in 1930s bespoke engineering

The 'best cars in the world' came about through the partnership of engineer Henry Royce and salesman Charles Rolls. Their 40/50 model of 1906, known as the Silver Ghost, was certainly worthy of this accolade: the famously silent Ghost was made right up until 1926, with many built at their US factory in Springfield, Massachusetts.

During the Great War, Rolls-Royce had begun to built V12 aero engines, though it was not until 1936 that this configuration of engine would appear in one on their cars. This meant that neither Royce nor Rolls were to see this ultimate development of their car: Rolls was the first Englishman to die in an air crash in 1910 and Royce died in 1933.

In 1926 came the Phantom I, with a new overhead valve 7,668cc six-cylinder engine. For 1929 it evolved into the Phantom II. There was also a smaller 20hp model, which developed into the 20/25 and the 25/30. It was the Phantom III, however, that was to be the pinnacle of pre-WW2 automotive engineering.

The aircraft and ship engines produced by Rolls-Royce were a major influence on the engine of the PIII, a 7,340cc overhead valve V12. Cadillac had tried to go one up with a V16, but it was a simple side-valve device, and not in the same engineering league as the PIII. The advantages of the V12 layout were sublime smoothness and considerable power: Rolls-Royce were always coy about power outputs, simply stating that they were 'adequate'. In fact, the V12 made something like 170bhp, which was more than adequate.

The PIII also had far more modern suspension than its predecessors. The independent front suspension used coil springs and wishbones, as developed by General Motors.

Unsurprisingly, the PIII was expensive. Not until after the war did RR build their own bodies, so having purchased the chassis a person then had to take it to their favourite coachbuilder. In the US, a complete car would have cost around $15,000 – the same amount that would have bought five Cadillac 75s!

Hostilities of 1939 halted production, which meant that the V12 never reached its development potential, and the era of hand-built bespoke engineering came to a close.

Incidentally, a Phantom III should never be referred to as a 'Rolls': any pre-war Rolls-Royce is more appropriately referred to as a 'Royce'.

Specifications

Production dates	1936-1939
Manufactured units	710
Engine type	V12, pushrod operated overhead valve
Engine size	7,340cc
Maximum power	170bph
Transmission	4-speed synchromesh
Top speed	Approx 92mph
0-50 mph time	N/A
Country of origin	UK

AFU 209

The streamlined Cord car and Cord the man: both American icons

Cord 810/812

It it said that Errett Lobban Cord knew nothing about cars – except how to sell them. He made more than half a dozen fortunes in his life (and lost a few of them), yet Cord is best remembered through the cars that bore his name.

Having bought and turned around both Auburn and Duesenberg, in 1929 he launched his own car. The Cord L-29 was radical in that it had front wheel drive. The Miller front-drive racing cars had been beating the Duesenbergs at Indianapolis, and Cord wanted it for his road car.

The car looked terrific, but transmission problems, a high price tag and a dull Lycoming engine meant that it was a flop. Something much better was needed.

In December 1935, the new Cord 810 debuted at the New York show. It was a sensation. There was still front wheel drive, but a far more sophisticated design. There was a also a new V8 engine, with the option of supercharging up to 190bhp, pushing the Cord to 110 mph. Gear changing was achieved via electric solenoids controlled by a tiny lever. All told, it was a completely new car – and one that drove a whole lot better than the L-29. In fact, its cornering ability was in a different class to anything else on the market.

Designer Gordon Buehrig had created a stylish masterpiece. Construction was unitary, with no separate chassis, which allowed the car to be very low to the ground. Headlights were hidden in the fenders, while louvers extended round the front and back to the doors, with a 'coffin nose' hood above. The interior was also spectacular, with an aircraft-inspired dashboard.

Convertible, phaeton and two sedan models were constructed. Unusually, it is arguably the sedans that are the most stunning of the lot, with lines that were cleaner than anything on American or European roads at the time.

For 1937, the Cords were retitled 812s. It was to be their last year. Cord had gone to England in 1934 due to investigations into his business practices. In 1937, a bill was filed against him and Cord production stopped.

These were hard times in the US, and sales of the revolutionary Cord were never strong, but Buehrig's shape is now recognised as one of the most beautiful and influential automotive designs of all time.

Cord himself went on to further fame and fortune in real estate, radio, TV and politics.

Specifications

Production dates	1936-1937
Manufactured units	2,320
Engine type	V8 side-valve, optional supercharger
Engine size	4,719cc
Maximum power	115bhp (190bhp supercharged)
Transmission	4-speed, electric gear selection, front wheel drive
Top speed	91mph (110mph supercharged)
0-50 mph time	N/A
Country of origin	USA

AG 25

Designer Gordon Buehrig gave the Cord some of the most original and beautiful lines ever seen. It was no less imaginative under the skin, with front wheel drive and electric gear selection.

INDIANA-37

The GIs' transport of choice that went from being a legend to an institution

In 1940, America was still some way from entering the war in Europe, but there was enough concern for the US Quartermaster Corps to issue an invitation in July to 135 US manufacturers, asking them to submit prototypes for a general purpose vehicle. There was a list of requirements including an 80in wheelbase, 50mph top speed and a very optimistic limit on weight. This put off many contenders, and it was the tiny Bantam company that met the deadline.

Jeep

Bantam had been making Austin Sevens under licence, but were not doing well. They enlisted freelance engineer Karl K Probst, and a prototype and drawings were duly delivered in an incredible seven weeks. Although overweight, it was considered to be a success. Ford and Willys Overland also submitted. They had access to the Bantam, and so their designs were very similar. Seventy vehicles from each company were made, after which the three companies were asked to build 1,500 vehicles for evaluation.

The Willys had the best engine, and was the best value at $739. The design was standardised, and due to concerns about Bantam's lack of capacity, the contract went to Willys. Sixteen thousand were ordered, but even Willys were unlikely to meet demand, so Ford were asked to build a further 15,000 to the Willys design. Poor old Bantam got to supply trailers, and never built another car, despite their initial success.

America entered the war and demand soared. At their peak, a Jeep was leaving the Willys production line every 90 seconds. By the end of the war, over 350,000 Jeeps had been supplied to US, British and Russian forces, making a huge contribution to the Allied victory.

The Jeep's 60bhp side-valve four-cylinder engine gave it a top speed of over 60mph. It had a three-speed synchromesh gearbox connected to a high/low transfer box and four-wheel drive. With minimal overhangs and good ground clearance, it took seriously rough terrain to halt its progress, and ended up being used as everything from a gun platform, to radio car, reconnaissance vehicle and ambulance. It was easy to drive, simple to maintain, and – most of all – extremely tough.

Willys went on to build a civilian version, and the Jeep has been an institution ever since. Others copied the formula, and the British Land Rover went on sale as early as 1948.

As to where that name came from – GP, for 'general purpose', is the most likely explanation.

Specifications

Production dates	1941 to present
Manufactured units	1941-1945 350,000
Engine type	4-cylinder side valve
Engine size	2199cc
Maximum power	60bhp
Transmission	3-speed sychromesh + 2-speed transfer box, 4-wheel drive
Top speed	65mph
0-50 mph time	N/A
Country of origin	USA

141 IBN-4

In the Jeep was a rightness found only when form follows function and purpose so completely. A very similar vehicle to the WW2 Jeep is still made in India.

TP30
USA

Old-fashioned and not very fast, but post-war America fell in love with the little MG

The 'Bullnose' was William Morris' first car in 1913. The cars were sold from a converted stable in Oxford, not far from the Abingdon works. This became known as Morris Garages, and from 1922 the retail side of the business was run by Cecil Kimber. It was Kimber who was to create the MG marque, MG standing for 'Morris Garages'.

The first MGs soon appeared, but it wasn't until 1929 that MG really got moving with the Midget.

MG TC

Based on the Morris Minor, it had a lively and modern overhead cam 850cc engine.

In 1930, 1,000 MGs were built, and success meant moving over to Abingdon. This was also the year that the famous slogan, 'safety fast', was coined. MGs were doing well on the race tracks, beating arch rivals Austin in the Brooklands Double Twelve – Britain's equivalent of the Le Mans 24 Hour – amongst many other victories.

1933 saw the creation of the J2 Midget, and this was to establish the styling of MGs all the way through to the 1950s: a radiator well set back, flowing wings, cut down doors, a fuel tank on the back and a folding windscreen.

In 1934 came the TA Midget, which was based on the Morris Ten saloon, and which used its pushrod 1,292cc engine. This seemed a retrograde step after the overhead cam unit of its predecessor. However, it was larger, so power did not suffer, and neither did sales.

In fact, the engine was more flexible, and, with softer suspension and modern hydraulic brakes, it was an altogether easier car to drive. The traditional MG styling had reached its perfection, and it is still many people's idea of what a real sports car should be.

With a revised engine it became the TB – at which point war stopped play. After 1945, there was a huge hunger for new cars, especially sports cars as a source of fun after the grim years of fighting. There had been no development of new cars since 1939, so most manufacturers dusted off their old models as best they could. The TC came to the market in 1946, and MG couldn't make enough of them. Little had changed from the TB: it remained archaic but extremely charming. Thousands of units went to America, starting the US love affair with British sports cars that has endured to this day.

Specifications

Production dates	1946-1949
Manufactured units	10,000
Engine type	4-cylinder pushrod OHV
Engine size	1,250cc
Maximum power	54bhp
Transmission	4-speed synchromesh
Top speed	78mph
0-50 mph time	N/A
Country of origin	UK

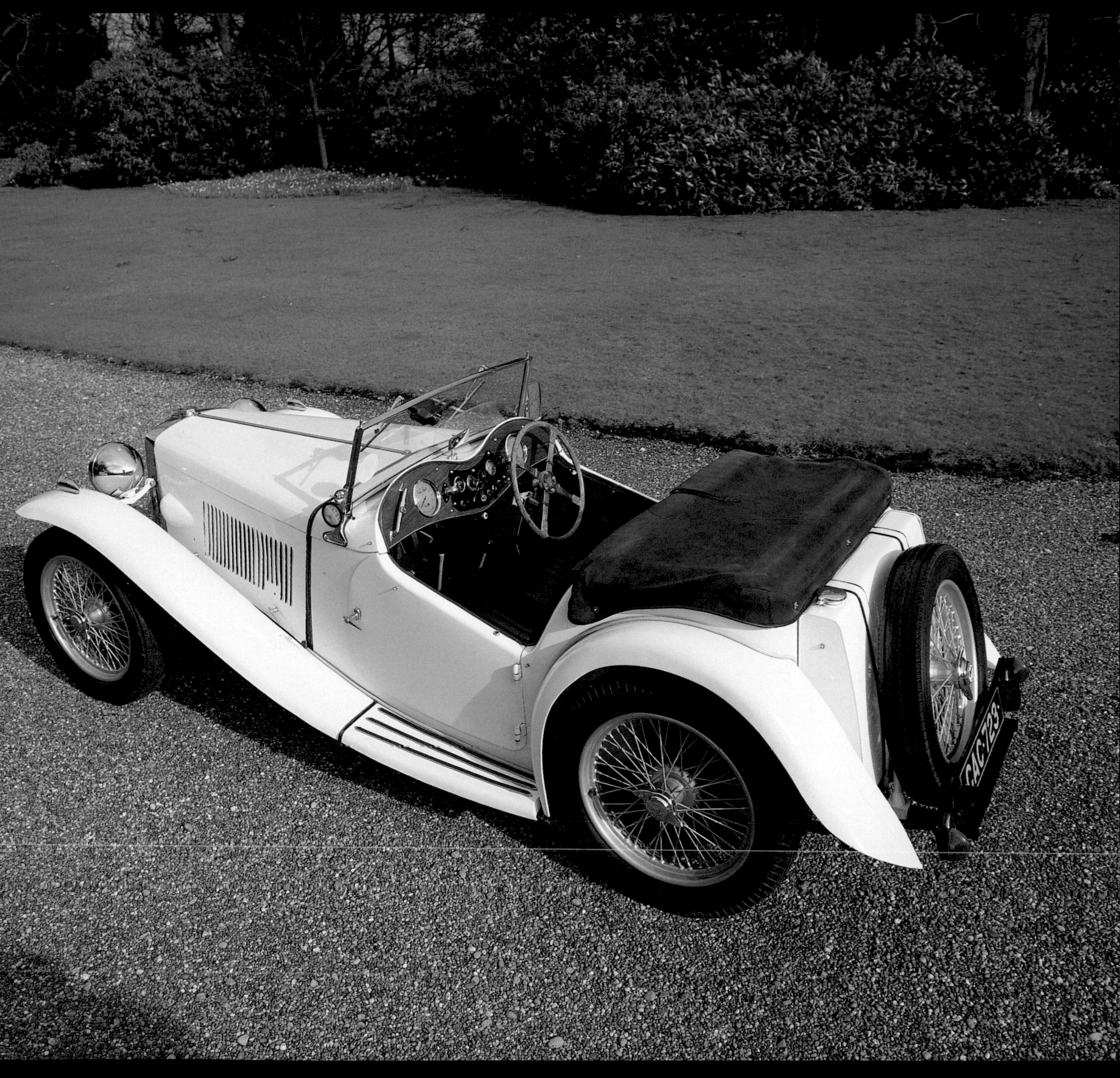
CAC 723

These were the vehicles that started the US' enduring love affair with British sports cars.

VW Beetle

The inimitable Bug has the strangest and longest story of any motor car in history

On July 30th, 2003, Beetle number 21,529,464 left the Puebla factory in Mexico. It was the very last one. The story of the world's most successful car had started an incredible 70 years earlier – and it's one of the most remarkable in the business.

Hitler is often credited with inventing the Beetle, but it wasn't really so. The idea came from Dr Ferdinand Porsche, and was brought to Hitler's attention in 1933, the year that he became chancellor. It was on June 22, 1934 that Porsche secured a contract to build a prototype for the 'people's car'.

There is much discussion over who contributed what to the design, but Czech Hans Ledwinka, from the Tatra company, is thought by some to have had much to do with it. By 1934 there was also a very Beetle-esque rear-engine Mercedes on the market.

With assistance from Mercedes Benz, three cars were built in 1936, and a further 30 pre-production cars in 1937. In 1938, Hitler laid the foundation stone of the factory near Hanover where the car was to be built. It was to be called the 'KdF-Wagen', or, 'strength through joy car'. The new factory spent the war making weapons and military vehicles, but in 1945 the tooling for the KdF-Wagen had survived.

The factory, and the town built to service it, ended up under the jurisdiction of the British Military Government, which at first failed to realise quite what it had. A young Major Ivan Hirst was appointed to sort out the factory, which had last been used to build rockets with slave labour, and which had been badly bombed. Hirst saw the potential, and persuaded the military police to place an order for 20,000 vehicles. He scrounged steel and supplies, and by 1946, 1,000 cars a month were being built. In 1949, the renamed Wolfsburg town and factory were handed over to the new West German government.

VW promoted the little car in the US, and against all preconceptions the Americans took the Bug to their heart, buying them in their millions.

The tiny 1,131cc engine grew in size and power, while the split rear window became one, and got bigger. Eventually, the windscreen became curved and the torsion bar front suspension gave way to modern struts. And yet the Beetle's character never really changed.

In 1972, it overtook the Model T Ford's record for production numbers, and it seems unlikely that any car will ever exceed the VW's 21.5 million examples built over its 57 years.

Specifications

Production dates	1946-2003
Manufactured units	21,529,464
Engine type	Flat 4, air-cooled, rear-mounted
Engine size	1131cc-1584cc
Maximum power	25bhp-50bhp
Transmission	4-speed synchromesh
Top speed	62mph-82mph
0-60 mph time	17.1 seconds (1303-1584cc)
Country of origin	Germany

KRY 724

'...against all preconceptions the Americans took the Bug to their heart, buying them in their millions'

Race track domination and fabulous looks couldn't save Hudson

Hudson Hornet

Hudson had been around since 1908 and, at times in the 1930s, had risen as high as number five in US sales, but remained a relatively small fish in an extremely big pond, and so life was never easy.

The war brought the production of Helldiver planes and parts for B29s, but following VJ Day in 1945, Hudson made enough cars to regain fifth place. The cars created between 1945 and 1947 were based on old designs, but for 1948 it had an all-new car. These were the 'Step Down' Hudsons, and the Commodore models made money for the old firm.

The nickname came from the way in which the main chassis members ran around the perimeter of the car, allowing the floor to be stepped down inside. Not only did this make the car extremely low, it also made it exceptionally safe.

There was a new engine as well. The Super Six was a side-valve 4,294cc unit, and was only marginally less powerful than Hudson's straight eight. By 1951 it had become rebranded as the 5,048cc Hornet engine. The Hornet looked much like the Commodore, but with a new grill. The lines were sensational and, while performance from the 145bhp motor was excellent, there was potential for more and the car became a tuner's favourite. Marshall Teague said he could get 112mph out of a car certified as stock by the racing authorities. The Hudson engineers developed 'severe usage' parts, which were really racing equipment. In 1953, the Twin H Power carburettor setup was offered. The ultimate '7-X' racing engine could make 210bhp.

Teague raced the Hornet in AAA and NASCAR stock-car events from 1951 and was simply invincible through to 1954, winning 12 out of 13 races in the 1952 AAA season. As late as 1955, after Step Down production had finished, the Hornet was still winning races.

The trouble was that the Hornet's modern unitary construction and fabulous lines made it impossible to restyle year to year in the way that most manufacturers did: all its designers could do was fiddle with the trim. It also hurt sales that however good the Hudson engine was, it wasn't a V8. Profits fell, and in 1954 came a merger with Nash – really more of a takeover by their rival. The 1955 Hudson used a Nash body, and was disparagingly referred to as a 'Hash'.

Specifications

Production dates	1951-1953
Manufactured units	106,785
Engine type	6-cylinder side valve
Engine size	5,048cc
Maximum power	145bhp, Twin H Power 160bhp
Transmission	3-speed manual, with options of overdrive and Drive-Master semi automatic. Hydra-Matic automatic gearbox optional
Top speed	105mph
0-60 mph time	12-14 seconds
Country of origin	USA

Could the 300SL be the world's most desired automobile?

Mercedes 300SL

The 300SL is seen by most as the greatest car Mercedes Benz ever built. And yet, without some very strong external persuasion, it would never have come into being.

Daimler Benz was all but obliterated by Allied bombing during WW2, and in 1945 its directors stated that the company had 'ceased to exist'. Miraculously, the tooling for the humble 170 saloon had escaped, and this little car went back into production, easing Germany's need for basic transport. In 1951, Mercedes brought out the big 300 saloon that became synonymous with chancellor Adenauer's government.

Mercedes wanted to go racing, but had nothing in the way of blueprints on which to base a sports car except the staid 300, the tall, heavy engine of which was not what was wanted in a cutting-edge competition vehicle. Tipping the engine over to 40° dealt with the height, and they built the rest of the car super-light to compensate for the engine's bulk: the answer was a space frame made of dozens of small diameter tubes.

The new car was a sensation, winning both Le Mans and the Carrera Panamericana in 1952. It was called the 300SL, but it was only a racing car – and that's the way it would have stayed if it hadn't been for New York car importer Max Hoffmann, who saw the potential of the 300SL as a road car in the US. The factory wasn't really interested until Hoffmann made a firm order for 1,000 cars.

In 1954, the 300SL became a road car. Where the racer had been aerodynamic but ugly, the road car was stunning. It kept the upward opening doors of the racer, and this led to its being universally called the 'Gullwing'.

It was the first road car with a fuel-injected engine, and with 195bhp it could top 150mph with a high ratio axle. However, this gem was not without its flaws: the suspension was taken from the 300 saloon, and at the back used a very old-fashioned swing axle design. This could cause a sudden breakaway, and the Gullwing killed a fair few drivers with more money than ability.

In 1957, the Gullwing gave way to the Roadster, which had large, one-piece headlights and regular doors. Most importantly, the rear suspension had been redesigned and the handling improved.

The 300SL created the SL tradition that lasts to this day, with the cars themselves more desirable now than at any point in their formidable history.

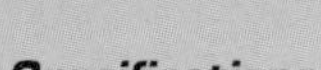

Specifications

Production dates	1954-1957 (Gullwing); 1957-1963 (Roadster)
Manufactured units	1,400 (Gullwing); 1,858 (Roadster)
Engine type	Straight 6 single overhead cam, fuel-injected
Engine size	2,996cc
Maximum power	195bhp (Gullwing); 215bhp (Roadster)
Transmission	4-speed
Top speed	125mph-150mph, dependent on final drive ratio
0-60 mph time	7-9 seconds, dependent on final drive ratio
Country of origin	Germany

SYN 126F

OSCAR

Values for the Gullwing are higher than for the Roadster, due to its overt racing heritage. In fact the Roadster is better to drive, just as fast, and you don't have to lift out the windows to keep cool!

Spaceship or goddess; to many the DS was both

Citroen had long been known for adventurous and innovative engineering. The Light 15 of 1934, also known as the 'Traction Avant', pioneered mass-produced front-wheel drive and unitary construction and, when the DS19 landed in an unsuspecting world on Octber 5th, 1955, it was by far the most advanced car in the world.

The DS and cheaper ID (sounding like the French for 'goddess' and 'idea', respectively)

Citroen DS

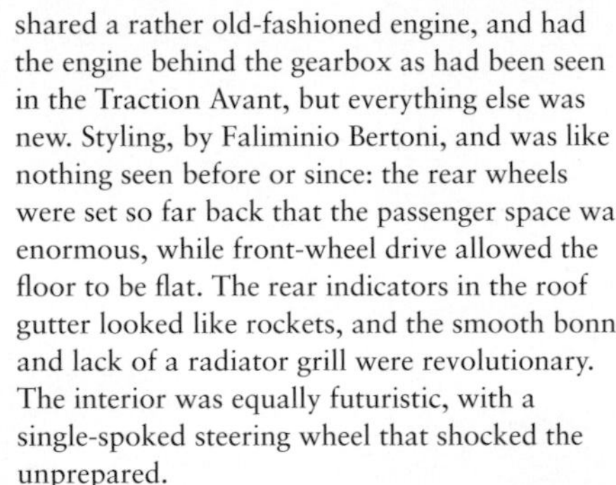

shared a rather old-fashioned engine, and had the engine behind the gearbox as had been seen in the Traction Avant, but everything else was new. Styling, by Faliminio Bertoni, and was like nothing seen before or since: the rear wheels were set so far back that the passenger space was enormous, while front-wheel drive allowed the floor to be flat. The rear indicators in the roof gutter looked like rockets, and the smooth bonnet and lack of a radiator grill were revolutionary. The interior was equally futuristic, with a single-spoked steering wheel that shocked the unprepared.

The car's life blood was its high-pressure hydraulic system. There were no steel springs and the suspension gave an unworldly soft ride, plus there was also the ability to adjust the ride height, although the DS's party trick was its ability to drive on three wheels (which allowed drivers to change a wheel without a jack). The brake pedal was a button, the sensitivity of which caught out every novice driver first time, while the power steering utilised hydraulics, and some models even had hydraulic gear and clutch engagement (although the simpler ID boasted only the suspension and braking systems).

On paper, the DS did not appear especially fast, but its handling ability, combined with a talent for keeping its passengers cosseted during spirited driving, made it a formidable A-to-B machine.

As time went by, its designers came up with increases in power and sophistication, such as swivelling head lights. Later models were designated the DS20, DS21 and DS23. The Pallas meanwhile, was a luxury model, the Safari was a cavernous estate, and there was even a coupé and a convertible by Chapron, both highly prized collectors' items with prices to match.

On the DS's 50th anniversary, Paris ground to a halt as thousands of DSs came to celebrate their birthday. There are few objects the French are more proud of than the DS, and enthusiasts everywhere display a loyalty verging on obsession

Specifications

Production dates	1955-1975
Manufactured units	1,456,115
Engine type	4-cylinder push rod OHV
Engine size	1,911cc; 1,985cc; 2,175cc; 2,347cc
Maximum power	109bhp (DS21)
Transmission	4-manual and semi-automatic, front-wheel drive
Top speed	106mph (DS21)
0-60 mph time	14.8 seconds (DS21)
Country of origin	France

AA
LVB 793K

Though most DSs provided everyday transport for the French middle classes, the convertible by Chapron was something rare and special. Today these wear a price tag that is truly exclusive.

'55-'57 Ford Thunderbird

For the T-Bird, first was best, as the purity of the two-seater cars was never fully recaptured

It was Chevrolet that made the Thunderbird happen. In 1953, it brought out the Corvette, and GM certainly weren't going to have anything that Ford didn't have. Ford wanted a more practical vehicle than the 'Vette, so, rather than calling the T-Bird a sports car, it termed its new creation a 'personal' car.

The T-Bird fused low-slung elegance with a thoroughly Ford look. It was not the out-and-out sports car that the early Corvette had tried and failed to be. It sat on the same 102in wheelbase, but there were proper wind-up windows, a power top and a lift-off hard top. Under the hood was a beefy 193bhp Mercury V8, while the 'Vette struggled with flappy side screens and a limp six pot. Under that gorgeous skin it might have run on standard Ford parts from lesser models in the range, but who cared?

On release in 1955 it was priced at an irresistible $3,000, and as a result managed to outsell the Corvette that year by an incredible 24 to one.

Detroit restyled its models every season in the 1950s, but the runaway success of the T-Bird meant that it was too good to change. For 1956 it received a 'continental' spare wheel on the back, a little more power and softer suspension. It also got the no-cost option of distinctive portholes in the hard top. Remember the mystery girl's white T-Bird in 'American Graffiti'?

For 1957 there was a light makeover, with a different bumper and grill, and a longer rear deck for more trunk space. Elegance was undiminished, and you could now get up to 285bhp if you ticked the right boxes. They even went racing with a 340bhp supercharged version – only 208 were built, and success was limited.

Ford wanted greater sales, and for 1958 the T-Bird became a four seater. The new car was so ugly that even its mother couldn't have loved it, but the American public did, and it sold twice as well as the two-seater cars had.

The T-Bird would never be a two-seater again, but the 1961 to 1963 cars regained a beauty and simplicity of line, and would later feature in the film 'Thelma and Louise'.

The 1964 model held on to some of its predecessors' looks, but from there on it was downhill all the way, with the T-Bird becoming a car for men wearing white shoes and plaid slacks.

Specifications

Production dates	1955-1957
Manufactured units	53,166
Engine type	V8 pushrod OHV
Engine size	4,785cc; 5,112cc
Maximum power	193bhp-285bhp
Transmission	3-speed manual with optional overdrive, or 3-speed automatic
Top speed	105mph-125mph
0-60 mph time	11.5-7.0 seconds
Country of origin	USA

KRV IP

'...the runaway success of the T-Bird meant that it was too good to change.'

Few cars have been as right as the '55 Chevy with its new V8. Except perhaps the '57

'55, '56, '57 Chevrolets

The '54 Chevy was upright, old fashioned and had a dull six under the hood. The all-new '55 Chevy, on the other hand, could not have been more different.

GM styling chief Harley Earl instructed his staff to 'go all the way, then back off'. The result was three years of Chevys that are affectionately known as the 'Tri Chevys', and remain revered the world over to this day.

There was a new lighter chassis frame underneath, but it was the clean, perfectly proportioned looks that got noticed. So did the engine: 1955 saw the birth of the 'Small Block' V8, super-modern in design and built for high revs and low weight.

There were two- and four-door cars, a four-door station wagon, a convertible, and three ranges – the One-Ten, Two-Ten, and the desirable Bel Air. Then there was the Nomad: a station wagon styling exercise on the Corvette was so well received at shows that the design was rapidly adapted for the '55 model. The two-door wagon was stunning: it cost more than the convertible and sold slowly, but Tri Chevy Nomads remain a collector's dream.

1955 was a boom year, and Chevrolet sold 1.7 million cars, taking a full 44% of the lower-priced market.

For 1956, there was a gentle restyle, and the pillarless two-door car was joined by a 'hard top' four-door pillarless sedan. The restyle was successful, but today the '56 is less sought after than its '55 and '57 cousins.

Perhaps they saved the best till last. Designer Carl Renner said they had tried to make the car, 'look like a little Cadillac'. It worked, and with tail fins and bumper bullets in the grill it was hard to believe that this was still the same basic hull as in the '55. It might have lost the unadorned simplicity of the '55, but it didn't matter.

In 1957, Chevy gave the option of fuel injection – a first on an American car, and not so far behind Mercedes Benz with the 300SL. It made 283bhp and blasted the '57 to 60 in eight seconds, but cost a whopping $500, so only 1,503 'Fuelies' got built.

No cars better epitomise the decade than the Tri Chevys. All of them are true classics, but if you find yourself a Nomad, convertible or a Fuelie, better talk to you bank manager first, as they tend to go for truly phenomenal prices.

Specifications

Production dates	1955, 1956, 1957
Manufactured units	'55 1,703,993 '56 1,563,729 '57 1,499,658
Engine type	straight 6 and V8 OHV
Engine size	straight 6 3,850 cc; V8 4,342cc/4,637cc
Maximum power	(V8) 162bhp-283bhp
Transmission	3-speed manual with optional overdrive, or 2-speed automatic
Top speed	(V8) 90mph-120mph
0-60 mph time	(V8) 11.4-8.0 seconds
Country of origin	USA

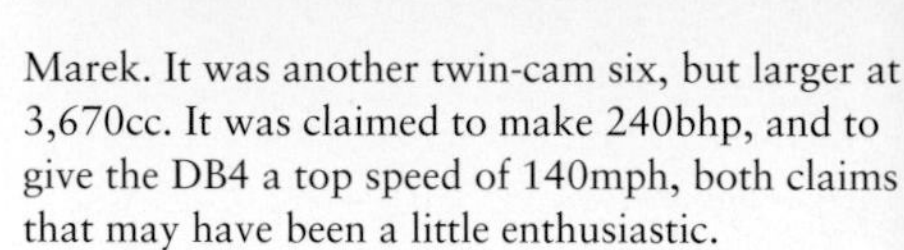

The DB Astons were the epitome of the post-war sports car, with exceptional lines and success on the track

Aston Martin got its name from the English village of Aston Clinton, where Lionel Martin had competed in hill climbs. The first Aston Martin appeared in 1914, and in 1921 came racing success at the Brooklands track. The company built small-engined, hand-made sports cars that were very special, but very expensive. It first went bust in 1924, and from then on was always on a shaky financial footing.

Aston Martin DB4/DB5

In 1947, the company was bought by tractor magnate David Brown. A four-cylinder engine had been designed, but Brown wanted more. He had also purchased Lagonda, and with it came a twin overhead cam six-cylinder unit, which had been designed by the great W.O Bentley, and was used to power his Astons.

The DB2 of 1949 was a sleek coupé along the lines of Ferraris at the time. Rather confusingly, it developed to become the DB2/4, DB2/4 Mk II, and the DB Mk III. The DB3 was a sports racing car, as were the DB3S and the DBR 1, which won both Le Mans and the World Sports Car Championship for David Brown in 1959.

The DB4 in 1958 was all new, including its engine, designed by Polish engineer Tadek Marek. It was another twin-cam six, but larger at 3,670cc. It was claimed to make 240bhp, and to give the DB4 a top speed of 140mph, both claims that may have been a little enthusiastic.

The styling was svelte and lithe, and the unique bodywork was handmade using the 'superleggera', or 'super light', technique of Carrozzeria Touring of Milan.

In 1962 there came a convertible. There was a faster Vantage version, and a very fast short wheelbase DB4 GT. Then there were 19 GTs with beautiful bodies built by Zagato in Italy.

In 1963 the DB4 became the DB5. It used the faired-in lights of the GT, but looked little different to the DB4. The engine was enlarged to 3,995cc and there was 282bhp available. The DB6 in 1965 was a heavier, less elegant motor car.

The DB5 shot to worldwide fame when Sean Connery's James Bond drove one in 'Goldfinger'. The Corgi toy sold in millions to small boys, and although they're all grown up, for most of them the DB5 remains as unattainable as ever.

Specifications

Production dates	1958-1963 (DB4); 1963-1965 (DB5)
Manufactured units	1,110 (DB4); 1,021 (DB5)
Engine type	Twin-cam 6-cylinder
Engine size	3,670cc (DB4); 3,995cc (DB5)
Maximum power	240bhp (DB4); 285bhp (DB5); 315bph (DB4 Zagato)
Transmission	4-speed sychromesh
Top speed	140mph+
0-60 mph time	8.1 seconds
Country of origin	UK

848 HYL

The Aston Martin DB4 sets the gold standard for classics. Beautiful, fast, rare and, above all, utterly desirable.

Facel Vega HK500

The exotic HK500 never quite fitted in, but remains one of the most romantic cars ever made

In the early 1950s, the Facel company of wealthy industrialist Jean Daninos was making everything from kitchen sinks to jet engine parts. Then it started making bodies for auto makers such as Simca, Panhard and Ford. The French Ford Comete of 1952 was a pretty coupé, but Daninos wanted to build his own car.

In 1954 he presented the Facel Vega FVS. Powered by one of the best engines of the day, the Chrysler 'Hemi' V8, it was fast and very beautiful. Its styling was truly 'transatlantic', with an unmistakable American influence filtered through European sensibilities, while the wrap-around windscreen and forward lean gave it a unique look. The Facel was the first of several British and Italian–American hybrids, but none achieved the perfect fusion of styles seen in the Facel.

The engineering was straightforward and heavy, following US practice with a hefty tubular chassis and solid rear axle – and with only drum brakes to slow it down, it was arguably better at speeding up than stopping!

A stretched four-door FVS called the Excellence arrived in 1958. With pillarless construction and suicide rear doors it looked incredible, but unfortunately it wasn't rigid enough, and if parked on anything other than a flat surface, the doors would refuse to open.

In 1959 the FVS became the HK500, with an even bigger 5,907cc Chrysler V8, while later cars had a 6,286cc engine with up to 390bhp! Unfortunately, the chassis wasn't really up to it, the steering said to be 'vega' than most. The styling was perfected, and the cars were equally spectacular on the inside. The aircraft style wrap-around dashboard appeared to be in heavily figured burr walnut, but in fact it was steel, painted by a talented tromp l'oeil artist.

Everything about the HK500 is romantic – even the legends that surround it. Nobel Prize-winning author and philosopher Albert Camus died in one during an accident near Paris. His friend and agent, who was driving, also perished.

In 1962 came the Facel II, with a totally different look. The big V8 cars were always slow sellers, but it was Daninos' ill-fated venture building his own small sports-car engine that eventually sank the company.

The HK500 isn't really a very good car, but with charisma and presence in spades, who cares?

Specifications

Production dates	1959-1961
Manufactured units	500
Engine type	V8 Hemi
Engine size	5,907cc; 6,286 cc
Maximum power	325bhp-390bhp
Transmission	4-speed manual or automatic
Top speed	140+ mph
0-60 mph time	8.4 seconds
Country of origin	France

FACEL
898 FKG

Beloved of both bank managers and bank robbers, the Mk II is still the greatest Jaguar saloon

William Lyons and William Walmsley set up their Swallow Sidecars business as very young men in 1922. By 1927, they had progressed to building bodies on Austin Seven chassis. They looked extravagant but were keenly priced, and sold well. In 1931 came their first proper car: the SS. In 1935, a new six-cylinder saloon and sports car were launched, both called the SS Jaguar. The cars looked to be in the same class as Bentleys, but at a quarter of the price.

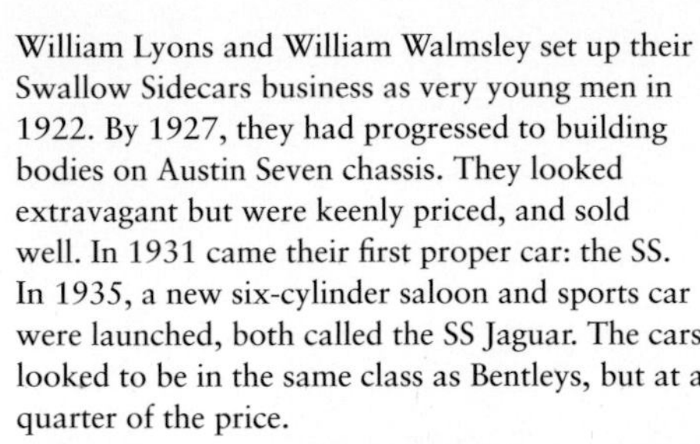

Jaguar Mk II

After the Second World War, the SS name could no longer be used due to its unpleasant connotations of Nazi stormtroopers.

There was soon a new Jaguar engine on the block. This was the legendary twin overhead cam, six-cylinder XK unit. It powered both the XK sports cars and the Mk VII, VIII and IX saloons. These were big cars, but the XK engine endowed them with remarkable performance.

Something sportier was needed, and in 1955 the much smaller Mk I was released. With the same 3.4-litre engine as its big brother, it was considerably quicker. It was an instant hit, but when Jaguar developed it into the Mk II in 1959, it created its most famous saloon ever.

There was a wider rear track, and the glass house was given much lighter styling. Under the bonnet you could have the 2.4 or 3.4 from the Mk I, but there was now a 3.8. This endowed the Mk II with quite extraordinary performance, and 125mph could be rung out of it on Britain's unrestricted motorways. There were new disc brakes all round, as pioneered by Jaguar on its competition cars. It handled well, but by modern standards the gearbox and steering were heavy and hard work. Inside was as much leather and wood as you would find in a Rolls Royce, and all this for the bargain price of £1,444 including tax, for the 2.4.

The Mk II dominated the new production saloon racing, but there were other, less salubrious characters who also appreciated its performance. The Mk II became infamous as the bank robber's get away car of choice, and no self-respecting 1960s cop drama was complete without a tyre-smoking Mk II.

Today, the Mk II is both archetypally British and a quintessential icon of the 1960s – as attractive a package now as it ever was.

Specifications

Production dates	1959-1967
Manufactured units	83,976
Engine type	Twin overhead cam 6-cylinder
Engine size	2,483cc; 3,442cc; 3,781cc
Maximum power	120bhp; 210bhp; 220bhp
Transmission	4-speed with optional overdrive
Top speed	125mph (3.8)
0-60 mph time	8.5 seconds (3.8)
Country of origin	UK

The Mk II was formidable on the track. Seen here cresting Paddock Hill and braking for Druids corner at Brands Hatch, the "BUY 12" registration gives the white car away as a 'Coombes' Jaguar, from John Coombes garage in Guildford.

MOTORMILES LTD
CARSAVERS
VCD 400

If ever a car proved that you don't have to go fast to have fun, it was the 'Frogeye'

Donald Healey had worked for various British car makers before and during WW2, and in 1945 was quick to acquire a factory in Warwick, England.

His first cars were powered by Riley engines, and as coupés, convertibles, and sports cars around 600 units were sold. A collaboration with Nash in America created the equally successful Nash-Healey, which sold only in the US.

Austin-Healey Sprite

In the early 1950s, boss of BMC Sir Leonard Lord, which included both Austin and Morris, was on the lookout for a sports-car design. He liked what Healey showed him and the Healey 100 was the result. Meanwhile, Healey was happy because he didn't even have to build the cars!

The 100 gained a six-cylinder engine, becoming the 100/6 and later the 3000. In the mid-1950s there was a gap in the market for a small, no-frills sports car, and Healey was asked to develop one: the Austin-Healey Sprite of 1958.

The designer responsible for the big Healey's lovely lines had departed, and the Sprite ended up with rather 'individual' styling. The headlights popping out of the bonnet gave rise to its enduring nickname of the 'Frogeye', but the quirky looks only added to the little car's charm.

Charm it had aplenty, and although its top speed was only 83mph, it was a hoot to drive. The little 948cc A-Series engine from the Austin A35 saloon had a lively and eager character quite at odds with its humble specification. The front suspension also came from the little Austin, but 1/4 elliptic rear springs located the axle much better. It was light, nimble, and had perfect balance – all thanks to its simplicity. There were no locks, no boot, no proper windows, and you had to reach inside to open a door.

A more conventional restyle came in 1961, and the Sprite was joined by the near-identical MG Midget. Engines got bigger and weight increased. The last Sprite was made in 1971, but the Midget soldiered on until 1980, by which time it was a rather overweight shadow of the first Sprite.

The Frogeye was the original cheeky little sports car, and still engenders enormous affection in its many devotees.

Specifications

Production dates	1959-1961
Manufactured units	48,987
Engine type	4-cylinder push rod OHV
Engine size	948cc
Maximum power	43bhp
Transmission	4-speed, synchromesh on top 3 gears
Top speed	83mph
0-60 mph time	18 seconds
Country of origin	UK

WGY 873

Cadillac

In the 1950s, the American dream had come true, and the '59 was perhaps its ultimate manifestation

Has there ever been a car so famed for just one feature? With the '59 Caddies it was all about those fins. For 1960 they'd been trimmed back, and by 1965 fins were just a memory for the American auto industry.

It was all their fault in the first place. Harley Earl, or 'Misterearl', as he was always referred to, had pretty much come up with the idea of car styling. At General Motors in 1925 he introduced the concept of annual model changes and – although he wouldn't have put it this way – designed obsolescence. When GM formed its Art and Colour section in 1927, Earl was in charge. It started with 50 people, but was to grow to 1,400.

Making cars look good, and making them different every year, made them sell. The rest of Detroit had to play catch up.

Come the end of WW2, the US was set to enter its golden decade. It was a unique time of economic boom, confidence, and cultural innocence, but the Bay of Pigs and Kennedy's assassination brought it all to an end.

This was the jet age, the TV age, the space age, and the greatest time there had ever been to be an American. Americans wanted their cars to reflect their dreams, and Misterearl obliged.

Back in 1941, Earl had seen the still secret P38 Lightning fighter plane. He took the beautiful tail fin shape and applied it to his '48 Cadillacs.

Throughout the 1950s, US styling grew more outrageous, as did the prominence of the fins. There were some biggies on Chryslers and Plymouths, but the '59 Caddie's beat them all. With twin bullet lights mounted half way up, looking like small rockets, style had completely triumphed over function.

The '59 wasn't even a very good car, but no-one noticed. It had a V8 under the hood, like any other Cadillac, but no-one asked any questions. Sure, the front end suffered from vibration and it handled badly. So what?

The '59 is the ultimate icon of rock 'n' roll Americana: a reminder of the good times when the good times were never going to end. Another way to see it might be as an old-fashioned, inefficient relic, heaving its last gasp while dressed up in preposterous fancy dress. Vietnam was just around the corner.

Specifications

Production dates	1959
Manufactured units	142,272
Engine type	V8 OHV
Engine size	6390cc
Maximum power	325/345bhp
Transmission	Hydra-Matic auto
Top speed	120mph
0-60 mph time	11.5
Country of origin	USA

'The '59 is the ultimate icon of rock 'n' roll Americana'

Mini

The Mini put more new ideas into 10ft than had ever been seen in one car before

Alex Issigonis was a genuine genius. During the fuel crisis of 1956, he put his extraordinary mind to creating a new sort of small car – and no small car has been packaged as well as the Mini. His first big idea was to turn the engine across the car. Most cars have transverse engines these days, but the Mini was the first. Then he put the gearbox under the engine, in its sump. This meant them sharing their oil, but developments in lubrication meant this wasn't a problem.

The suspension used rubber for springs, which saved space again. Issigonis didn't like wasting space on a boot that was seldom used, so the lid to the tiny boot opened downwards, and larger loads could be carried with the boot open. This left more room for passengers, and the Mini was something of a Tardis. To make manufacture cheaper, the body's seams were turned outwards, welded together and covered with trim.

And all this innovation came in a 10ft package. Issigonis' previous small car, the Morris Minor, had been a full 28in longer!

The car was so light that, on its release in 1959, the engine size was reduced from 950cc to 850cc, because it was too fast! It was the first classless car, driven by Peter Sellers and his cleaning lady alike. It was immediately super trendy and stayed that way, epitomising Cool Britannia and the swinging '60s.

The Mini was a blast to drive, and pretty soon there were faster Cooper and Cooper S versions available. They were unbeatable on the track or rally stage, and giant killing became routine, including a triple on the Monte Carlo Rally. Anyone who has ever driven a Cooper S will know that it's impossible to drive one slowly!

The Mini's place in every British heart was sealed when three Mini Coopers starred in 'The Italian Job' in 1969, which featured Michael Caine and a seemingly endless supply of unforgettable lines.

The Mini came as a van, a pickup, and a Traveller estate with wood trim. There were luxury Riley Elf and Wolseley Hornet versions, and later the Clubman and 1,275GT. No other car ever approached its dimensions and still carried four in reasonable comfort. Its unique status meant it looked as though it would last forever, but time was finally called on October 4th 2000, when the last Mini rolled off the production line.

Specifications

Production dates	1959-2000
Manufactured units	5,387,862
Engine type	4-cylinder transverse
Engine size	848cc-1,275cc
Maximum power	34bhp-76bhp
Transmission	4-speed in sump
Top speed	72mph-96mph
0-60 mph time	29.7-10.5 seconds
Country of origin	UK

S
AUSTIN COOPER
JUY 232D

123

ACY 25B

Ferrari 250GT SWB

No other car has combined everyday roadability and weekend track talent like the SWB

In 1928, Enzo Ferrari founded Scuderia Ferrari, a racing team competing in the fabulous Alfa Romeo racing cars of the time. He built a couple of cars in 1940, but the Ferrari name didn't appear on a car until after WW2.

Throughout the 1950s, 'Il Commendatore', as Enzo was known, was only really interested in racing – his road cars were simply a way to finance the competition programme.

The first Ferrari appeared in 1946 with a 2.0-litre V12 engine designed by the great Gioacchino Columbo, and was winning races by 1947. The first road cars came a year later, powered by versions of the V12. The trouble was that Enzo was giving his attention to winning Grand Prix, something his team were pretty good at. They lifted the World Championship in 1952, 1953, and 1958, with further titles in 1961 and 1964. They also won Le Mans in 1949, 1954, 1958, and 1960 straight through to 1965.

The 1950s road cars were beautiful, fast, and certainly exclusive. But they were also under-developed and often too close to competition models to be practical. Many were raced in sports-car events, but unless you had a works car you were unlikely to win.

In 1956 came the first 250 (the number relates to the cylinder capacity, so x12 gives you 3 litres). Derivatives followed, including the Tour de France, or TDF. A short chassis development appeared in 1960, and the 250GT Short Wheel Base Berlinetta was born. Bodywork was styled by Pininfarina and built by Scaglietti. You could have it in steel or aluminium, and no two cars were exactly the same. In spite of this, it was the first real series-produced Ferrari.

Production-car racing was very popular, and the 250SWB was the car to drive if you wanted to win. What was unique about the SWB was that it really could be driven to the shops, then driven to the track, raced, and driven home again. You wouldn't have wanted to go shopping in a TDF, and the 250GTO that followed the SWB was a pure racing car with little pretence of being domesticated, but otherwise the principles of the cars remained the same.

The GTO may be more famous, but the SWB is still the greatest dual-purpose car ever built.

Specifications

Production dates	1960-1962
Manufactured units	165
Engine type	60-degree V12
Engine size	2,953cc
Maximum power	220bhp-280bhp
Transmission	4-speed synchromesh
Top speed	145mph-155mph
0-60 mph time	6.3 seconds
Country of origin	Italy

'The GTO may be more famous, but the SWB is still the greatest dual-purpose car ever built.'

The 180 made Mercedes a major manufacturer. But is it a classic?

After WW2 Daimler Benz started building a small pre-war model, and it proved to be its salvation. This model had a clever cruciform separate chassis, and even the company's new 300 limousine shared this design. Something more modern was needed, and it would have to embrace the new unitary body construction techniques.

In 1953 came the 180. It was simply styled, perhaps even a little dumpy. The engine and front

Mercedes Benz 180

suspension was carried on a separate subframe – a little like a pontoon bridge – which led to this shape of Mercedes always being referred to as the 'Pontoon'. Volvo claims to have pioneered crumple zones but, in fact, the 180 was the first car to incorporate the concept.

Engines were the slow, wheezy, diesel, and side-valve petrol units from the old 170. Not until 1957 did the 180 get a detuned version of the overhead cam engine from the 190SL, and decent performance.

The model shown here (the author's car) has been to Spain twice, France several times, and has visited Italy, Sicily, Belgium, Holland, Luxembourg, Switzerland, and Wales. On these journeys it cruised at 75mph, even though the top speed is only 84mph. There have been one or two problems, but nothing that stopped it from getting home. Just to prove that using an old car doesn't do it any harm, it has also won its class in the Mercedes Benz Club national concours. It might have a few stone chips, but it wears them with pride.

But is it a classic? The public's reaction speaks for itself – in Italy, the car was greeted with cries of, 'Bella, bella' and in south London West Indian guys shout, 'Cool car man'...

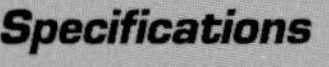

Specifications

Production dates	1953196262 (189b 1959-1961)
Manufactured units	271,217 (all types)
Engine type	4-cylinder petrol, OHC (180b)
Engine size	1,897cc (180b)
Maximum power	68bhp (180b)
Transmission	4-speed synchromesh, column change
Top speed	84mph
0-60 mph time	18 seconds
Country of origin	Germany

857 TPD

Jaguar E-Type

America loved it so much that they bought most of them. No export has done more for Britain's image than the E-Type Jag

Few cars have caused a storm like the one at the unveiling of the E-Type in 1961. The XK120 of 1948 had been cutting edge, but by now it had developed into the XK150 and was fairly antiquated. With a heavy separate chassis it was tall and old-fashioned. Its replacement could not have been more different.

Jaguar had been extremely successful in sports-car racing during the 1950s, with Le Mans victories in 1951, 1953, and 1955 through to 1957. First there had been the C-Type, with the brand new technology of disc brakes. Then came the D-Type with its aerodynamic form and unitary chassis. All the lessons learnt at the La Sarthe track were used in the design of the E-Type.

There were Dunlop disc brakes all round, and the body was of unitary, or monocoque, construction. This allowed it to be low, and it's hard to think of a car that looks lower than the E-Type. It plainly owed much to the lines of the D-Type, but that was a racing car and didn't have to sell. The E-Type shared the same small oval grill and faired-in lights, but it was styled to please – and please it did. The roadster and the fixed-head coupé vied to be the most beautiful car in the world.

A press car was tested to 150.4mph. Though it may have had a little extra care in its preparation, customers' cars could get very close to this magic number. The same car reached 60 in 6.9 seconds.

It wasn't just fast and beautiful. With sophisticated independent rear suspension it handled well and rode like no sports car before it. This was a car in which to cross continents.

The E-Type had one more trump card up its sleeve – it was cheap. Jags had always been good value, and combined with great performance, this had created a slightly unwelcome image. A derogatory term for the middle classes was 'the Jag and gin brigade'. All this was forgotten with the E-Type – it was just too good to knock.

Its unique combination of qualities mean the E-Type will never go out of fashion, yet even now it's remarkable value next to an Aston or Ferrari.

Specifications

Production dates	1961-1973 (all types)
Manufactured units	72,584 (all types)
Engine type	6-cylinder twin overhead cam
Engine size	3,781cc (pre-1964)
Maximum power	265bhp
Transmission	4-speed sychromesh
Top speed	150mph
0-60 mph time	7.1 seconds
Country of origin	UK

With world-beating performance and looks to die for, it's hard to believe that the E-type was also cheap.

The MGB was a sports car for every man. The MGB GT was a sports car for every man and his dog

Ever since the end of WW2, MG seem to have been selling old-fashioned cars to old-fashioned people. With the release of the MGB in 1962, that was to change – at least for a while.

The MGA had been a direct development of the T series cars, with their pre-war roots. In spite of this, it was too modern for many British sports-car enthusiasts – who would have been shocked by its replacement, the thoroughly modern B.

MGB

The B was of monocoque construction. This wasn't exactly ground breaking, but the Austin-Healey and Triumph opposition were still built on separate chassis. The mechanical bits came from the rather mundane Austin and Morris saloons. The B series engine was tuned to 95bhp and that meant 100mph. It was enough to make the B an instant bestseller.

In 1965 came a coupé version with small back seats. The clever bit was an opening rear hatch, considerably pre-dating the hatchback boom. The MGB GT's back seats weren't very useful, but there was plenty of room for the dog and the shopping. Practicality meant excellent sales.

By the 1970s, the B was long in the tooth, and MG were back to selling simple outdated cars to those who could not embrace modernity. In 1974, the disastrous decision was made to fit all MGBs with the US spec 5mph impact bumpers. The MGB became a bit of a joke – in fact, with hindsight, the rubber bumper cars drive almost identically to earlier cars, but they do look awful.

Management indifference and incompetence meant that no successor to the B was developed, and, with complete inevitability, the MG factory closed in 1980.

There had been interesting variations on the MGB theme, but none were properly developed or marketed. The MGC of 1967 was powered by a modernised version of the 3.0-litre Healey's engine. Unfortunately, it was underpowered, and the great weight of the engine ruined the B's tidy handling. The MGB GT V8 of 1973 was much better. The lightweight Rover V8 meant 125mph and 0 to 60 in just 8 seconds, but only 2,591 of these misunderstood coupés were made.

It's no road burner, but as a sports car to live with, the B still takes some beating.

Specifications

Production dates	1962-1980
Manufactured units	365,000 (MGB); 150,000 (MGB GT)
Engine type	4-cylinder push rod OHV
Engine size	1,798cc
Maximum power	95bhp
Transmission	4-speed sychromesh, optional overdrive, optional automatic – avoid!
Top speed	105mph
0-60 mph time	12.1 seconds
Country of origin	UK

ARENA

With excellent performance and a V8 rumble, the MGB GT V8 was the best of all the Bs. It was never built as a roadster, and poor management prevented it from achieving its potential.

V8

Record sales plus record victories made the Mk I 'Tina an all-time classic

In the early 1960s, the choice of mid-range cars made in Britain was grim. Ford's Consul Classic was plain ugly, and sales were slow, but the Cortina of 1962 was as right as the Classic was wrong.

The name came from the 1956 Winter Olympics venue, Cortina di Ampezzo, in the Italian Dolomites. It was initially to be called 'Caprino', but this was shelved when it became apparent that in Italian this meant 'goat dung'!

Ford Cortina

There was nothing revolutionary about the car, as all of its mechanical parts came from other Fords, but the sum of its parts was greater, and the crisp-looking 'Tina was just what the British family man wanted – and at £639, he could afford it.

There soon came a 1500 to add to the 1200, with the option of two or four doors, or an estate. The product planners knew what people wanted, and in 1963 came the GT. This was the first sporty British Ford, and was the start of a dynasty that continues to this day. With 78bhp, it was capable of reaching 90mph, and with lower suspension and wider wheels it was every boy racer's dream – or it would have been, if the Lotus Cortina hadn't come along.

'Race on Sunday, sell on Monday', was an ethos never better expressed than in the Lotus Cortina. Colin Chapman's company developed a twin-cam version of Ford's 1500 engine for its Elan, and this was to power the new car. There was much modified running gear, including a rear suspension that often fell apart, but such things were easily overlooked: after all, the car was a sensation on the track. Driven by masters such as world champion Jim Clark, it seemed to have at least one wheel off the ground on every corner. All but unbeatable then, it remains so today in historic saloon-car racing. The Lotus cost twice the price of a basic 1200 when new, but you'd have to pay a lot more for one now.

In 1966 came the Mk II Cortina, and the final Mk V 'Tina finally bowed out in 1982, being replaced by the Sierra.

The Cortina was the UK's best-selling car for two decades, and continues to occupy a unique place in British popular culture.

Specifications

Production dates	1962-1966
Manufactured units	1,013,391
Engine type	4-cylinder, twin cam (Lotus)
Engine size	1,198cc; 1,498cc; 1,558cc (Lotus)
Maximum power	1,200 50bhp; 1,500 61.5bhp; 78bhp (GT); 105bhp (Lotus)
Transmission	4-speed manual with automatic option
Top speed	78mph-107mph
0-60 mph time	8 seconds (Lotus)
Country of origin	UK

JTW 498C

The Lotus Cortina was a giant killer in its day, its glory on the track reflected in the imagination of every salesman who drove a 1200 Deluxe.

For some, too much is never enough. The Cobra is the car for them

AC (which stands for Autocarriers), had been building cars in Thames Ditton, south of London, since 1904. After WW2, they resumed production by putting the six-cylinder engine they had been making since 1921 into a rather ungainly saloon. Things improved when they adopted a design by John Tojeiro, based rather closely on the contemporary Ferrari Barcetta. This was the AC Ace of 1954, and as well as fitting their own engine, AC also used Bristol and Ford units later on. The Ace, particularly with Bristol power, was quick, good looking, and handled a treat.

In 1961, Bristol stopped making their engine, preferring to utilise the easy power of an American V8, and AC soon followed suit.

Texan racing driver Carroll Shelby fitted a Ford V8 to an Ace, and the rest, as they say, is history. Starting with a 4.2-litre, it was soon the 4.7, or 289 cubic inch, that was used. The old chassis coped manfully with twice the power it was designed for.

Even the 350bhp that the 289 could be persuaded to push out wasn't enough, and Shelby set about squeezing in the 7.0-litre 427 big block. This time, some big changes were needed to give the chassis a fighting chance. The antiquated transverse leaf springs were gone in favour of wishbones and coils. The chassis tubes were also enlarged.

The 289 was an animal, but the 427 was a monster. To accommodate much fatter rubber, the wheel arches were widened, giving the appearance of a body builder's biceps. No car has ever looked tougher, or had more muscle to back it up. If the 425bhp of the standard 427 wasn't quite enough, you could order up a 485. 'Motor' magazine tested such a car, accelerating to 100mph in a phenomenal 10.1 seconds!

There was success on the track, as one might expect, and there were several beautiful Daytona coupés built just for racing.

No car has been as copied as the 427 Cobra, its brutish good looks making it irresistible to kit car builders. And yet, opinions divulge wildly. There are those who say that the Cobra's chassis could never really cope, making the handling twitchy and difficult. Amongst the acolytes there are also those who say it's the most overrated car in history. Unfortunately, few of us will ever have the chance to find out.

Specifications

Production dates	1962-1969
Manufactured units	560 (289); 510 (427)
Engine type	V8 puhrod OHV
Engine size	4,727cc (289); 6,997cc (427)
Maximum power	270bhp-485bhp
Transmission	4-speed manual
Top speed	160mph
0-60 mph time	4.6 seconds (427)
Country of origin	UK, engine USA

GTM 777F

If imitation really is the sincerest form of flattery, then the Cobra should be the greatest car of all time. Fibreglass kit car replicas have made the shape familiar, but it's still a fabulous-looking car.

The Avanti was a heroic failure, but one that refused to just lie down and die

Studebaker had been around for a long time – in fact, longer than any other auto maker, as the brothers Studebaker first built covered wagons back in 1852! Fifty years later, they started on cars – but only electric ones. They didn't get around to a petrol car until 1911.

Like most independent car makers, they usually had a hard time. Poor management in the 1920s and 1930s, followed by the Depression, meant receivership in 1933 and the suicide of Studebaker's president. The vice president was a better businessman, and with help he nursed the company back to health.

In 1938, we saw the first alliance with the creator of the Coke bottle, brilliant industrial designer Raymond Loewy. He was to be involved in all of Studebaker's finest moments – and, as a result, 1939 was a record year.

Loewy Studios styled the whole post-war range, and they looked so good that 1950 was another record year. The cars were great, but fighting the Big Three was always going to be a losing battle.

In 1953, Loewy's legendary Starlight coupé was born, which became the Hawk. It was a fabulous car, but circumstances were against it, and 1956 saw the unfortunate end of the Loewy Studio contract with the company.

By the early 1960s, sales were in the doldrums. Loewy was invited back to create an exotic sports car and revitalise the old company's image, and the result was the Avanti, with styling more innovative than any US car since the Cord. Nothing looked like the Avanti, and although it had never been near a wind tunnel, the sloping front and high tail meant that it was exceptionally slippery. It was powered by the Studebaker 289 cubic inch V8. It gave 240bhp, but it was possible to order a supercharger providing 290bhp.

They took a modified car to Bonneville and broke a hatful of records, including running 170.78mph in the flying mile. Unfortunately, problems in making the Avanti's fibreglass body held up its release – deposits were withdrawn and people bought Corvettes. Only a small number were sold before the company moved from its famous South Bend Indiana factory to Ontario and by 1966 Studebaker was no more.

The Avanti was just too good to die, however, and was taken back into successful production as the Avanti II. The new company was run by enthusiasts, and although it has changed hands a few times, you can still buy a brand new Avanti today.

Specifications

Production dates	1963-1964
Manufactured units	4,643
Engine type	V8, optional supercharger
Engine size	4,733cc
Maximum power	240bhp-290bhp
Transmission	3-speed
Top speed	120mph
0-60 mph time	7.9 seconds
Country of origin	US

Avanti

'...with styling more innovative than any US car since the Cord.'

Chevrolet Corvette Stingray

The Stingray was a piece of automotive sculpture – with a V8!

America's first sports car debuted in 1953. It was innovative in being the first mass-produced car with a fibreglass body. Unfortunately, the oily bits were less inspired, with the old-fashioned, 'Stovebolt' six engine, and two-speed powerglide transmission. It was slow, and so were sales. It nearly expired in 1955, but then along came the excellent new Small Block V8, and suddenly it was a real sports car.

For 1956 came a smart restyle, and in 1957 a four-speed gearbox and the option of fuel injection. Only 240 'Fuelies' were bought, but they could hit 60mph in 5.7 seconds. In 1958 there was another restyle, creating more weight, but more power too. In 1961, the rear end got a makeover, giving a subtle hint of what was to come.

The fabled Harley Earl had retired as head of GM's Art and Colour section, and Bill Mitchell's era had begun. The 1961 took its back end from a Mitchell styling exercise called the 'Stingray'.

For 1963 there was the first all-new Corvette since 1953 – the Stingray. Mitchell and his team had taken full advantage of the opportunities offered by fibreglass construction to sculpt a truly beautiful body. Design cues were all from the amazing Stingray concept car, while the roadster was now joined by an even more stunning coupé. This dramatic shape had the doors cut into the roof, and the 1963 models had a divided rear screen. These cars are highly sought after.

Under the plastic skin was a new chassis, and a first on a US production car – independent rear suspension. Engines were all 327 cubic inch V8s, with up to 360bhp available.

From the headlights hidden in its pointy nose, to its delicate rear quarter bumpers, it was a hit. Production doubled on the previous year, with around 20,000 cars sold.

Looks were too good to change, and there were only detailed differences year to year. Power went up and up, with a 427 big block for 1966. The ultimate was the L88, with wild 12.5:1 compression ratio and 560bhp, but only 20 were built. Thankfully, disc brakes were now an option.

There was plenty of success on the track, spawning the ferocious Grand Sport racing car, but a US industry-wide ban on racing meant that only five got built.

In 1968 a new Corvette was born, and although handsome, it lacked the unique visual magic of the Stingray.

Specifications

Production dates	1963 - 1967
Numbers made	117,964
Engine type	V8 pushrod OHV
Engine size	5358 cc/6997 cc
Maximum power	250 bhp to 560 bhp
Transmission	4 speed, optional automatic
Top speed	140 mph - 427
0-60 mph time	4.9 seconds - 427
Country of origin	USA

So often first is best, and many would say that about the Stingray. The split rear window on the early coupé may have had a cool reception when new but, today, these cars are a collector's dream.

Was there ever such a showroom sensation as the '64 Mustang?

Ford Mustang

Ford had been badly burnt by their first experiment with market research. There hadn't really been anything wrong with the Edsel, but the ripples from its belly flop in the market would take some time to die down. Ford's second dalliance with market research, however, was significantly more successful.

Ever since the Thunderbird had become a fat four-seater there had been pressure to build something sporty again. The ambitious and able Lee Iacocca had become Ford vice president at the age of 36 in 1960. With the success of the Corvette and imported British sports cars, he saw the opportunity for Ford.

The first result of his commitment to a new kind of Ford was the Mustang I. It was an impractical, mid-engined concept car, but the public loved it. It didn't take long for the idea to develop into the production Mustang.

Mustang hit the showrooms on April 17th 1964, and it caused a stampede. Demand was beyond the wildest predictions. In fact, demand exceeded supply by 15 to 1. The Mustang became the fastest-selling car in history. Before August 1965, 680,989 had been sold, and the million mark was soon passed.

Ford never called it a 'sports car': the term was 'personal car', and every opportunity was given to buyers to personalise their Mustang. There was a six and a V8, a hard top and a convertible. These were soon followed by a 2+2 fastback. The options list was huge, and Mustangs could be completely different cars depending on which boxes were ticked at the sale.

The 260 V8 (4,260cc) was soon replaced by the 289 (4,735cc). Bigger and bigger V8s were optioned, including the powerful 390bhp 428 (7,013cc) in 1968.

The most famous Mustangs were built by Carroll Shelby, creator of the Cobra. His package of modifications brought the 289 up to 306bhp in the Shelby GT-350. Usually white with blue stripes, they are a performance icon. All had four-speed manuals except the 936 cars ordered by Hertz. Many cars got rented on Friday, only to be returned after a weekend on the track.

There were styling changes, but the car remained largely unspoilt until 1969. The new Mustang for 1969 was bigger, heavier and uglier. The glory days were over.

The Mustang spawned a whole new genre and many imitators, but the 1964 to 1969 Mustangs will always be the genuine 'Ponycars'.

Specifications

Production dates	1964-1969
Manufactured units	2,078,082
Engine type	Straight 6 / V8
Engine size	2,785cc-7,013cc
Maximum power	271bhp (HiPo 289 4735cc)
Transmission	3- or 4-speed manual, optional overdrive / automatic
Top speed	142mph (HiPo 289)
0-60 mph time	6 seconds (HiPo 289)
Country of origin	USA

G.T.350
MAXIMA RADIAL

Never has a car left the showroom floor as quickly as the '64 Mustang. It was the fastest-selling car in history, and it's not hard to see why.

Big engine, little car. Simple enough, but with the Tempest GTO, the muscle car was born

In the late 1950s, Pontiac had built itself an image based on performance and competition. NASCAR domination worked wonders, but then came the Detroit-wide 'no racing' edict. A new way to preserve the youthful brand image was needed.

For 1964, there was the all-new Tempest compact. It was ad man Jim Wangers who dreamed up the idea of shoe-horning the big 389 V8 into the more usually six pot motivated little Tempest.

Pontiac GTO

It broke all the industry rules about power to weight ratios and had to be put together in secret. When presented to the board, they said it would never sell, but the word was out and dealer orders were already rolling in. Reluctantly, the authorities gave the green light, although it was not to be a model in itself, but simply an option – down around 320 on the list.

Pontiac quite deliberately raised a digit to the whole sports-car world by stealing the name from Ferrari. GTO stood for 'gran turismo omologato', and the 250 GTO was Ferrari's most illustrious sports racer. In typically American fashion, the Tempest GTO was soon affectionately dubbed the 'Goat'. In a straight line, the $3,800 Goat would outrun the $20,000 Ferrari with ease. Corners would have been a different matter. So would braking, as there wasn't even an option of disc brakes. But at that price, who was complaining?

The GTO Pontiac almost single-handedly invented the muscle car. It was the simple hot-rodding practice of dropping the biggest V8 into the smallest compact sedans and convertibles.

The car that would never sell became the company's fastest-selling new model ever.

Acceleration was sensational. With a single carb, the GTO could hit 60 in 6.9 seconds. With the 'Tri-Power' three-carb setup it was 5.7, hitting 104 in the quarter mile at 14.1 seconds. Nobody much bothered with recording top speeds.

For 1965 there was a restyle, then another for 1966. The 1966 GTO was larger but very good looking, and was now a series all on its own. Jan and Dean sang about it, and its image received another boost when a customised version became the Monkeemobile. The Monkees all got GTOs, and Mike Nesmith was caught speeding on the Hollywood Freeway at 125mph – priceless publicity for Pontiac!

The GTO was a completely different car for 1968 – another great one, certainly, but that's a different story altogether.

Specifications

Production dates	1964-1967
Manufactured units	286,470
Engine type	V8
Engine size	6,374cc (389 cubic inch)
Maximum power	360bhp
Transmission	3- or 4-speed manual, or 3-speed Hydra-Matic
Top speed	Approx 130mph
0-60 mph time	6.9 seconds
Country of origin	USA

GTO

Porsche 911

Few would argue against the 911 being the greatest, and the most enduring, sports car ever

The Porsche 911 is a car that shouldn't work. Hanging the engine out the back might be okay in a 35bhp Beetle, but physics says it isn't going to work in a sports car.

In 1948, Ferdinand Porsche's son, Ferry, looked to his father's creation, the VW, as the basis for a sports car – the first production Porsche was the 356 of 1950. It started out with a tiny 1,100cc engine, but from the very start the Porsche identity was set.

The 356 got bigger and better engines, and the upturned bathtub styling was refined. Porsche didn't bother with advertising and just went racing instead. The number of wins was unparalleled and, where the cars were too small for overall victory, class wins became the norm, starting with Le Mans in 1951. Unfortunately Dr Ferdinand Porsche had died of a stroke in January of that year.

When the time came to replace the 356, the job of styling went to the third Porsche generation – 'Butzi', in fact another Ferdinand. The new car broke with its Beetle roots through having six cylinders. However, it was still air-cooled, rear-engined, and very recognisably of the breed.

Starting as a 2.0-litre, it graduated to a 2.2, 2.4 and 2.7 in the ultimate RS models of 1973. Later engines carried on getting bigger. There was a basic T, fuel injected E, and the S was the quickest.

Engineering and design had overcome physics, and the 911 is held as a paragon of balance and handling. Having said that, it has always demanded a certain committed style of driving, and lifting off in a bend is ill-advised.

The 911 carried on winning like the 356, with dominance in everything from rallying to endurance racing. By now Porsche were building pure racing cars, no longer developed from the road cars, and these were all but unbeatable at Le Mans and in World Sports Car events. The 911 metamorphosed for the track into the mighty 935, which dominated its class to the point of tedium.

The ultimate early 911 was the 2.7RS of 1972/1973; 210bhp might not sound that impressive, but the RS encapsulated every fine sports-car quality in concentrated form. Fast and raw, with the sharpest steering and perfect balance, the RS has become something of a Porsche holy grail.

Specifications

Production dates	1964-present
Manufactured units	78,872 to 1973
Engine type	Flat 6, air-cooled, rear-mounted
Engine size	1,991cc; 2,195cc; 2,341cc; 2,687cc
Maximum power	210bhp (2.7RS)
Transmission	5-speed manual or 4-speed Sportmatic
Top speed	153mph (2.7RS)
0-60 mph time	5.5 seconds
Country of origin	Germany

Carrera

'Engineering and design had overcome physics, and the 911 is held as a paragon of balance and handling.'

Alfa Romeo Duetto

No car has quite embodied 'la dolce vita' like the little Alfa Spider

Before WW2 Alfa Romeo's road cars were exotic, exclusive, and only for the super rich. The economic realities of post-war Italy meant that another sort of car was needed.

Pre-war racing success continued and Alfa proved unbeatable in the first two years of Formula 1. Its 158 and 159 Alfetta cars took the World Championship in 1950 and 1951; Alfa then bowed out of top-line racing to concentrate on its road cars.

The first mass-produced Alfa was the 1900 of 1950. It was a rather dull-looking saloon, but had a powerful twin-cam engine. In 1955 it was replaced by the smaller, sharper Giulietta, a range of cars of which each model was to be based on the same mechanicals. These cars were very advanced for 1955, with twin overhead cam all-alloy engines, five-speed gearboxes and clever, lightweight monocoque bodies. The engines, in modified form, were to last over 40 years.

First to surface was the Giulietta Sprint. It was an achingly pretty coupé designed by Bertone, and even though it was only a 1,300cc it could crack 100mph. There was also a saloon, and in the summer of 1955 came the Giulietta Spider. The open car had a different look to the coupé because it was designed by another of Italy's great studios: Pininfarina. Just as lovely as the Sprint, it was a very sophisticated little car, and Alfa Romeo sold all that it could make. In 1962 it got a 1,570cc engine and became the Giulia Spider.

For 1966 the Giulia Spider was given a completely new look, once again by Pininfarina. At the time, the jury was out on the new styling, some thinking it lacked the finesse of the old shape, some saying it wasn't modern enough. As the most popular and enduring of all Alfas, it now seems hard to believe.

Released without a name, a competition was held and 'Duetto' was the winner. Unfortunately it was also the name of a well-known snack, so it only lasted a year. The car lasted rather longer. With a sharply cut-off tail that arrived in 1967, the Spider carried on well into the 1980s.

The Duetto will forever be associated with the carefree 1960s, as lovestruck Dustin Hoffman's car in 'The Graduate'. You just can't see one without hearing Simon and Garfunkel.

Specifications

Production dates	1966-1967
Manufactured units	6,325
Engine type	4-cylinder twin overhead cams
Engine size	1,570cc
Maximum power	109bhp
Transmission	5-speed synchromesh
Top speed	111mph
0-60 mph time	11.3 seconds
Country of origin	Italy

'The Duetto will forever be associated with the carefree 1960s, as lovestruck Dustin Hoffman's car in "The Graduate."'

Lamborghini Miura

Ferruccio's Miura set the standard for supercars, and remains the most beautiful in perpetuity

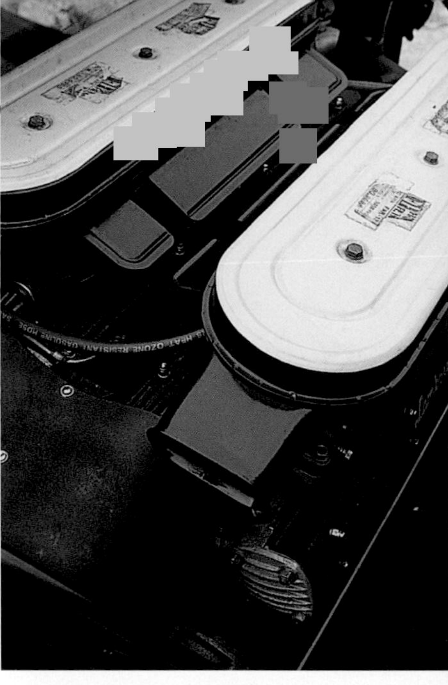

In 1961 there was something of a walkout at Ferrari. Enzo was infamous for his conservatism. He had, for instance, resisted using British-invented disc brakes to the point where his cars looked ridiculous. Frustration at their inability to realise their ideas led to the departure of six of 'Il Comendatore's' top designers and engineers.

There were unhappy customers as well. One was Ferruccio Lamborghini. Producing tractors and air-conditioning systems had made him wealthy, and now he decided to beat Enzo at his own game. Ford were to do just that on the race track, but Lamborghini was only interested in building a better road car.

Giotto Bizzarrini, who had designed the immortal Ferrari 250 GTO, designed a fabulous new engine for Lamborghini. Ferrari used a single cam per bank of their V12; his V12 would have two. This wonderful four-cam engine powered the first Lamborghini, the 350GT, which was unveiled in 1963. It was technically what Bizzarrini had wanted the GTO to be, but the styling was a little dubious and sales were disappointing. A similar 400GT followed, but it was in 1966 that Ferruccio staked a genuine claim on immortality.

His engineers still wanted to go racing. The mid-engined layout was now ubiquitous on the track, but the length of the V12 engine was a problem. Dallara and the other Ferrari renegades came up with the brilliant idea of placing the engine transversely, across the car behind the driver. Ferruccio said, 'Great, but we're not going racing – make it a road car'.

Design house Bertone were keen to come on board, as rivals Pininfarina were cosy with Ferrari. The young and ambitious Macello Gandini was given the job and penned the most flowing and sensuous lines that would ever be seen on a mid-engined car.

The Miura P400 took the 1966 Geneva Motor Show by storm. It was a technical marvel, with the engine block, gearbox, and final drive all made in one complex casting. It performed as good as it looked, completely rewriting the sports-car rules.

There followed a more powerful S model, and the ultimate SV in 1971, capable of over 170mph. In 1974 the Countach took over. It was shocking and sensational, but it wasn't beautiful.

What a shame that the nearest most of us will come to driving a Miura is watching the opening sequence of 'The Italian Job'.

Specifications

Production dates	1966-1972
Manufactured units	765
Engine type	V12 4-cam, transverse rear-mounted
Engine size	3,929cc
Maximum power	350bhp (SV 385bhp)
Transmission	5-speed in unit with engine
Top speed	171mph
0-60 mph time	5.5 seconds
Country of origin	Italy

Lamborghini
Miura
ZA
805 GY

The muscle car's flowering was short but vibrant; the R/T Hemi Charger was brightest of them all

Dodge Charger

In the US in the 1950s, horsepower became a seriously marketable commodity. Chevrolet took the top sales spot in 1955 because of its new 'Small Block' V8 and even unlikely manufacturers, such as Rambler, got in on the horsepower race.

Things really got serious in 1964 with Pontiac's GTO. Until then big engines were for big cars and small engines were for small cars; GTO turned that on its head. Petrol was cheap, octane was high, and the likes of Ralph Nader were yet to climb on their environmental and safety bandwagons.

In 1966 the Dodge Charger was born. It was built, 'to bite deep into the Pontiac GTO belt'. The Charger was based on the mid-sized Coronet, but with a distinctive fastback roof line and hidden headlights. The standard engine was the 318 cubic inch V8, but there were options. Top of the list came the fabled 'Hemi'. Developed by Chrysler in the mid-1950s, and named after its hemispherical combustion chambers, the Hemi had taken on almost mythical status. Bolted into the Charger it would get you to 60mph in 5.3 seconds. Perhaps a little too quick for most customers – only 468 of the 37,344 '66 Chargers were 426 Hemis.

In 1967, the 440 cubic inch engine became available. Bigger but simpler and cheaper, it made 'only' 375bhp against the Hemi's advertised 425bhp (really closer to 500bhp).

In 1968 the second-generation Charger was created – a shape known to those who watched 'The Dukes of Hazzard'. More memorably, it was the bad guys' car in the greatest car chase ever filmed, seen pursued by Steve McQueen's Boss Mustang in 'Bullitt'.

The sleek new shape could now be seen wearing an R/T badge if a 440 or a 426 cubic inch engine was lurking under the hood. The Hemi was still too rich for most – only 475 '68s got sold.

The Charger didn't do as well in NASCAR as had been hoped, so for 1969 a homologation special was made with an outrageous aerodynamic package. A wing towered feet above the trunk and the nose was long and tapering. Less obviously the rear window was different, to make it work better at the 200mph that stock cars were reaching.

For 1971 the Charger got an ugly restyle, and very soon the muscle-car breed was legislated out of existence.

Specifications

Production dates	1966-1970
Manufactured units	238,936
Engine type	V8
Engine size	6,980cc (Hemi); 7,210cc (440 Magnum)
Maximum power	425bhp (Hemi); 375bhp (440 Magnum)
Transmission	4-speed or Torqueflite automatic
Top speed	Approx 140mph
0-60 mph time	5.3 seconds
Country of origin	USA

3 VVO
GR60-14

DAYTON

'...for 1969 a homologation special was made with an outrageous aerodynamic package. A wing towered feet above the trunk and the nose was long and tapering.'

The world's first high-speed estate makes the perfect classic... but nobody's noticed

Scimitar GTE

The reliant Scimitar GTE was innovative, had high profile royal patronage, and it makes a fast, stylish, and remarkably practical classic. The fact that it is the most undervalued classic on the market probably has much more to do with Reliant's other products than it does with this model itself.

Reliant made three-wheelers. Horrid, dangerous, uncomfortable, ugly things that were made simply because a loophole in the law allowed you to drive one on a UK motorcycle license. Del Boy from the British TV sit-com 'Only Fools and Horses' drove one. If only they had called the four-wheelers 'Scimitar' and dropped 'Reliant'.

The nasty three-wheelers were constructed from fibreglass and, due to their expertise with the new material, Reliant helped develop a car for the Israelis. The first car was a version of this called the Sabre. Although horrid and slow, with a restyle and a six-cylinder Ford engine, it was better, even if rather old-fashioned, cramped, and expensive.

Ogle Design had built a show car on the Daimler SP250 sports-car chassis; although Daimler didn't want it, Reliant did. It was mated to a revised Sabre 6 chassis, and when it appeared in 1965 Reliant had a beautiful car on their hands. Christened the Scimitar, it was a 2+2 coupé. Ford's new 3.0-litre V6 of 1966 made it even better. There were some rough edges due to Reliant's lack of experience in building expensive cars, but the Coupé was a rather nice car.

Sales were hampered by the lack of proper rear seats, and Ogle were asked to come up with an answer. There had been a Triplex Glass show car with a glass estate rear grafted onto the coupé. This proved the inspiration for a whole new kind of car.

In 1968 the GTE was unveiled. It shared its running gear with the Coupé, but the chassis was new, as was the fibreglass body. The styling, however, was still plainly related. There were four proper seats and a glass hatchback, and yet it was still most certainly a sports car – and an elegant one at that.

Princess Anne was a loyal and vocal supporter of the marque, owning several examples. The GTE sold well, and with 1975 came a redesign. Although a bigger, less attractive car, it still sold. Unfortunately there was never the investment to develop a successor and in 1986 the GTE died.

Specifications

Production dates	1968-1986
Manufactured units	14,273
Engine type	V6
Engine size	2,994cc
Maximum power	138bhp
Transmission	4-speed optional overdrive; automatic
Top speed	121mph
0-60 mph time	9.3 seconds
Country of origin	UK

SCIMITAR
TBB 32M

As the British dropped the sports car baton, the Japanese picked it up, and the 240Z became the best-selling sports car of all time

Datsun 240Z

The Americans loved the sports cars that came from across the Atlantic. The trouble was that by the late 1960s the British sports car was on its knees. A chronic lack of vision and investment meant that the old favourites were all well past their sell-by date and emerging emissions legislation was about to finish off the last of the dinosaurs.

In the whole of the first decade after WW2 the Japanese motor industry exported a grand total of 22 cars. Another decade later and the situation was very different, although there was still a huge resistance to the eastern product. Cheap and tinny was the perception, but with the Japanese about to annihilate the British bike industry simply through offering far superior machines, respect for Japanese engineering was growing.

Following the release of the MGB in 1962, Datsun started making a very similar-looking car, the Fairlady SP310. It was soon sending 3,500 units a year to the States. With rumours of a six-cylinder Toyota sports car, Datsun decided to retaliate.

The Japanese were still happy to copy the best, and the engine they had put together for their saloons was uncannily similar to Mercedes' six-cylinder unit. With suitable running gear from the Bluebird, they were now in search of a body. It was to be no larger than a Porsche 911, and concern over increasingly paranoid US safety legislation meant that an open car was ruled out.

There is much discussion over who actually styled the car. The Austrian count, Albrecht Goertz, certainly had a lot to do with it. The car took its cues from all the best sources: there was a good deal of E-Type, some 911, and maybe some Aston in there. The resulting 240Z was unoriginal, but very pleasing.

The engineering was equally conventional, but again, it came from the best sources. Many compared the driving experience to the recently deceased, and much missed, Austin Healey 3000.

The 240Z not only took over from where the Healey stopped – it took over and took off. The Americans loved it so much that the 240Z and its successors became the best-selling sports cars in history. In 1973, the 240Z was replaced by the similar 260Z, but from there on the Z cars got bigger and softer. First is still best.

Specifications

Production dates	1969-1973
Manufactured units	172,767
Engine type	Straight 6
Engine size	2,393cc
Maximum power	151bhp
Transmission	4-speed or automatic (USA); 5-speed only (Europe)
Top speed	125mph
0-60 mph time	8.0 seconds
Country of origin	Japan

240Z
DATSUN

BMW 3.0 CSL

A fabulous road car, the 'Batmobile' was to make the European Touring Car Championship its own

Although having been around since 1916, BMW's first car of 1928 was the Dixi – a humble Austin Seven built under licence. The manufacturer's engineering advanced rapidly, and by the late 1930s it was building some very advanced cars.

The division of Germany following WW2 left the factory in the east, so a new factory was built in Munich. BMW struggled through the 1950s making unwieldy, large saloons, together with the odd sports car that lost them yet more money. Only building the Isetta bubble car kept them afloat.

It was the 'Neue Klasse' 1500 of 1961 that was to set the future direction for the company. There was a single overhead camshaft engine and independent suspension all round. It was a sharply styled, thoroughly modern car, and it sold. In 1966 came the 1602, soon joined by the 2002 – the small saloons that were to establish BMW as a volume manufacturer.

A 2.0-litre coupé appeared in 1966; initially odd-looking, it became a beauty in 1968 with a new nose and a six-cylinder engine. In 1971, the 2800CS became the 3.0CS, with fuel injection available on the CSi, offering 200bhp and 130mph. It was a great road car... but BMW wanted to go racing.

Ford were having it all their own way in European Touring Car Racing with the Capri – BMW wanted to beat them. Tuners such as Alpina had been competing in the 3.0CSi with some success, but the cars were too heavy to really bother the Capris. So in 1972, BMW built the CSL, a homologation special, to give the racers the parts they needed. These included alloy body panels, minimal trim, and a reduction in weight wherever it could be made. Engines were 3,003cc, and later 3,153cc. Most striking were the aerodynamic modifications. There was a deep front air dam, and odd little 'fences' on the tops of the wings. But what everybody remembers is the rear wing. This enormous device provided enough downforce to stop the cars getting loose at the back at high speed. It also gave the CSL its nickname of 'The Batmobile'.

In 1973, the CSL was victorious in Touring Cars. Ford were back for 1974, but the Batmobile ruled from 1975 all the way to 1979 – that's a record six times, and it still stands.

Specifications

Production dates	1972-1975
Manufactured units	1,039
Engine type	Straight 6-single overhead cam
Engine size	3,303; 3,153cc
Maximum power	206bhp (400+ for racing)
Transmission	4-speed
Top speed	137mph
0-60 mph time	7.4 seconds
Country of origin	Germany

BMW ALPINA
53
BMW ALF
53
Castrol

3.0 CSL

The BMW 3.0 CSL road car – the everyday version of the 'Batmobile' that took Touring Cars Racing by storm.

MERCEDES
BENZ

SUPERCARS

Mercedes 300SL Gullwing (1954–1957)

This is not a true supercar, but it is one that showed the way forward because of its incredible technology and performance; the 3-litre engine, producing 240bhp, could make the sprint from 0-60 in 8.8secs and hit a top speed of 145mph.

Innovations in technology saw the 300SL become the first ever production car to have fuel injection, and the car featured a space-frame chassis which, because of the chassis running down either side of the car, meant the 300SL had to have those now-famous gullwing doors. Furthermore, the 300SL also happens to be one of the most beautiful cars ever made – very much a supercar then.

Specifications:

Engine	2996cc
Max power	240bhp at 6,100rpm
Max torque	217lb ft at 4,800rpm
0-60mph	8.8secs
Top speed	135mph +

Ford GT40 MkIII (1967)

Ford's race car version of the GT40 humiliated Ferrari at Le Mans in the latter half of the 1960s (see page 60). It also spawned a road-going version in 1967 that was panned by critics for its sloppy road manners. But real drivers didn't care about its manners, because the GT40 MkIII could see off its competitors in a straight line with the 306bhp produced by its 4.7-litre V8 engine – and boasted 0-60 in 5.5secs. Its top speed of 170mph also hinted at what the future held for true super-cars. Only seven GT40s (MkIII) were ever built.

Specifications:

Engine	4736cc
Max power	306bhp at 6,000rpm
Max torque	229lb ft at 4,200rpm
0-60mph	5.5secs
Top speed	170mph

Lamborghini Muira (1966–1972)

Unveiled to a stunned audience at the Geneva Motor Show, Switzerland, in 1966, the Muira is what many believe to be the planet's first true supercar, partly because its mid-mounted engine was a world first. Just as importantly, the engine's placement had a direct effect on the car's appearance – and those looks are still stunning. The greatest version of Muira is the SV produced at the beginning of the 1970s, which saw the original's 350bhp increased to 385bhp. The only problem with the Muira is that the front end is prone to lift at high speeds because of the engine layout – so handle with care.

Lamborghini Muira SV specifications (1971–1972):

Engine	3929cc
Max power	385bhp at 7,850rpm
Max torque	294lb ft at 5,750rpm
0-60mph	6.0secs
Top speed	180mph

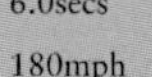

Other key cars from the 1960s: Jaguar E-Type, Ferrari 275 GTB, Ferrari 365 GTB Daytona, Corvette Sting Ray, De Tomaso Mangusta.

Lamborghini Countach 25th Anniversary (1989–1990)

Lamborghini Countach (1974–1990)

It's one of the defining shapes in car history – the prototype Countach, which was shown for the first time in 1971, was greeted with rapture by the crowds. The replacement for the Muira, the sleek, sensual lines had been supplanted with dramatic lines and a wedge shape that would come to dominate the supercar world for the next ten years. The first Lamborghini Countach to be released (the LP400) featured a 3.9-litre V12 engine that could make the sprint from 0-60 in 5.6secs. Several incarnations of the Countach, which included the celebrated 5-litre Countach QV in 1985, followed over its illustrious 17-year reign as the king of the supercars. It has to be said though that the Countach represents the ultimate old-school supercar – it offered a driving experience that had to be learned; simply getting behind the wheel and flooring it was not to be recommended. After all, you can't tame a bull.

LP400 specifications (1974–1982):

Engine	3929cc
Max power	375bhp at 8,000rpm
Max torque	268lbft at 5,000rpm
0-60mph	5.6secs
Top speed	180mph +

BMW M1 (1978–1981)

The M1 is one of the unsung heroes of the 1970s. It was BMW's first (and, so far, only) foray into creating a mid-engined supercar, and it could have worked out if the project hadn't been besieged by problems. It was intended that the M1 would be styled and built by Lamborghini, but because the raging bull was experiencing money woes, Bauer, in Germany, produced the car for BMW. More trouble was to strike – the car had been intended for the track but these plans fell through. It's a tragedy because the road-going M1 put the wind up its Italian rivals by offering the same levels of grip but pairing it with forgiving handling and bullet-proof reliability – not exactly a forte of Italian supercars at the time.

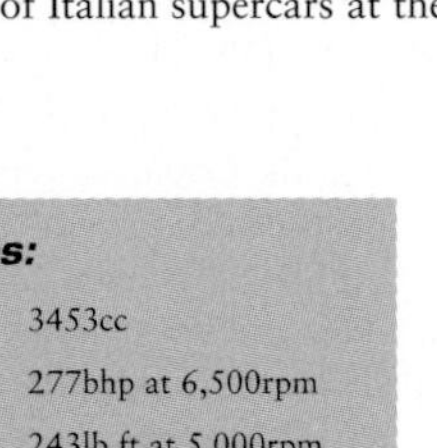

Specifications:

Engine	3453cc
Max power	277bhp at 6,500rpm
Max torque	243lb ft at 5,000rpm
0-60mph	5.6secs
Top speed	162mph

Other key cars from the 1970s: Maserati Bora, Porsche 911 2.7 RS, Porsche 911 Turbo, Aston Martin V8 Vantage.

Lotus Turbo Esprit SE (1989)

Lotus Turbo Esprit (1980–1992)

The Lotus Esprit has had a long and illustrious history dating back to when the car was first introduced in 1976. One of the most revered versions was the Turbo that first surfaced in 1980 and featured a four-cylinder aluminium engine that could produce 210bhp. The Esprit's 'credentials' were further increased thanks to a movie appearance – the Turbo was James Bond's vehicle of choice (both on the road and underwater) in The Spy Who Loved Me. Over the decades there have been numerous incarnations of the Esprit, but its production run (that spanned an incredible 28 years) came to a close on February 21st, 2004. Fans needn't worry though – Lotus are already designing its replacement.

Specifications:

Engine	2174cc
Max power	210bhp at 6,250rpm
Max torque	200lb ft at 4,500rpm
0-60mph	5.6secs
Top speed	150mph

Ferrari 288 GTO (1984–1985)

The mid-engined GTO is actually the forefather of the classic F40, but this 1980s supercar has earned its rightful place in the history books because its body was manufactured from composite materials such as carbon fibre – making it one of the very few cars to feature such race-developed technology. These lightweight materials coupled with a twin-turbo 2.8-litre V8 engine meant that the GTO was an extremely quick car with handling that was, let's just say, best exploited by the 'experienced driver'.

Specifications:

Engine	2855cc
Max power	400bhp at 7,000rpm
Max torque	466lb ft at 3,800rpm
0-60mph	4.7secs
Top speed	188mph

Ferrari Testarossa (1984–1992)

Aimed at being more of a GT than a hardcore road racer, the Testarossa ('Red Head') showed Ferrari heading in a more refined direction while retaining the astonishing speed and acceleration that all supercar owners demand. And the flat-12 engine saw to that with its 390bhp.

Specifications:

Engine	4942cc
Max power	390bhp at 6,300rpm
Max torque	354lb ft at 4,500rpm
0-60mph	5.3secs
Top speed	180mph

Porsche 959 (1987–1991)

Trust Porsche to come up with a world-class supercar – the 959 was able to hit 0-60 in under 4secs. This phenomenal acceleration was achieved with typical German efficiency using a rear-mounted twin-turbo flat-six engine that produced 450bhp. To get such power down onto the road, the 959 featured four-wheel drive paired with a six-speed gearbox, and the kind of stability needed to hit a cool 197mph.

Specifications:

Engine	2850cc
Max power	450bhp at 6,500rpm
Max torque	369lb ft at 5,000rpm
0-60mph	3.6secs
Top speed	197mph

Other key cars from the 1980s: Aston Martin Bulldog, Aston Martin Vantage Zagato, Ruf CTR Yellowbird.

Ferrari F40 (1987–1992)

Released to celebrate the company's 40th anniversary, the F40 was the last road car that the marque's creator, Enzo Ferrari, commissioned before he passed away – but what a swansong. It looked more like a racing car than a supercar and it featured a 2.9-litre V8 engine that would see a brave driver propelled to over 200mph. The car is, of course, not for the faint-hearted but its position as one of the iconic supercars of any age is indisputable.

Specifications:

Engine	2936cc
Max power	478bhp at 7,000rpm
Max torque	425lb ft at 4,000rpm
0-60mph	3.9secs
Top speed	201mph

Bugatti EB110 (1992–1995)

It was supposed to be the rebirth of the Bugatti brand and, at first, the future was looking bright for the marque. While the EB110's looks may have been controversial, the Bugatti was a true supercar with staggering performance; it featured, thanks to the chassis and four-wheel drive, a colossal amount of grip to make the most out of all that power. Two versions were available – the 'humble' GT with 553bhp and the Supersport which boasted 603bhp. But alas, the Bugatti dream imploded in 1995 when the company went bust, mainly because of the global recession.

EB110 Supersport specifications:

Engine	3500cc
Max power	603bhp at 8,250rpm
Max torque	479lb ft at 4,250rpm
0-60mph	3.1secs
Top speed	218mph

Jaguar XJ220 (1992–1994)

Quite frankly, the Jaguar supercar was something of a debacle. Back in 1988 customers were bedazzled by promises of a huge V12 engine, coupled with a four-wheel drive, when the XJ220 prototype was unveiled. Down went the deposits as (very rich) people waited for the car's arrival in 1992. The trouble was that Jaguar replaced the engine with a V6 and dumped the four-wheel drive. Some angry customers withdrew their orders and demanded their deposits back; legal wranglings ensued. Add to this a world recession, and Jaguar's supercar foundered. The sad fact is that on its release, the XJ220 was still a fantastically fast car boasting supreme handling (in the dry) – and then there were those striking looks.

Specifications

Engine	2498cc
Max power	542bhp at 6,500rpm
Max torque	472lb ft at 5,000rpm
0-60mph	3.6secs
Top speed	210mph +

McLaren F1 (1993–1997)

Until recently, the McLaren F1 was the fastest car on the planet. Its BMW 6.1-litre V12 engine produced a staggering 627bhp and could propel the car up to 240mph. And never mind the 0–60 time – the F1 could hit 100mph in just 6.3secs. The key to the McLaren's success was the fact it was created entirely from carbon fibre and built on a philosophy that demanded it be put together with absolute precision. The resulting car can seat three people – the driver in the middle with two passengers to the side and back of him. The McLaren's production came to an end when customers decided that the price tag of £635,000/US$1,000,000 was perhaps stretching even them a little too much. The McLaren would also carve out a name for itself on the track by winning the Le Mans 24-hour race in 1995. The F1 then remains the supercar that all others are judged by.

Specifications:

Engine	6064cc
Max power	627bhp at 7,400rpm
Max torque	479lb ft at 4,000rpm
0-60mph	3.2secs
Top speed	240mph

Ferrari F50 (1995–1997)

What happens when you put a Formula One engine into a production car? Well, trust Ferrari to be the ones bold enough to try it – and, of course, to get it right with the F50. The 4.7-litre V12 lump featured in the supercar was a direct descendant of the engine that nearly earned Alain Prost top honours in the 1990 F1 World Championship. Just as important to the F50's achievement as a true race car made for the road was its easy-to-access driving experience – the F50 left its forefather the F40 for dead on a twisty track, so sweet and accessible was its handling. Perhaps the car's ungainly looks and zero practicality were the only thorns in its side – but those issues apart, the F50 was yet another classic Italian stallion from the Ferrari stables.

Specifications:

Engine	4698cc
Max power	513bhp at 8,000rpm
Max torque	347lb ft at 6,500rpm
0-60mph	3.7secs
Top speed	202mph

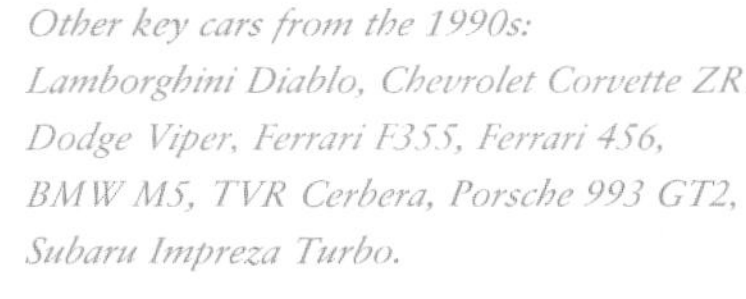

Other key cars from the 1990s: Lamborghini Diablo, Chevrolet Corvette ZR1, Dodge Viper, Ferrari F355, Ferrari 456, BMW M5, TVR Cerbera, Porsche 993 GT2, Subaru Impreza Turbo.

Aston Martin Vanquish S

The arrival of the original Vanquish and this, its more powerful brother the Vanquish S, has ushered in a new era for Britain's most iconic sports car company…

When Aston Martin unveiled the Vanquish in 2001, first impressions had to count – after all, here was a car that needed to make an impact. The Ford-owned company was coming out of the recession-ridden 1990s and needed an all-new flagship car to show the world that they were more than their classic DB7 coupe. Thanks to Ford's vision for the company and car designer maestro Ian Callum, the Vanquish hit its mark. Jaws dropped to the floor when the car was first shown – the Vanquish was that striking; that poised; that menacing; that… British.

Featuring a V12 6-litre engine pumping out 460bhp, those bold good looks were backed up with an equally impressive driving experience – supremely comfortable on long cruises while being able to kick up its heels on the twisty stuff. Any concerns about the future of Britain's premier car brand had been well and truly kicked into touch. Another key element of the Vanquish's success story was the way it was built. Ford wanted Aston Martin to become the home of new car technology – the Vanquish featured a body combining both aluminium and carbon fibre, which was lightweight enough to put itself in range of serious supercar territory.

But the car marque's crowning glory is the Vanquish S. The S came into existence to push the car further into Ferrari territory, and to appeal to the driver looking for a car that combines handcrafted tradition with the latest innovations from the world of Formula One and aerospace technology.

Debuted at the Paris Motor Show, France, in 2004, the S is the fastest production model Aston Martin has ever made. The 48-valve V12 6-litre engine now produces 520bhp over the previous Vanquish's 460bhp, and it can top 200mph. The S also features stiffer springs and dampers, plus shorter steering arms to give drivers the ultimate handling package.

As the flagship for Aston Martin, the Vanquish S is a true GT cruiser able to devour continents in style and comfort. Some nitpickers might argue that it's not a supercar in the strictest sense of the word, but with the Vanquish S's intoxicating mix of power and grace, it's the only word suitable to sum up its incredible talents.

VX04 MMJ

AM 520

'...the fastest production model Aston Martin has ever made.'

Copyright Aston Martin

From Start To Finish

It takes 396 hours for Aston Martin's engineers at the Newport Pagnall factory, in the UK, to hand-build the Vanquish S; the interior alone takes more than 70 hours to craft, and features eight hides of leather.

Nip And Tuck

Cosmetically the S has been given subtle tweaks over the original Vanquish; as well as changes to the car's nose, it has also a raised lip on the boot to aid stability and balance while reducing lift.

What Lies Beneath

The Vanquish was always intended to show off Aston Martin as a hotbed of cutting edge technology. This is perfectly reflected by the materials that make up the car – aluminium is used for the bulkheads and floor while the windshield pillars and centre tunnel are made from carbon fibre.

Something Old, Something New

Designed by car industry legend Ian Callum, the Vanquish manages to blend perfectly the old and the new into a modern and fresh look. Callum is reported to have said that it was the DB4 GT Zagato from the 1960s that fuelled his vision for the Vanquish.

Well Engineered?

For the original Vanquish launched in 2001, Aston put 50 prototypes through hellish tests across several continents to nail reliability – and managed to clock up an impressive 1,000,000 miles between them in the process.

Aston Martin Vanquish S: The Specifications

Engine	Fuel injected 48-valve V12
Valvetrain	DOHC 4 valves / cyl
Displacement	5935cc
Maximum Power	520bhp at 7,000rpm
Maximum Torque	425lb ft at 5,800rpm
Transmission	Six-speed manual with paddle shifting
0–60mph	4.7secs
0–100mph	9.8secs
Maximum Speed	200mph +
Steering	Rack and pinion with variable power assist
Brakes Front	Ventilated & grooved with six callipers/378mm/15in
Brakes Rear	Ventilated & grooved with four callipers/330mm/13in
Suspension Front	Double wishbones with monutube dampers, coil springs & anti-roll bar
Suspension Rear	Double wishbones with monutube dampers, coil springs & anti-roll bar
Kerb Weight	1875kg/4134lbs
Length	4665mm/184in
Width	1923mm/76in
Height	1318mm/52in
Wheels Front	9 x 19in
Wheel Rear	10 x 19in
Price	£174,000/US$255,000

While the Vanquish showed the world where Aston Martin's future lay, it's the DB9 that has further secured their place as one of the most desirable brands on the planet...

Any car enthusiast knows that the DB7 was an iconic British car, and one of the most beautiful in the world. The problem was that the DB7 had been around for a while and was beginning to show its age. It needed an all-new replacement – something that would put the wind up Ferrari and Porsche; while the Vanquish demonstrated that Aston had its eye firmly on the future, they still needed a lower priced car that would help the company shift 5,000 cars a year. The DB9 is that car – built at Aston Martin's all-new factory in Gaydon, UK, it is regarded as one of the greatest GTs ever built.

Aston Martin DB9

Seeing it in the flesh for the first time with its low, sleek and muscular looks is enough to make you want to sign on the dotted line there and then. Those looks can be credited to design maestro Ian Callum who handed over the baton to Henrik Fisker to complete what many argue is the most beautiful car on sale today. But the DB9's beauty isn't merely skin deep – under the exterior is a wholly new platform.

Named the VH (Vertical and Horizontal), it's constructed from aluminium, and all the major mechanical and body components have been engineered from aluminium, magnesium or lightweight composite materials. This means that with its V12 450bhp engine, the DB9 is able to propel itself at a fierce pace on the straights because of its relative lightness but also to corner confidently because of its rigidity. Most importantly, the driver never feels left out, or scared, by the DB9.

While some supercars can feel like they'll make for the nearest hedge if you show them a moment's lack of concentration, the DB9 is renowned for its user-friendliness and its approachable and exploitable driving experience. This accessibility is easily managed by either a manual six-speed gearbox or a six-speed ZF automatic with paddle shifts that, while shaving 0.2secs off the car's 0–60 time, is highly regarded for its suppleness and smoothness.

The DB9's interior is more than a match for its elegant exterior – like any supercar should, it makes you feel special but let's face it, no one does leather and wood like Aston, and the DB9 is no exception with its elegant and seductive blend of materials.

While its predecessor the DB7 will always hold a special place in the history of the supercar – and be credited as the product that was key to Aston Martin emerging from the dark old days of global recession – the DB9 has proven itself to be a worthy successor. It's a car that has made Aston Martin a true 21st century supercar creator.

Many argue that the DB9 is the most beautiful car on sale today.

DB9 V12

Punishing The Prototypes

53 DB9 prototypes were made and put through their paces to ensure that the cars could cut it in extreme climates – from the gruelling conditions of Death Valley and the Arctic Circle through to its mechanics being stretched on the Nürburgring in Germany.

Delight In The Details

The DB9's cockpit has a wealth of quality touches – the glass starter button in the centre console shimmers red when the ignition is switched on, and once the engine is turned on the button lights up blue.

VH–Very Handy

From the 'old school' DB7 to the innovative, cutting edge DB9 and beyond – just how did Aston Martin afford it? By creating the über-flexible VH (Vertical and Horizontal) platform–this unique chassis lets Aston change the length of its wheelbase so it can be used on different models (i.e. the larger DB9 or the shorter V8 Vantage).

Personalised For Perfection

Customers have a host of options to choose from when ordering their DB9 – there are 29 colours available but Aston Martin will let you choose any you want at an extra cost. As well as a multitude of different leather options, four different woods are also available for the Aston's interior – mahogany, walnut, bamboo and piano black.

Taking A Different Tach

The rev counter featured in the DB9 actually runs anti-clockwise which echoes early Aston Martins such as the Atom and DB2. You won't find a red line on the tachometer either – instead a red light appears once the maximum revs are hit. The reason is another sign of how Aston Martin has moved the game on – electronics detect when that red light should come on depending on ambient temperature, the engine's mileage and how long ago the engine was turned on.

Swan Song

The DB9's doors don't open like the average coupe's – they actually pull upwards at a 12° angle to help the driver gain easier access to the cabin.

Aston Martin DB9: The Specifications

Engine	Fuel injected 48-valve V12
Valvetrain	DOHC 4 valves / cyl
Displacement	5935cc
Maximum Power	450bhp at 6,000rpm
Maximum Torque	420lb ft at 5,000rpm
Transmission	Six-speed manual or six-speed auto
0–62mph	4.7secs (manual) 4.9secs (auto)
0–100mph	4.9secs (manual) 5.1secs (auto)
Maximum Speed	186mph
Steering	Rack and pinion with Servotronic speed-sensitive power-assist
Brakes Front	Ventilated & grooved with six callipers/355mm/14in
Brakes Rear	Ventilated & grooved with four callipers/330mm/13in
Suspension Front	Double wishbones with monutube dampers, coil springs & anti-roll bar
Suspension Rear	Double wishbones with monutube dampers, coil springs & anti-roll bar
Kerb Weight	1710kg/3770lbs (manual) 1800kg/3968lbs (auto)
Length	4710mm/185in
Width	1875mm/74in
Height	1270mm/50in
Wheels Front	8.5 x19in
Wheel Rear	9.5 x 19in
Price	£103,000/US$155,000

Aston Martin DBR9

Aston Martin has wanted to return to the international motor racing scene for decades and this is how they are doing it – with the DBR9. Based on the DB9 and featuring the same aluminium chassis, the racing car has had some major modifications to make sure it's up to the job of winning major competitions – like they did at Le Mans back in 1959.

The DBR9's engine produces 600bhp compared to the DB9's 450bhp while the suspension set-up boasts up-rated components plus a revised geometry. The car now features carbon brakes and a six-speed sequential gearbox mounted on the rear axle. The DBR9's aerodynamics have been optimised to produce the best possible performance on the track and the panels of the racer are also handmade from carbon fibre composite to ensure the car meets competition weight regulations – it now weighs in at featherweight 1,100kg/2425lbs compared to the DB9's 1710kg/3770lbs.

Aston Martin Racing is making 12 cars to compete in races across North America, Europe and the Far East, and the DBR9 has already experienced major success on its debut at the 53rd Annual 12 Hours of Sebring, Florida in March where Aston's team gleaned itself a GT1 class victory. If you fancy a slice of the action, do bear in mind that 20 of the DBR9s are also being made available to private buyers.

This is what everyone is calling the new 'baby' Aston, but it's destined to make one very big splash when it finally touches down...

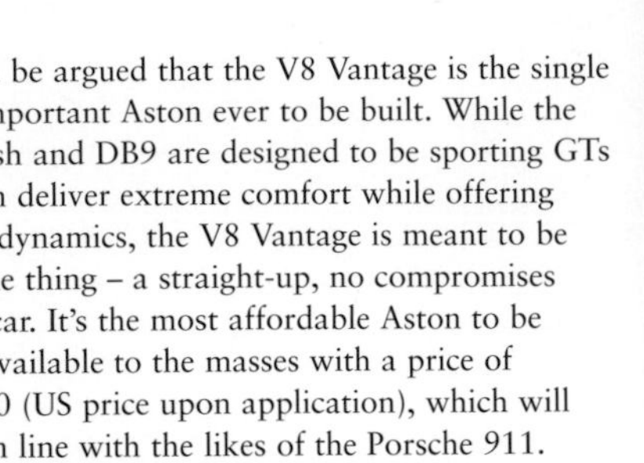

It could be argued that the V8 Vantage is the single most important Aston ever to be built. While the Vanquish and DB9 are designed to be sporting GTs that can deliver extreme comfort while offering superb dynamics, the V8 Vantage is meant to be only one thing – a straight-up, no compromises sports car. It's the most affordable Aston to be made available to the masses with a price of £74,500 (US price upon application), which will put it in line with the likes of the Porsche 911.

Aston Martin V8 Vantage

That's virgin territory for Aston Martin, but by all accounts, they are all set to hit the mark right on the bulls-eye. Using their unique aluminium VH platform, as used by the DB9 but shortened with stiffer suspension, the V8 Vantage has a howling 4.3-litre engine providing the firepower. While the V8 Vantage 'only' features a V8, it can match the V12-driven DB9 because it's lighter –giving it a 0–60 time of 4.8secs and a top speed of 175mph; the V8 Vantage owner won't feel inferior in the company of Ferrari or Lamborghini either, never mind its bigger brother.

Unsurprisingly of course, the interior of the two-seater is up to the typical Aston high standards – the alloy fascia with instrument panel features beautifully finished aluminium. But diehard wood fans won't be disappointed – like the DB9, optional mahogany, walnut or bamboo can be included.

As for the build quality, 78 prototypes have been clocking up 1,500,000 miles between them – suffering the searing temperatures of 48°C in Dubai, and enduring –30°C in Sweden. The Nürburgring, Germany, and the Nardo test track, Italy, have been used to develop and hone the V8 Vantage's handling and performance to ensure that the car delivers on its hype while not breaking down after the first quarter of a mile – in fact, one V8 Vantage was challenged with the task of racking up 5,000 miles round the Nürburgring, which it did without breaking its stride.

While it's not strictly a supercar, as is the case with all Astons, there is something about the V8 Vantage that propels it into that category – perhaps it's the perfect styling created by Henrik Fisker – that long nose, the perfect cut lines and its unquestionable presence. It's exotica defined, and put up against its competitors you have to ask yourself – which one is the more desirable? Which one has that 'X factor' which elevates it beyond mere sports car? The answer is staring you in the face...

It's perhaps telling that if this book had been written five years ago, we may have been hard pushed to feature one Aston Martin, let alone three. Perhaps the reborn Aston Martin shows that the amassed talent based in Modena, Italy, has a new direct competitor for making the ultimate exotica that boasts near-unparalleled desirability – and that new region is known as Gaydon, UK. The name will grow on you, we promise.

The Aston Martin V8 Vantage 'is exotica defined, and put up against its competitors you have to ask yourself – which one is the more desirable?

Which one has that 'X factor' which elevates it beyond mere sports car?

The answer is staring you in the face...'

Wait-y Issues...

To make sure the V8 Vantage keeps that important air of exclusivity, production of the car will be capped at 2,500 per year. Expect epic waiting lists – for the driver slapping down his deposit today, you can expect to wait until 2007 before it appears on the driveway.

Designer Departed

The good-looking V8 Vantage was designed by Henrik Fisker (who also designed the DB9). He has since departed Aston Martin and moved to California to set up an automotive design and customization company.

Weight A Minute...

The front-engined V8 Vantage has the spot-on weight distribution and offers the ideal set-up for any self-respecting sports car. The Aston's dry-sump lubrication system means that the engine can be placed lower in the body, meaning a lower centre of gravity. The result – better balance and stability.

Aston Martin V8 Vantage: The Specifications

Engine	All alloy quad overhead camshaft 32 valve V8
Valvetrain	DOHC 4 valves / cyl
Displacement	4280cc
Maximum power	380bhp at 7,000rpm
Maximum torque	302Ib ft at 5,000rpm
Transmission	Six-speed manual
0–60mph	4.8secs
Maximum speed	175mph
Steering	Rack and pinion with power assist
Brakes front	Ventilated & grooved steel discs with four- piston monobloc callipers/ 355mm/14in, ABS
Brakes rear	Ventilated & grooved steel discs with four- piston monobloc callipers/ 330mm/13in, ABS
Suspension front	Independent double aluminium wishbones with coil over aluminium monutube dampers & anti-roll bar
Suspension rear	Independent double aluminium wishbones with coil over aluminium monutube dampers & anti-roll bar
Kerb weight	1570kg/3461lbs
Length	4383mm/173in
Width	1866mm/73in
Height	1255mm/49in
Wheels front	8.5 x 18in
Wheel rear	9.5 x 18in
Price	£74,500 US price upon applicaton

When Bugatti crashed and burned in the 1990s, a small group of ex-employees decided to take their destiny into their own hands and produce a supercar...

The Edonis is unusual. Not just in the way it looks with its bizarre lines and curves; it's different because B Engineering, the company behind this supercar, isn't interested in becoming a major player that produces exotic machinery. After all, the Edonis is their first and last car. All B Engineering ever wanted the supercar to be was a showcase for cutting edge technology that represented the excellence of both the company and the region where it is built – Modena, Italy, home of the supercar.

B Engineering Edonis

The number of staff may be small but many have worked for some of the greatest supercar makers of all time – Ferrari, Lamborghini and Maserati, to name but a few. In fact, the owner of the company, Jean-Marc Borel, used to be the vice chairman of Bugatti. With such an esteemed collection of experts and engineers under one roof, it's hardly surprising that the Edonis is such a special machine.

B Engineering's links with Bugatti form the core of the Edonis–when Bugatti declared bankruptcy in 1995, 21 leftover carbon fibre tubs from the Bugatti EB110 were acquired by B Engineering to create the Edonis. At the heart of the car's hand-built aluminium body is an extreme engine, an evolution of the EB110's – a 3.7-litre V12 with twin turbochargers, plus a six-speed manual gearbox.

With such power under your right foot, it's hardly surprising that the Edonis is blisteringly quick. How the supercar handles such horse power is also a revelation; with project director, Nicola Materazzi, who is famous for the classic handling of the Ferrari, it's perhaps predictable that the Edonis should become renowned for its precision steering and abundant feel.

Equally important to the car's handling are the tyres that were designed by Michelin. Called the PAX system, the Edonis-specific tyres have shorter than normal sidewalls to aid the supercar's handling.

B Engineering set out to showcase just why the Italians are still regarded as the masters of the supercar – and in the eyes of the supercar aficionados, the Edonis has done just that. While B Engineering won't become an everyday name (or the Edonis the star of teenage males' bedroom walls all over the world), the company has added yet another layer of prestige to Modena, the home of the supercar.

Edonis

'The Edonis is B Engineering's first and last car. All the company ever wanted the car to be was a showcase for cutting edge technology'

Record Breaker

A 720bhp version of the Edonis managed to break the circuit record of the Nardo race circuit in Italy by lapping at 223mph.

Named And Famed

The word Edonis is actually the Greek word for pleasure. And only a select few will be privileged enough to experience the car – just 21 will be made. B Engineering decided to make 21 because the Edonis is the first car of the 21st century.

Keeping It In The Family

B Engineering has stayed true to its vision of creating a supercar that uses all the incredible resources of the Modena area – local body builders, casters, upholsterers, pattern makers and others were called in to produce the Edonis.

Perfect Supercar CV

The Edonis's project director, Nicola Materazzi, has a resumé that screams supercar pioneer – he was the main contractor for the likes of Bugatti, and then from 1980, he worked for Ferrari on projects such as the GTO Evoluzione and F40. He was also top dog at Ferrari's F1 research and design division.

B Engineering Edonis (720bhp version): The Specifications

Engine	Twin turbocharged V12	**0–100mph**	8.2secs	**Suspension Front**	Double wishbones with coil springs, gas dampers & anti-roll bar	**Width**	1998mm/79in
Valvetrain	DOHC, 5 valves / cyl	**Maximum Speed**	223mph	**Suspension Rear**	Double wishbones with coil springs, gas dampers & anti-roll bar	**Height**	1120mm/44in
Displacement	3760cc	**Steering**	Rack and pinion with power assist	**Kerb Weight**	1500kg/3307lbs	**Price**	£450,000 US price not available
Maximum Power	720bhp at 8,000rpm	**Brakes Front**	Cross-drilled & ventilated discs, ABS/355mm/14in	**Length**	4350mm/171in		
Maximum Torque	590lb ft at 5,250rpm	**Brakes Rear**	Cross-drilled & ventilated discs, ABS/335mm/13in				
Transmission	Six-speed manual						
0–60mph	4secs						

Is it beauty or the beast? It doesn't really matter, the Enzo defines what the supercar moniker is all about...

Explosive, aggressive, uncompromising – these are just some of the words that roar into your mind when you first see the Ferrari Enzo. Where do you start with such bold statement in supercar design? On its release in 2002, it was perhaps intended as a boast; a flipping of the finger at all the other supercar manufacturers that had been snapping at the heels of Ferrari since the marque began making cars back in 1947.

Ferrari Enzo

Named after the company's founder Enzo Ferrari, who died in 1988, the Enzo is the marque's fastest ever road-going car with a top speed of over 217mph, and the looks penned by Pininfarina are pure Formula One drama. There are no luscious curves that one normally associates with a exotic supercar; the Enzo makes its intent clear; that F1 nose, the angular body and those venturis shout to even the most casual of observers that this car is the closest a driver will ever get to feeling like Michael Schumacher.

But being a Ferrari, the Enzo is not all show – it also goes like a beast. With 660bhp produced by an ultra lightweight aluminium 6-litre V12 engine, the Enzo can devour many of its modern day competitors with a 0–60 time of 3.5secs. It almost has enough torque to stop the Earth rotating if you should happen to floor the gas while heading in an easterly direction.

Ferrari have made sure that the Enzo makes the most of its gigantic power by using its hi-tech ASR traction control system and an F1-style six-speed paddle shift that can snap through the gears in milliseconds. The Enzo's handling is legendary as well – its chassis is constructed from carbon fibre and Kevlar honeycomb, which provides the Enzo with its extreme rigidity and strength; while that F1 nose, with its three air intakes, helps to keep the car glued to the road as it increases in speed, while keeping the V12 cool. Stopping capability is vital for such explosive thrust – and the carbon ceramic brakes with ABS are more than a match for such a punishing job.

Open the Enzo's scissor doors and there's easy access to the carbon fibre and leather cabin. The steering wheel is a F1 fan's idea of paradise with a multitude of F1-style buttons mounted on it for controlling everything from race settings to turning off the ASR (if the driver is feeling brave enough). And for that extra Grand Prix touch, there are LEDs running along the top of the wheel, which act as a rev counter.

The Ferrari Enzo is currently regarded as the most technologically advanced supercar available. There's no question that the Enzo is an evolutionary step towards bringing road and track cars closer together. Perhaps the only concern is how Ferrari will top this.

The Enzo is Ferrari's fastest ever road-going car with a top speed of over 217mph.

Going, Going, Gone

Like any respectable supercar, limiting the numbers that can be bought is paramount. Initially, only 349 Enzos were made to order, and Ferrari sold every single one of them before they'd even shown a single picture or spec list of the car. The final figure for the number of Enzos assembled is 400 – one more than planned, with the extra car being auctioned off to raise money for the 2004 Asian tsunami appeal.

F1 Champ Elevates Enzo

Formula One champion Michael Schumacher had a firm hand in developing the Enzo. He drove several prototypes of the supercar and gave his thoughts on all aspects of the Enzo, from its performance to the driving position. In fact, thanks to Schumacher, there are 16 different pedal settings available to choose from.

Sky's The Limit

It would appear that the Enzo's value doesn't depreciate – hardly surprising considering the number Ferrari has actually ended up building. But if you want proof–in 2004, the Enzo became eBay Motors' most expensive car ever sold when a Swiss man (bidding from Brazil) made a winning bid of £544,000/US$1,038,227 – a brand new Enzo is worth £450,000/US$670,000.

Pulling Power

A survey by the RAC Foundation, based in Britain, discovered that 86 percent of British men would rather spend the weekend with a Ferrari Enzo than hang out with former *Baywatch* star Pamela Anderson. Well, at least the Enzo features more natural materials!

Ferrari Enzo: The Specifications

Engine	Aluminium V12
Valvetrain	DOHC, 4 valves /cyl with Continuously Variable Timing
Displacement	5988cc
Maximum Power	660bhp at 7,800rpm
Maximum Torque	485lb ft at 5,500rpm
Transmission	Six-speed sequential gearbox
0–60mph	3.5secs
0–100mph	6.5secs
Maximum Speed	217mph +
Steering	Rack & Pinion with power assist
Brakes Front	Ventilated carbon-ceramic discs with 6-pot callipers, ABS/380mm/15mm
Brakes Rear	Ventilated carbon-ceramic discs with 4-pot callipers, ABS/380mm/15in
Suspension Front	Double wishbones with pushrod links, coil springs, gas dampers & anti-roll bar
Suspension Rear	Double wishbones with pushrod links, coil springs, gas dampers & anti-rollbar
Kerb Weight	1365kg/3009lbs
Length	4702mm/185in
Width	2035mm/80in
Height	1147mm/45in
Wheels Front	9 x 19in
Wheel Rear	12 x 19in
Price	£450,000/US$670,000

The Lamborghini Gallardo, the Ford GT and the Aston Martin V8 Vantage... yes, Ferrari may have been facing increased competition over the past couple of years but trust them to come out fighting...

The F430 had a tough act to follow – Ferrari's illustrious reputation for creating exceptional sports coupés is unrivalled. Think 355 and 360 and mental images of what a sports car should look like pop into your mind immediately. But Ferrari have topped both of these – after all, just in visual terms, it's almost impossible to tear your eyes away from these pictures, isn't it? Some pundits may have complained about the Enzo's angular lines but even they must surely be happy with the F430. Designed by Pininfarina, the 360 Modena replacement is a masterclass in mixing the sensual with the angular, and blending such seemingly diametric elements into a alluring body shape; the back is very Enzo while the front is all scoops and curves.

Ferrari F430

The successor to the acclaimed 360, the F430 is constructed entirely from aluminium and features a brand new 4.3-litre V8 engine that boasts far more torque than its forebearer and produces 483bhp – the car has a 0–62 time of 4secs and a top speed of 195mph. The F430 features a six-speed manual as standard and, as an option, a F1 paddleshift that can now move through those gears quicker than the previous incarnation found in the 360.

The F430 also has some new Formula One-sourced tricks up its sleeve for the driver to indulge in.

The most obvious is mounted on the steering wheel – the 'manettino' – which is a switch that can be flicked between various different modes – Ice, Wet, Sport, Race and CST – and, as any F1 driver will be familiar with, lets you, with a simple flick, automatically alter the F430's settings such as dampers, traction control plus the speed of the F1 gearshifts (if you have opted for one).

It's clever stuff but that's not all – the F430 also features an electronic differential. A smart alternative to four-wheel drive, this e-diff aids torque distribution to the rear wheels, so if over-keen driving sees the back end starting to slide out, the clutches inside the e-diff quickly send torque to the wheel that has the most traction. Thanks to this unique e-diff, the F430 has none of the on-the-limit tail happiness that the 360 Modena was sometimes known for, and it has been acclaimed for its benign handling and the ability to conquer corners with absolute and utter controllable ease. Not surprising really when you take into consideration the fact that Michael Schumacher had a hand in the car's development.

The interior of the F430 is spot-on for such a thoroughbred – it's all plush leather plus carbon fibre or alloy for the centre console. The red starter button can be found on the steering wheel along with that 'manettino' dial. Creature comforts include air-conditioning and a stereo–though how you'd ever get sick of hearing that glorious V8 howl from behind you is quite frankly unimaginable.

The F430 is a genuine step up from the 360 – Ferrari knows it can't rest on its laurels with the competition encroaching on its space, but as usual, the Italian stallion has stepped up and thrown down the aluminium gauntlet to its 'foe'. We wonder how the likes of Lamborghini will take to such a challenge.

The F430 is acclaimed for its benign handling and its ability to conquer corners with absolute ease.

Back To The Future

The F430 features a host of styling cues from Ferrari's rich heritage – the air scoops at the rear pay homage to the 250 LM's, and the two elliptical air intakes at the front are inspired by Ferrari's 1961 F1 racing cars. Even the wing mirrors are similar to the Testarossa of the 1980s. Of course, the Enzo heavily influences the rear layout – the only elements that have remained from the 360 to the F430 are the doors, bonnet and roof. It's just a shame then that there's a three year waiting list for this fabulous Ferrari.

Wind Up

The F430 is undeniably a beautiful car but, as with any serious supercar, the form follows function. The development of the F430 saw Ferrari's engineers spending over 2,000 hours in a wind tunnel making sure that the aerodynamics of the car were honed to perfection.

A Big Downer

The F430 features a 50 percent increase in downforce when compared to its successor, the 360 Modena. That means stability and safety at high speeds is now vastly improved.

Devil In The Details

It's obvious that Ferrari want owners to bespoke the F430 to their hearts content. Not only can customers turn up with a colour sample that they want their car painted in but they can also decide on the tiny details, such as the thread colour used inside the car and even the spacing of the actual stitching. And of course, like all supercars, the F430 has its very own luggage set that has been tailored specifically for the car.

Tops Off

A rag top, the F430 Spyder, has joined the F430. While there are always worries about cutting off the roof of a supercar, leaving it structurally compromised, the Spyder has been getting thumbs up all over the media for still being a thrilling drive. And the soft top is electrically operated and so offers quick and easy access to those summer rays.

Ferrari F430: The Specifications

Engine	Aluminium V8
Valvetrain	DOHC, 4 valves / cyl with variable timing and variable intake tract
Displacement	4308cc
Maximum power	483bhp at 8,500rpm
Maximum torque	343lb ft at 5,250rpm
Transmission	Six-speed manual (optional F1 paddleshift available)
0-62mph	4secs
Maximum speed	196mph
Steering	Rack & pinion with power assist
Brakes front	Carbon-ceramic discs (optional) with 6-piston callipers / 380mm/15in, ABS, EBD
Brakes rear	Carbon-ceramic discs (optional), 4-piston callipers/ 350mm/14in, ABS, EBD
Suspension front	Double wishbones with coil springs, electrically adjustable tube shocks & anti-roll bar
Suspension rear	Double wishbones with coil springs, electrically adjustable tube shocks & anti-roll bar
Kerb weight	1450kg/3197lbs
Length	4512mm/178in
Width	1923mm/76in
Height	1214mm/48in
Wheels front	7.5 x 19in
Wheel rear	10 x 19in
Price	£118,500/US$170,000

The Ferrari-beating Le Mans racing legend is reborn and the motoring world falls in love all over again...

It must have been tough for Ferrari when they upset Henry Ford II. After all, the great man was all set to buy the Italian stallion in the early 1960s but alas, the premium sports car marque had a change of heart – and walked away. Bad idea. Ford's reaction to the pullout was the desire to humiliate Ferrari at Le Mans with the creation of the Ford GT40. Built for revenge, Ford managed to thrash Ferrari at its own game by winning the Le Mans 24-hour race four times in a row – from 1966 to 1969.

Ford GT

After such a public dressing down of the world's top supercar, the GT40's legacy was talked about for decades to come. But fast forward to the Detroit Auto Show, USA, in 2002 – where the concept of its successor is unveiled – and everyone starts talking again. The world does a double take, pinches itself to make sure that it isn't dreaming and then scrabbles for its chequebook – you see, there's presence and then there's *presence.*

While some woolly-minded critics whined that Ford was merely doing a retro retake on the GT40 and not coming up with any new and fresh ideas for their flagship cars, the rest of us quite frankly couldn't have cared less – the original GT40 was a beautiful car; but the Ford GT is quite simply stunning.

Sitting close to the ground on its low profile tyres, the GT epitomizes how a proper sports car should look and, with a Ford-claimed 500bhp nestled behind the driver, how it should go as well. With a 0–60 time of 3.7secs and a top speed of 200mph, this is no lukewarm or cynical attempt to cash-in on Ford's heritage by pilfering their classics to make a quick buck – this is a thoroughly updated take on the legendary supercar.

The GT may look dimensionally like the original at first glance but the car is actually 84mm/3.3in taller than its forbearer, and it's wider. And underneath that fine looking exterior is a thoroughly modern all-aluminium spaceframe. Providing the fireworks is a supercharged 5.4-litre V8 mid-engine lump with enough torque to rip tarmac from the road. Or at the very least, rip the rubber off those 19in tyres on the back. After all, the Ford features no traction control or fancy stability systems; driver and passenger air bags and anti-lock brakes are the only concessions to modern 'safe' motoring.

But this really shouldn't be a problem for the driver who treats the GT with the respect it deserves – because the car is renowned for being an absolute cinch to drive through rush hour as well as at full speed. Unlike some of its more 'highly strung' supercar competitors, this car also enjoys being on the limit, and with the GT's chassis, spot-on steering and entertaining handling, has the driving experience to match those damn fine looks too.

Ultimately, what the Ford GT has shown the world is that the blue oval is not just about mass produced people carriers, city and rep cars – it can also mix it up with the very best in the sports car business and still come out on top.

STOP

'The original GT40 was a beautiful car; but the Ford GT is quite simply stunning.'

MICHIGAN
112M20
FEB
MANUFACTURER
PLATE
04

As Good As Old

Like the exterior, the GT's cockpit is a modern take on the old GT40 featuring toggle switches, seats with ventilated seat backs and squabs, and a speedo located above the transmission tunnel.

Fast Forward

To make sure that the GT was ready for their centennial celebrations in 2003, Ford managed to turn the concept car into a production model in a record-breaking 16 months.

Last In Line

Of the 5,000 GTs made, Ford allowed only 85 cars to be shipped over to Europe. The poor old UK had only 24 allocated – so you can only begin to imagine the scrambling of potential purchasers as they tried to get on the fabled shortlist.

The Past Made New

The GT is actually part of Ford's Living Legends range – cars from yester-year given a fresh reworking. Other cars in the series include the glorious-looking Ford Mustang and Thunderbird.

Size Matters

The original GT40 was named so because it was 1016mm/40in tall. The GT has crept up in height to accommodate taller drivers and now stands at 1100mm/43.3in. The height difference aside, if you're wondering why Ford didn't simply stick with GT40 as the name, well, it's because they don't actually own the copyright to it.

Inspired Driving

It has been reported that the designers at Ford wanted the car to offer the image of a Ferrari 360 while retaining the sheer usability of a Honda NSX.

Ford GT: The Specifications

Engine	All-aluminium V8, supercharged
Valvetrain	DOHC 4 valves / cyl
Displacement	5409cc
Maximum Power	500bhp at 6,000rpm
Maximum Torque	500lb ft at 4,500rpm
Transmission	Six-speed manual
0–60mph	3.7secs
0–100mph	8.3secs
Maximum Speed	200mph
Steering	Rack & pinion
Brakes Front	Cross-drilled and ventilated with four-piston callipers, ABS/356mm/14in
Brakes Rear	Cross-drilled and ventilated with four-piston callipers, ABS/335mm/13in
Suspension Front	Double wishbone, mono tube aluminium dampers & anti-roll bar
Suspension Rear	Double wishbone, mono tube aluminium dampers & anti-roll bar
Kerb Weight	1519kg/3349lbs
Length	4643mm/182in
Width	1953mm/77in
Height	1125mm/44in
Wheels Front	9 x 18in
Wheel Rear	11.5 x 19in
Price	£125,000/US$141,000

Ford GT (2003)

Ford GT40 (1966 Le Mans)

A supercar? From Japan? If you think that only the Europeans make supercars, think again. Honda has been producing one of the world's finest for the past 15 years...

Snobbery is always a terrible thing, but it is the only explanation as to why Honda hasn't been on the receiving end of the kudos it deserves since the NSX was introduced to the world 15 years ago. What you are looking at after all is one of the world's easiest-to-drive supercars. The trouble is that it has a Honda badge on the front and back which, for those with more money than sense, is something of a no-no in a world of Porsches and Ferraris.

Honda NSX

And what a shame – because the mid-engined, rear-wheel drive aluminium-bodied NSX is remarkable. Designed with extensive help from the world's greatest Formula One driver, Ayrton Senna, the car was launched in 1990 to critical acclaim. With a normally aspirated and highly tuned V6 engine (i.e. no turbo or other 'trinkets') welded on, it offered a rev-hungry and thrilling driving experience – when you wanted it.

After all, here's a supercar that can be guided round crowded urban streets at low revs without ever giving you the feeling that it wants to rip your arm off in impatience. Start redlining the NSX though and you'll know why it's a supercar – as with all Honda VTECs, using the full range of the engine rewards the driver with a frenzy of power the higher up the rev range they go. This power delivery is coupled with a rewarding chassis that offers huge grip and balance.

Then there's the reliability – while exotic supercars can demand deep pockets for unexpected 'temperamental' breakdowns, the NSX is Japanese – therefore, reliability comes as standard because Honda know how to screw a car together whether it be a 1.4 Civic or a 276bhp supercar.

The current NSX was introduced in 2002 and has seen the original's pop-up headlamps replaced by fixed headlamps. The current car also has two engines to choose from – the 3.2-litre V6 with a six-speed manual producing 276bhp, and the 3-litre V6 F-Matic version that produces 256bhp.

For the hardcore driver though, the Honda NSX-R is available but only to those willing to import it directly from Japan – a variant that while producing the same 276bhp as the standard car has been completely stripped down. Out has gone the stereo, sound insulation and power locks, to be replaced by race-track stiff suspension, Recaro bucket seats and a smaller battery to name but a few of the changes.

For the supercar driver who wants to experience a (relatively) cheap, comfortable and reliable supercar, the Honda NSX still remains after all this time, the perfect solution. Snobs not welcome.

'The NSX – designed with extensive help from the world's greatest Formula One driver, Ayrton Senna.'

David Versus Goliath

It's worth bearing in mind that the NSX was the first time a Japanese car manufacturer had dared to take on the likes of Ferrari – and many would argue that they succeeded.

Senna Sense

While Ayrton Senna was over in Japan in 1989, he was asked to drive a prototype of the original NSX to glean his expert thoughts. According to Honda, he told their engineers: "I'm not sure I can really give you appropriate advice on a mass-production car, but I feel it's a little fragile". Because of that input, the Honda team ended up increasing the car's rigidity by 50 percent.

Going Topless

The NSX is available with a targa top roof as well – the NSX-T – but critics do say that this affects the car's rigidity and that purists should stick to the coupé version. After all, what would Ayrton Senna say?

World First

The NSX was the first production car in the world to feature all-aluminium construction for the chassis, suspension components and chassis, and it is still the only true mid-engine two-seater supercar to come out of the Land of the Rising Sun.

Splitting Hairs

A debate has raged for many years about whether the NSX is a true 'supercar' – detractors believe that it is not powerful enough to warrant the label, while supporters vehemently argue that because of its handling and styling, it most certainly is.

Fighting Talk

The NSX's sleek looks have their origins in the air, not on the road. The original sketches drawn up for the Japanese supercar were actually based on an F16 fighter jet.

Hand-Assembled Heaven

To reflect its special position within Honda, the NSX is hand-assembled in Japan. To make sure the engineers are good enough to put together the supercar, they have to go through a rigorous testing process before being allowed to work on the NSX.

Honda NSX Coupe 3.2 V6 / Acura NSX: The Specifications

Engine	24-valve V6
Valvetrain	DOHC VTEC 4 valves / cyl
Displacement	3179cc
Maximum Power	276bhp at 7,300rpm
Maximum Torque	220lb ft at 5,300rpm
Transmission	Six-speed manual or six-speed Auto
0–60mph	5.7secs (manual) 4.9secs (auto)
0–100mph	4.9secs (manual) 5.1secs (auto)
Maximum Speed	168mph
Steering	Rack and pinion with Servotronic speed-sensitive power-assist
Brakes Front	Ventilated & grooved with six callipers/355mm/14in
Brakes Rear	Ventilated & grooved with 4 callipers/330mm/13in
Suspension Front	Double wishbones with monutube dampers, coil springs & anti-roll bar
Suspension Rear	Double wishbones with monutube dampers, coil springs & anti-roll bar
Kerb Weight	1710kg/3770lbs (manual) 1800kg/3968lbs (auto)
Length	4430mm/174in
Width	1810mm/71in
Height	1160mm/46in
Wheels Front	7 x 17in
Wheel Rear	9 x 17in
Price	£59,995/US$90,000

Ferociously fast, perfectly composed and luxurious... ladies and gentlemen, meet Sweden's McLaren F1 slayer with the world's most unpronounceable name...

There's one prerequisite for a supercar – it has to go like hell; and like Hades goes the Koenigsegg. Made in Sweden, the Koenigsegg CC, the dark horse of the supercar world, first broke cover in 2000 and blew the socks and anoraks off the motoring world.

The car is the brainchild of Christian von Koenigsegg who set up the supercar project back in 1993 with a small, dedicated group of enthusiasts. From such humble beginnings emerged the record-breaking monster that you're looking at now. With its latest incarnations, the CC8S and the CCR, that power is now the stuff of legend – the top of the range CCR is officially the fastest production car in the world and can propel you to McLaren F1-vanquishing speeds of beyond 242mph.

Koenigsegg CC

But making a record-breaking car means precious little if the car can't handle such colossal power – thankfully though, Koenigsegg has done its homework here as well. The chassis, made from carbon fibre composite, is renowned for its communicative feedback whether the car's hurtling along at 200mph plus, or being threaded through pot-holed city streets. Then add in the factor that

this car is unflappable and perfectly composed on the road – it manages to mix suppleness with practically zero body roll. The end result is a driving experience that never makes the driver feel left out of the loop with what is going on underneath.

While the 'base' model – the CC8S – offers 655bhp, its big brother, the CCR launched in 2004, has a staggering 806bhp on tap and can make the dash from 0–62 in only 3.2secs. This 'extreme' version of the Koenigsegg is achieved by boosting the 'standard' 4.7-litre V8 engine with a bi-compressor centrifugal supercharging system.

You would expect with such explosive power in a hardcore form that you'd find the interior somewhat lacking – that the Koenigsegg options would be limited to a cassette player at best or a floor carpet at worst. Not so with this Swedish supercar – as well as a full leather interior and CD player, the driver can indulge in a wide range of luxuries such as GPS navigation, a rear-view camera, a telephone system and even bespoke suitcases (where you'd put those is another issue altogether). And for those drivers who like the feel of the wind through their hair, open-air thrills are also available because the car comes with a removable roof panel that can be stored under the front bonnet.

The Koenigsegg offers that rare blend of incredible but utterly exploitable power, and genuine luxury to make the drive of your life the most comfortable possible. Yes, the price tag of £407,000 plus (US price based on customer specification) is a huge amount of cash – but the Koenigsegg is worth every penny. A truly remarkable supercar and virtually unbeatable; never has the phrase 'from zero to hero' been quite so true.

The 2002 Koenigsegg CC 8S

'A truly remarkable supercar and virtually unbeatable; never has the phrase 'from zero to hero' been quite so true."

Full House

The Koenigsegg headquarters are housed in a large fighter jet facility and there are 30 full-time staff. At the moment, seven vehicles can be assembled simultaneously and one car – bearing in mind there are 300-plus carbon fibre parts per car – takes 1,000 hours to assemble.

Door To Door

The carbon fibre doors of the CC open by swinging upwards and resting at a 90° angle. Thanks to gas struts, this operation can be done with a gentle push and also means that the car is easily accessible even in confined spaces.

Record Breaker

In the 2004 edition of the *Guinness Book Of Records*, the Koenigsegg CC8S is listed as the most powerful production car on the face of the planet. This has now been smashed by the 806bhp CCR, which currently holds the world record for the planet's most powerful streetcar.

Have Car, Wheel Travel

The five-spoke magnesium alloy rims featured on the CCR have been specifically designed for Koenigsegg, and the tyres are guaranteed to withstand the strains and stresses of travelling at over 240mph.

Not Too Hot To Handle?

The engineers at Koenigsegg have implemented KACS (Koenigsegg Advanced Control System) as standard on the CCR – this allows the driver to adjust the car's suspension, aerodynamics, road holding and braking components for their preferred set-up.

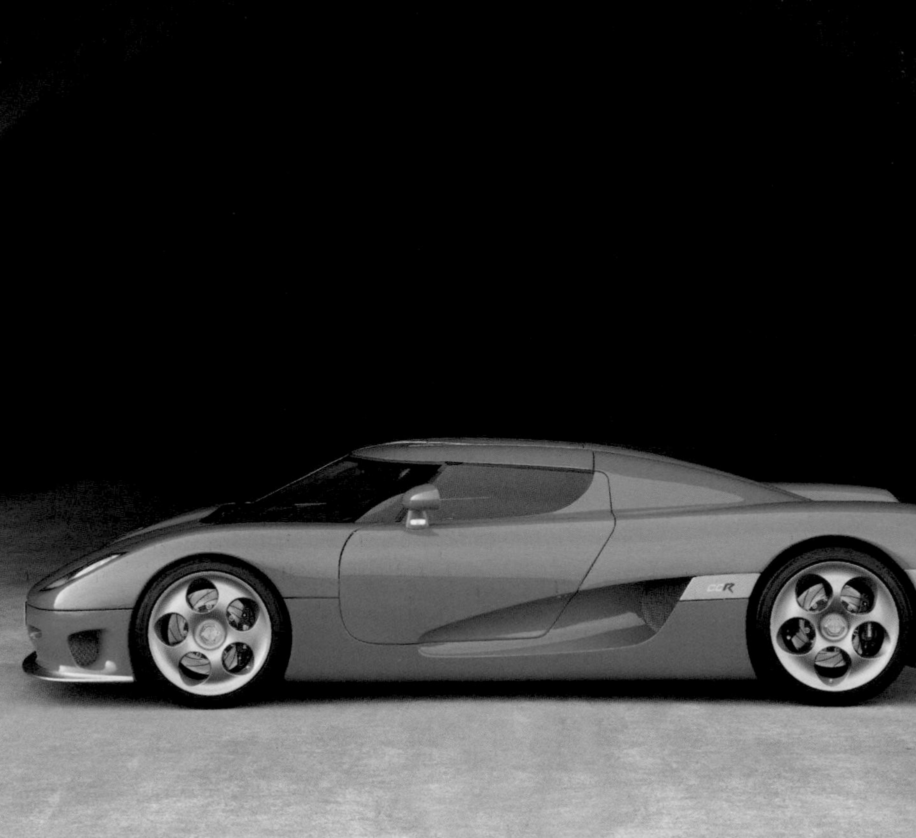

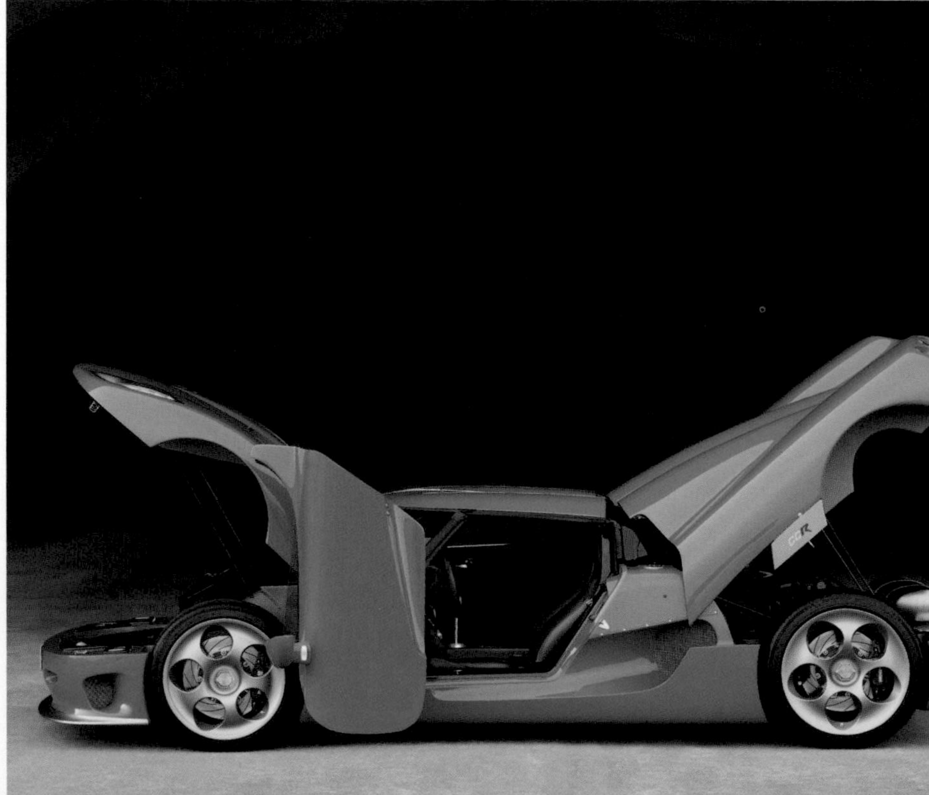

Koenigsegg CCR: The Specifications

Engine	V8 cast aluminium, supercharged
Valvetrain	DOHC 4 valves / cyl
Displacement	4700cc
Maximum Power	806bhp at 6,900rpm
Maximum Torque	678lb ft at 5,700rpm
Transmission	Six-speed manual
0–62mph	3.2secs
0–1/4 miles	9secs
Maximum Speed	242mph +
Steering	Rack and pinion with power assist
Brakes Front	Ventilated with six-piston light alloy callipers, ABS/362mm/14in
Brakes Rear	Ventilated with six-piston callipers/362mm/14in
Suspension Front	Double wishbones, adjustable VPS custom racing shock absorbers, pushrod operated & anti-roll bar
Suspension Rear	Double wishbones, adjustable VPS custom racing shock absorbers, pushrod operated & anti-roll bar
Kerb Weight	1230kg/2711lb
Length	4190mm/164in
Width	1990mm/78in
Height	1070mm/42in
Wheels Front	9.5 x 19in
Wheel Rear	12.5 x 20in
Price	£407,000/ US price based on customer specification

German build quality partnered with Italian passion... it's an intriguing concept but one that has paid off for the raging bull...

There were some bated breaths in the car community when Audi bought out Lamborghini in 1998 – yes, the idea of a car manufacturer known for making bullet-proof pluto barges was a welcome one; perhaps they could temper the sometimes unforgiving nature of Lamborghini's previous cars such as the classic Diablo. But could such a company evolve the iconic supercar marque but keep what makes any Lamborghini so special – the rawness, and the sheer scariness. Or could we end up with a supercar that lacked a certain something? In other words, would the bull be tamed?

Lamborghini Murcielago

All was revealed in 2001 when the result of Lamborghini's and Audi's mating rolled out in front of the public eye. But they need not have worried themselves.

The Murcielago is, yes, more refined and better built but don't start worrying that the Lamborghini has been sanitized. While Audi has ensured that the car has improved safety features and is better built than its predecessors, the Murcielago still has more than enough go to put a cold sweat on the foreheads of even the most experienced driver when taking the car to the limit.

The engine alone will see to that – with 580bhp, the aluminium 6.2-litre V12 is blisteringly quick, and with its four-wheel drive with a central vicious coupler plus traction control, the steel and carbon fibre-built Lamborghini's huge power can be placed down on the road with more ease than its predecessors. The Murcielago also represents a first for the Lamborghini with the inclusion of a six-speed manual gearbox. The car's rear spoiler adjusts depending on the speed, and those fabulous air intakes mounted on the car's rear shoulders open and close to cool the mammoth engine. And for the show-offs, there's also a dash-mounted button to activate that 'Variable Air-flow Cooling System'.

Lamborghini purists may be slightly disappointed with the car's exterior – but while the aggressive, melodramatic styling of previous Lamborghinis looked like testosterone wrought in metal, the more subtle Murcielago still demands your attention with its clean, simple and muscular lines – it's a thoroughly modern reimagining of the Lamborghini spirit penned by Belgian designer Luc Donckerwolcke.

All this handling and visual drama is backed-up by Audi's obsession with build. The Murcielago was put through a series of punishing tests to make sure that its reliability was up to scratch – while the previous Diablo had only five prototypes racing round the Nardo race track and Sant'Agata in Italy, twelve Murcielagos were taken as far a field as the USA to see how they would bear up under such scorching and harsh temperatures.

It's with this new mindset – the passion of Lamborghini and the build quality of Audi – that the company has matured into a true 21st century supercar marque. With the arrival of the even more desirable and critically acclaimed Roadster version of the Murcielago, the bull is all set to bear down on its competition well into the future.

'The Murcielago demands your attention with its clean, simple and muscular lines. It's a thoroughly modern reimagining of the Lamborghini spirit.'

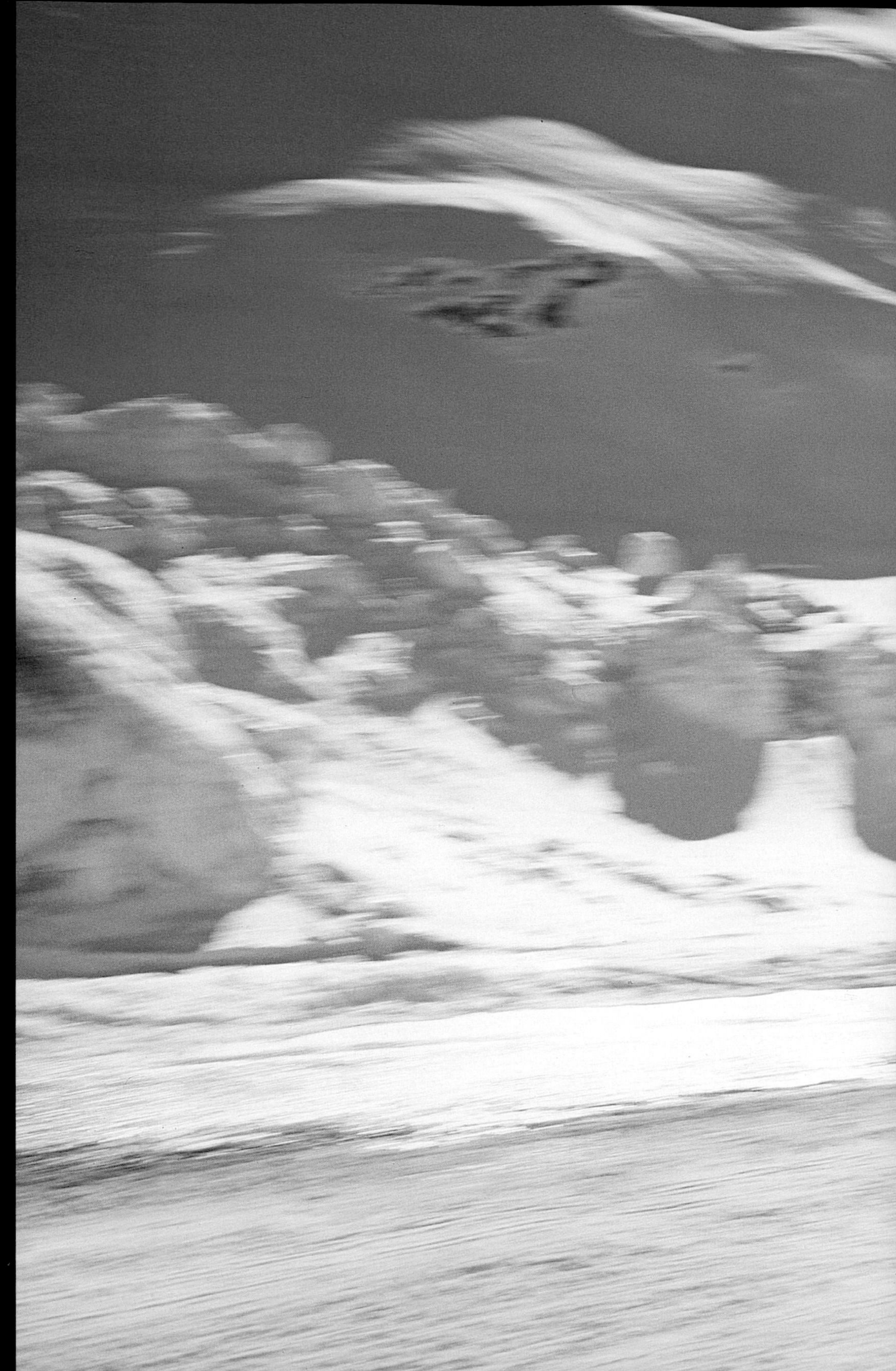

CC 807WT

What's In A Name?

The Murcielago is named after a bull that fought with the famous matador Rafael Molina 'Lagarttijo' on October 5, 1879. The aforementioned bull fought so bravely – and withstood being stabbed 24 times – that the great matador decided to honor the bull and spare its life. The bull was given to a top breeder and the Murcielago lineage continues to this day.

Bullet Proof?

Build quality and reliability were issues that sometimes hovered over the Lamborghinis of old. The now Audi-owned company say that Murcielagos are being driven over 10,000 miles a year by some customers with no problems.

Off With Its Head

Unlike the Diablo Roadster, which horrified the critics on its release, the Murcielago Roadster has taken their breaths away – not only incredible to look at but also a true zero-compromise supercar as well.

All-Wheel Thrills

Lamborghini wanted all the Murcielago's power put firmly down on the road so the driver could enjoy it, and not simply destroy the car's tyres. Subsequently, any excess torque on the rear axle is moved to the front axle to aid the Murcielago get the best traction.

Lamborghini Murcielago: The Specifications

Engine	Aluminium alloy V12
Valvetrain	DOHC, 4 valves / cyl with variable-geometry intake system and variable valve timing
Displacement	6192cc
Maximum Power	580bhp at 7,500rpm
Maximum Torque	479lb ft at 5,400rpm
Transmission	Six-speed manual / Optional E-Gear
0–60mph	3.8secs
0–125mph	8.6secs
Maximum Speed	205mph
Steering	Rack & Pinion with power assist
Brakes Front	Vented discs with 4-pot callipers, ABS/355mm/14in
Brakes Rear	Vented Discs with 4-pot callipers, ABS/335mm
Suspension Front	Double wishbones with coil springs, gas dampers & anti-roll bar
Suspension Rear	Double wishbones with coil springs, gas dampers & anti-roll bar
Kerb Weight	1650kg/3638lbs
Length	4580mm/180in
Width	2045mm/80in
Height	1135mm/45in
Wheels Front	8.5 x 18in
Wheel Rear	13 x 18in
Price	£162,000/US$228,000

So, you can't stretch to a Murcielago? There's no need to worry because its baby brother is just as convincing...

Lamborghini Gallardo

Taking on Ferrari and Porsche at their own game is not for the faint-hearted but then again Lamborghini isn't known for pulling any punches. With the backing of owner Audi, the Gallardo was designed to go up against the likes of the Ferrari F430 and Porsche 911. In other words, the Gallardo is supposed to be about potent power on tap with the handling to wring the most out of the 500bhp on offer, all for a price that undercuts its big brother the Murcielago, by a third.

There's no doubt that the Gallardo shares its genes with its big brother but the mini supercar looks more muscular and purposeful with its aluminium bodywork. The car maker wanted to ensure that the Gallardo could be used as a genuine everyday proposition – not simply to be taken out for a spin at the weekend. You won't be surprised to read that Lamborghini pulled it off.

That commute has never been quite so much fun – indeed, this car is easy to manage in the chaos of the rush hour but like any Lamborghini, the Gallardo is designed to be pushed, and heavy-footing the accelerator shows that this bull hasn't lost its horns. That V10 bellows its way up the rev range, easily managed with the six-speed manual or the optional e-Gear sequential gear shifting system that lets the driver flick through the paddles mounted on the steering column.

This power is delivered by a mid-mounted V10 5-litre engine, which produces 493bhp. Neck-snapping acceleration is mandatory with any Lamborghini, and the Gallardo won't disappoint either with a 0-62 time of 4.2secs and a top speed of 192mph. If anything, there's almost too much power on offer – finding a road long (and legal) enough to work your way up the gears is nearly impossible unless you're hurtling down a German autobahn or flexing the car's muscle on a track.

What's so revered about the Gallardo, and so different to the Countachs of yesteryear, is the sheer controllability of the car – with its low centre gravity and all-wheel drive featuring Lamborghini's Viscous Traction system distributing the power between the front and rear wheels depending on road conditions, the Gallardo isn't the kind of supercar that will catch you off guard. Even in the wet, that four-wheel drive system means that the Gallardo rarely has a problem finding traction. Couple such huge grip with the feedback pouring out from the steering wheel and the seat, and the Gallardo driver can make startling progress without feeling intimidated by what they are sitting in.

And sitting in the Gallardo offers no nasty surprises either – Audi-build quality seeps out of the cockpit; with its fully adjustable, electrically operated leather seats, there are enough creature comforts, such as air-conditioning and even optional satellite navigation, for the long-distance driver. The only blot on the landscape is actually accessing that cabin, which may disappoint if you are expecting scissor doors that sweep elegantly up into the air. No, these are, dare we say, just hinged conventional doors – it's obvious that Lamborghini wanted to reserve the fancy stuff for the company's flagship, the Murcielago.

What's most striking about the Gallardo is just how successful Lamborghini has been at muscling its way into traditional Ferrari territory without any compromise in Lamborghini's philosophy. The baby Lamborghini is the most sorted car the company has ever released.

DUNLOP
LJ53 KVO

The Gallardo is designed to be pushed, and heavy-footing the accelerator shows that this bull hasn't lost its horns.

LJ53 KVO

Winging It

The Gallardo's rear wing is able to change its angle depending on how quickly the car is moving. Below 50mph, the wing remains flush with the rest of the Gallardo's bodywork but at 80mph, it shifts upwards to create more downforce. After all, with 500bhp, the Gallardo needs all the stability it can get.

Audi Aluminium

To keep the Gallardo light on its toes, and to ensure rigidity, the supercar's chassis and body are made entirely from aluminium. Audi, pioneers in the use of aluminium in car production, have obviously brought their wealth of knowledge to the creation of the Gallardo.

The Lamborghini A8?

Audi didn't just stipulate the Gallardo's build quality, they also lent their air-conditioning system and stereo; you can normally find them residing in the Audi A8. This might be a cost-cutting exercise for Lamborghini but, at the end of the day, both of the Audi elements are of a very high quality, so Gallardo owners needn't be disappointed.

Instant Hit

It's a blessing for any keen driver who's just taken delivery of their new pride and joy – unlike many cars, the Gallardo's engine needs no 'breaking-in' period before unleashing the car's huge potential. To ensure that drivers can start wringing the most out of the V10's huge power, the engine is actually run in at the factory before being mounted in the Gallardo.

Lamborghini Gallardo: The Specifications

Engine	Aluminium V10
Valvetrain	DOHC, 4 valves / cyl with variable intake system & continuously variable valve timing
Displacement	4961cc
Maximum power	493bhp at 7,800rpm
Maximum torque	376lb ft at 4,500 rpm
Transmission	Six-speed manual (optional E-gear system available)
0-62mph	4.2secs
0-100mph	9.0secs
Maximum speed	192mph
Steering	Rack and pinion with power assist
Brakes front	Ventilated discs with 8-piston callipers/365mm/14in, ABS
Brakes rear	Ventilated discs with 8-piston allipers/335mm/14in, ABS
Suspension front	Double wishbones w/anti-roll bar with coil springs, dampers & anti-roll bar
Suspension rear	Double wishbones w/anti-roll bar with coil springs, dampers & anti-roll bar
Kerb weight	1530kg/3373lbs
Length	4300mm/169in
Width	1900mm/75in
Height	1165mm/46in
Wheels front	8.5 x 19in
Wheel rear	11 x 19in
Price	£115,000/US$166,000

The car you're looking at is a Ferrari Enzo. Well, it isn't. But it is. Let us explain...

Maserati's heritage is steeped in racing but it's been a long time since the revered marque headed back out onto the track – nearly four decades ago in fact. This road-going MC12 exists in order for a racing version to compete in the FIA Grand Tourer racing class; to qualify, Maserati had to sell 25 road-going versions before it could unleash its GT racetrack car. But how do you go about creating a racing thoroughbred in just a year without breaking the bank?

Maserati MC12

Up until recently, Maserati was in partnership with Ferrari and thanks to the Italian stallion, the MC12 has its engineering roots in the legendary Ferrari Enzo. It features the same carbon monocoque, the same V12 engine (albeit detuned), and even the same basic steering wheel and windshield. But before someone mentions 'the emperor's new clothes', the MC12 is aerodynamically superior to the prancing horse. After all, it's 610mm/24in longer and it features extended overhangs at both the back and rear. That means the engineers have been able to optimise how the air flows over (and exits) the MC12's body.

While the MC12 available to the public isn't the actual car that will race round tracks scooping up awards, it's close enough. Surprisingly though, it's been noted just how well behaved the MC12 is – easy gear changes, light steering and a ride that doesn't jar. But hit the accelerator and any illusions of being in a user-friendly runabout vanish quicker than the car hitting 0–60 in 3.8secs. The MC12 boasts an even power delivery so the driver is constantly pinned back in his racing seat as the car thunders its way up to 205mph. The Maserati's stellar progress aided amply by the gear changes made from the paddles situated behind the steering wheel. And needless to say, with a car based on the Enzo, the car handles, offering grip and feedback with perfect body balance.

The interior of the MC12 is an elegant but functional cockpit with lightweight carbon fibre used in abundance, plus striking Milan fashion house-sourced fabric mesh featured liberally on the dashboard. The carbon fibre seats feature full harnesses, and a large rev counter dominates the MC12's dials.

Those hoping to have a back window to glance out of will be disappointed because there isn't one. But you can always whip off the targa top and turn the MC12 into a Spyder – and poke your head up when reverse parking at your local shopping mall.

What's incredible about this supercar is what Masearti managed to achieve in 12 months – it's nothing short of a miracle. Yes, there may be a lot of Enzo genes in the MC12, but thanks to Maserati's exceptional design and engineering, they've created a truly unique supercar, which should help them propel the Trident back into the racing limelight all over again.

'The Maserati MC12 has its engineering roots in the legendary Ferrari Enzo.'

Long Time Coming

Maserati, a name synonymous with racing excellence, achieved its last victory way back in 1967 with the Cooper Maserati F1 at the South African Grand Prix. The last time the marque had its very own dedicated Grand Prix team was ten years before that.

Design Guru

While the MC12 was built for functionality rather than creative form, the supercar still has the kind of road presence that shames many of its competitors – it was designed by Frank Stephenson whose last job before joining up with the Ferrari Maserati Group was to design the Mini Cooper.

What's In A Colour?

The MC12 is available only in a two-tone white and blue livery. This colour scheme is in homage to the Maserati Tipo 60–61 'Birdcages' from the early 1960s.

Keeping Up With The Jones'es

The MC12 is surely the last word in exclusivity – only 50 will ever be made. While the price tag is colossal, you shouldn't be surprised to hear that most have already been sold. Time for interested purchasers to head to eBay then...

Hooked On Air

Like a true Le Mans racer, the MC12 features a large snorkel on its roof and rear grille to shove air down on to the Ferrari Enzo-sourced V12 engine.

Speedy Production

It's claimed that to get the MC12 from the drawing board to the finished car took a year. In fact, every element of creating the car was done at light speed – the alloys took a mere 15 days to go from design to the prototype wheel.

Maserati MC12: The Specifications

Engine	V12
Valvetrain	DOHC, 4 valves / cyl
Displacement	5998cc
Maximum Power	622bhp at 7,500rpm
Maximum Torque	480lb ft at 5,500rpm
Transmission	Six-speed sequential manual
0–60mph	3.8secs
Maximum Speed	205mph
Steering	Rack and pinion with power assist
Brakes Front	Cross-drilled & ventilated discs with 6-piston callipers, ABS/380mm/15in
Brakes Rear	Cross-drilled & ventilated discs with 4-piston callipers, ABS/335mm/13in
Suspension Front	Double wishbones with push-rod links, steel dampers & coil springs
Suspension Rear	Double wishbones with push-rod links, steel dampers & coil springs
Kerb Weight	1335kg/2943lbs
Length	5143mm/202in
Width	2096mm/82in
Height	1205mm/47in
Wheels Front	9 x 19in
Wheel Rear	13 x 19in
Price	£515,000 US$770,000 approx..

The three-pointed star wanted to make an impact with their first true supercar. Here's how they pulled it off...

Mercedes-Benz McLaren SLR

With hindsight, it's hard to think how Mercedes could have failed with the SLR. They're not exactly known for producing the four-wheeled equivalent of turkeys in the first place. Then you have Mercedes' racing heritage, which has directly influenced the SLR – its legacy dates back to the 1950s when the company was scooping up racing trophies left, right and dead centre with the original SLR Coupe.

And like its forefather, the new SLR pushes out the technological envelope too – a process helped by teaming up with their Formula One partners, McLaren, who are rather well known for producing what is arguably still the greatest supercar of all time – the McLaren F1.

So with impeccable credentials on both sides, it was perhaps inevitable that the new SLR is a classic, managing to straddle the gap between the ferocious performance of a supercar and the luxuries of a GT. But this is no watered-down compromise – just look over the long dart-like form of the car and its arrow-shaped nose, and it's not hard to see how the SLR's design elements are clearly inspired by the Formula One Silver Arrows. That full carbon fibre body encases cutting edge mechanics – a hand-assembled supercharged 5.5-litre V8 engine, producing 626bhp (and enough torque to beat its chief rival, the Ferrari Enzo) is mounted towards the front of the chassis. Power delivery is borderline insane–it's been compared to being shot out of a cannon as the car rips its way towards the horizon; the five-speed automatic gearbox effortlessly slicing up through the gears.

Handling is sublime with huge levels of grip coupled with that seemingly endless power delivery – coming out of corners and going hell for leather has never been quite so fast. While the suspension is, of course, firm, the SLR won't send the driver's spine into a jarring spasm – the car effortlessly deals with uneven road surfaces while offering the razor-sharp responses.

The only chink in the SLR's formidable armour is its ceramic brakes – they've been regularly criticized for their complete lack of feel, leaving the driver having to learn how to use the SLR's electronically regulated braking power – not something that you particularly want to do in a supercar that can hit 0–60 in 3.7secs. That said, once mastered, they are highly effective at slowing down in an emergency; a process helped by the SLR's spoiler turning into an airbrake under heavy braking.

Opening the gull wing doors of the SLR reveals a snug interior more in keeping with a luxurious GT rather than a hairy-chested supercar – an optional claret-red leather-swathed interior can be ordered, a colour arrangement inspired by the 1950s SLR's interior. Electronically adjustable carbon-frame seats, chronometer-style instruments and the use of carbon fibre and aluminium create an environment that should see drivers happily clocking up hundreds of miles in style.

The SLR is perhaps the best of both worlds – more than enough power and handling for the keen driver to exploit and, more importantly, enjoy while keeping said driver cosseted in GT-style comfort and refinement. It all sounds terribly Mercedes – and that's no bad thing.

D
S LR 2020

'The new SLR is a classic, managing to straddle the gap between the ferocious performance of a supercar and the luxuries of a GT.'

Smooth Operator

Based on Formula One technology, the SLR's underbody is virtually smooth. That coupled with a six-channel diffuser at the rear means that there is minimal drag and more downforce produced when hitting higher speeds. Even the exhausts have been moved to the side to ensure that aerodynamics aren't affected – those sidepipes also pay tribute to those featured on the 1950s SLR.

Sudden Impact

If an SLR driver should find themselves about to go nose first into an immovable object, they can seek solace in the car's long carbon fibre body and front end crash structure, offering the kind of energy absorption in crashes that has saved many lives on the Formula One circuit.

Acronym Explained

During the SLR's heyday in the 1950s, the SLR stood for Sporty Light Racer.

"How do I start this?"

Like all classic supercars, the SLR has the obligatory starter button. Instead of being mounted in the central console, the glowing red starter button is actually located on the end of the gear lever – simply flip back the cover and push down.

Geared For Action

The five-speed auto gearbox sourced from the Mercedes-owned luxury limo, the Maybach, comes with two automatic settings and three manual ones. The manual settings can be accessed via the gear lever or the steering wheel-mounted buttons.

Mercedes 'First' Supercar

The SLR isn't in fact Mercedes' first supercar. Back in 1991, Mercedes were all set to unleash the C112, a supercar with 500bhp that could break the 200mph barrier. Alas, the company eventually decided that the car simply wasn't right for the Mercedes' image and it was canned.

Mercedes-Benz SLR: The Specifications

Engine	AMG V8
Valvetrain	SOHC, 3 valves / cyl
Displacement	5439cc
Maximum Power	626bhp at 6,500rpm
Maximum Torque	575lb ft at 3250–5000rpm
Transmission	5-Speed Auto with Speedshift System
0–60mph	3.7secs
0–125mph	10.7secs
Maximum Speed	208mph
Steering	Rack & pinion with power assist
Brakes Front	Fibre reinforced ceramic discs with eight piston callipers, ESP, SBC/ 370mm/14.5in
Brakes Rear	Fibre reinforced ceramic discs with 4 piston callipers, ESP, SBC/360mm/14in
Suspension Front	Double wishbones with coil springs & gas dampers
Suspension Rear	Double wishbones with coil springs & gas dampers
Kerb Weight	1768kg/3898lbs
Length	4656mm/183in
Width	1908mm/75in
Height	1261mm/50in
Wheels Front	9 x 18in
Wheel Rear	11.5 x 18in
Price	£313,465/US$455,000

While supercars can trace their DNA back to the race track, the Evo range was born out of the mud, gravel and pot holes of rallying...

The Mitsubishi should probably be reserved for the final chapter about cars that boast supercar performance for a fraction of the cost; but the models found lurking in the Mitsubishi Lancer Evolution VIII range offer such outrageous performance and spot-on handling, that they make the Evo a genuine (if left-of-centre) supercar contender.

The VIII range features the VIII 260 'base' model, which is more than enough for most of us to enjoy on a regular basis. Mitsubishi though is famous for 'tweaking' its cars and has subsequently produced upgraded VIIIs, including the FQ-300 and FQ-340.

Mitsubishi Lancer Evolution VIII 400

The latest edition – the Evo VIII FQ-400 – can produce a G-force that would give the sort of Hollywood facelift that an aging actress would kill for. In the 3.5secs it takes to hit 60mph, your skin is pulled back so far that you'll look ten years younger; the trouble is that it could also age you if you're not up to handling the Evo's huge power.

While the FQ-400 may be easy to handle driving round town at low revs, hit the magic power band at 5,000rpm, and the turbo kicks in properly – well, 'kicks off' actually. Once the turbo is churning out its power through the rally-sourced four-wheel drive, you won't be able to believe that it's all coming from a 2-litre turbo-charged engine. Look at the spec list and you'll see that this car produces a whopping 405bhp. Not bad considering what is under the skin – a humble saloon car.

Of course, being a rally car designed for the road, the Evo can do the twisty stuff as well as the 0–100mph assault on your senses – with neutral handling, tidy body control and colossal grip, the Evo can devour corners with unnerving confidence. Many argue though that the FQ-400 is simply too extreme and that FQ-340 version will give you great performance but of the sort that can be used more frequently on the average trip to the supermarket. But perhaps the FQ-400 harks back to the good/gory old days of the supercar when zero fear of losing your driving licence (and spending long stretches in prison) was required to fully exploit the car's talents.

But for all the raw power on offer in the FQ-400, you might be surprised to hear that the makers of Evo have put their money where their mouth is when it comes to warranties. Remember that this is a Japanese car so reliability comes as standard – but this extreme engineering of the Evo has the benefit of being backed-up by a cast-iron three year/36,000 miles warranty – that even includes drivers who've taken to tearing their Evos round tracks on a regular basis.

While Europe may be seen as the home of the supercar with its exotic design and elegant engineering, the Evo is the Japanese equivalent of putting a single finger up to such svelte stallions. There's no pretension, no disillusions of grandeur – this is hardcore.

WX54
MFZ

'...being a rally car designed for the road, the Evo can do the twisty stuff as well as the 0–100mph assault on your senses. With neutral handling, tidy body control and colossal grip, the Evo can devour corners with unnerving confidence.'

Frightfully Quick

The MR stands for 'Mitsubishi Racing' but ever wondered what the FQ in the MR FQ-400 stands for? Hmm, tough question – we can confirm that the Q stands for 'quick', but the 'F'? Perhaps it means 'frightfully' or 'freaking', or perhaps something decidedly cruder. We'll leave it to your imagination...

Number Crunching...

The Pagani Zonda cranks out a very respectable 76.12bhp per litre. The Porsche Carrera GT manages 106.75. The FQ-400 claims 202.5bhp per litre. The Japanese certainly know how to get the most from their engines. And knowing Mitsubishi, they will at some point in the very near future top that too. They really can't help themselves, thankfully...

Need For FQ Speed

The FQ-400 is not only the fastest road-going car that Mitsubishi has ever made (for the UK market at least) – it also has the honour of being the fastest accelerating four-door sedan, from a major manufacturer, ever to grace public roads.

Ready To Launch

To keep the FQ-400's immense power welded to the road, instead of coming off at the first corner, Mitsubishi's engineers have made sure that the car remains stable at high speeds with the inclusion of a carbon fibre front lip spoiler, Ralliart aero mirrors and the rather menacing rear vortex generator – the 'shark's teeth' that can be found poking out of the rear of the roof.

So Little, So Much

Just how did Mitsubishi manage to get so much brake horse power out of a 2-litre engine? The most important element is the Garrett turbocharger made especially for the FQ-400, and the engine has also been strengthened to withstand the huge forces needed to develop 405bhp.

How To Handle Yourself...

Mitsubishi don't want customers simply roaring off into the distance in their new purchase – they offer free driver-training courses as part of the asking price so that customers know how to exploit the car's potential safely. Driving instructors are on hand to show how to corner the Evo without ending up at the top of a tree...

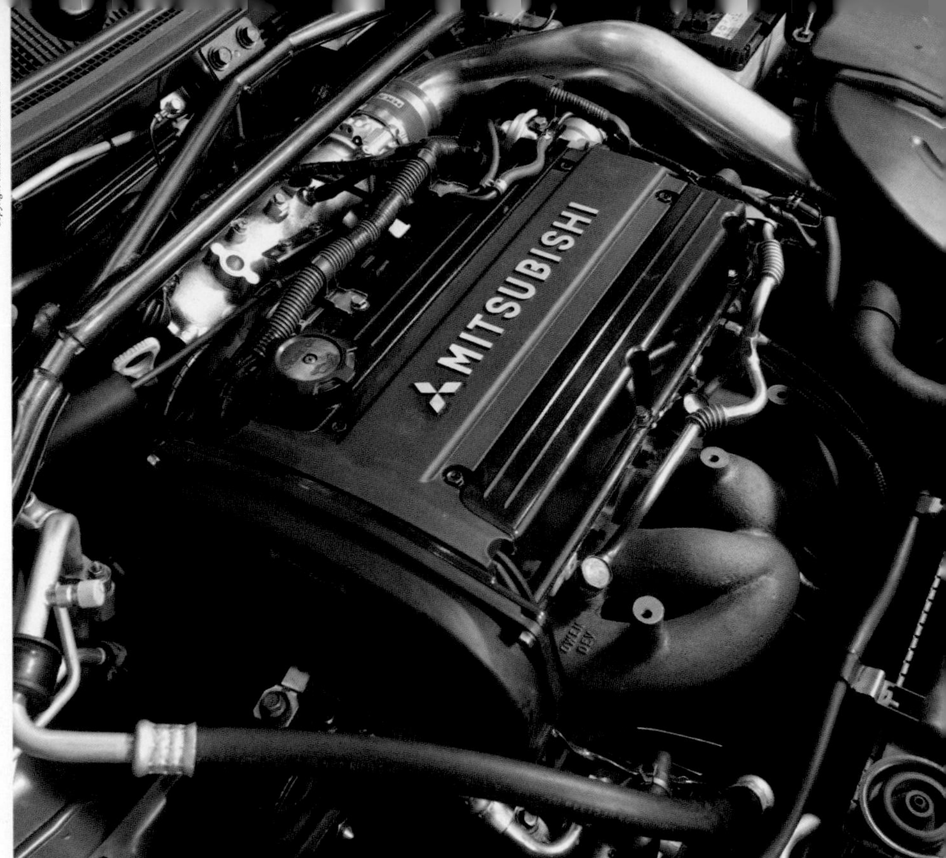

Mitsubishi Lancer Evo VIII MR FQ-400: The Specifications

Engine	Inline-4
Valvetrain	DOHC turbo with intercooler
Displacement	1997cc
Maximum power	405bhp at 6,400rpm
Maximum torque	355lb ft at 5,500rpm
Transmission	Six-speed manual
0-60mph	3.5secs
0-100mph	9.1secs
Maximum speed	175mph
Steering	Rack and pinion with power assist
Brakes front	Alcon 6-pot monobloc brake kit / 343mm/13in
Brakes rear	Ventilated discs with 2-pot aluminium callipers/ 300mm/12in
Suspension front	McPherson strut suspension with inverted shock absorbers, stabilizer bar & aluminium front lower arms
Suspension rear	McPherson strut suspension with inverted shock absorbers, stabilizer bar & aluminium front lower arms
Kerb weight	1400kg/3086lbs
Length	4490mm/177in
Width	1770mm/70in
Height	1450mm/57in
Wheels Front	8 x 17in
Wheel Rear	8 x 17in
Price	£46,999 Not available in the US

Exotic, outlandish, eccentric... the Zonda is the most individual supercar the world has ever seen...

Pagani Zonda

It looks more than modern – in fact, the Zonda looks like it could have been plucked straight from the pages of some sci-fi magazine, so vividly different does it look from its road-going competitors. But the origins of the car actually date back decades – after all, its Argentinean creator Horacio Pagani was only 12 when he first began making models of supercars from wood and moulded clay, and by the age of 20, he had already constructed his first race car for Renault.

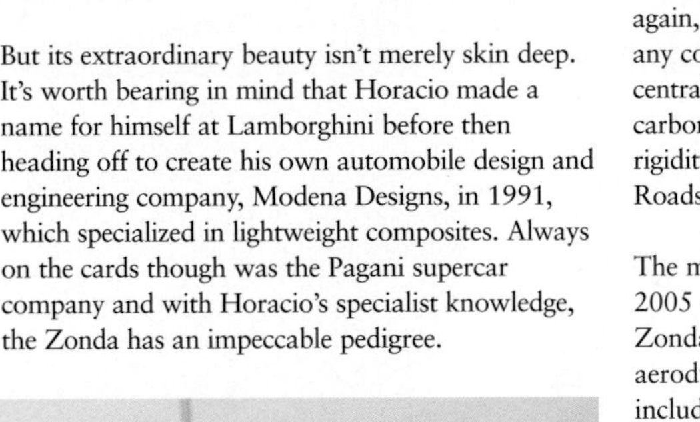

Now firmly ensconced in the 21st century, the lucid teenage dreams of Horacio have managed to create what many argue is the world's finest supercar. First revealed at the Geneva Motor Show, Switzerland, in 1999, the prototype of the Zonda was always going to cause a fuss – with those alien looks, it simply couldn't fail not to.

But its extraordinary beauty isn't merely skin deep. It's worth bearing in mind that Horacio made a name for himself at Lamborghini before then heading off to create his own automobile design and engineering company, Modena Designs, in 1991, which specialized in lightweight composites. Always on the cards though was the Pagani supercar company and with Horacio's specialist knowledge, the Zonda has an impeccable pedigree.

Unsurprisingly then, at the heart of the car is its unique use of composite materials with a carbon fibre chassis and body, ensuring an incredibly lightweight and rigid structure. Add into that a bullet-proof, smooth-revving Mercedes-Benz AMG V12 – after all, those Germans know how to build a reliable engine that won't blow up when you're attempting to top 200mph. The original five-speed C12 had 389bhp on tap in 6.9-litre form and has been constantly evolving ever since. The six-speed Zonda C12 S which is shown here has now evolved into the S 7.3 – all 555bhp of it boasting a 0–60 time of 3.6secs. Traction control is included, which is mighty handy for nailing all that power to the road in wet conditions

Perhaps the most keenly anticipated Pagani was the 555bhp Roadster – but there was a genuine concern among fans that chopping off the roof of the Zonda would leave its handling horribly compromised. But again, Pagani and his team managed to blow away any concerns by introducing a new carbon fibre central chassis structure, and a roll bar made from carbon and chrome-molybdene to ensure that rigidity remained at the heart of the Zonda Roadster's winning formula.

The most extreme Zonda was introduced in 2005 – the F version. Built alongside the standard Zonda, it features a lighter chassis and better aerodynamics courtesy of a host of changes including a larger front splitter. That monster Mercedes engine is now even more powerful thanks to a new induction system which means you've got a whopping 602bhp under your right foot – the power-hungry driver wanting even more face-stretching acceleration can of course settle for the Clubsport edition that boasts 650bhp.

For all its firepower though, what makes the Zonda supercar truly exceptional is that while it can lap tracks with the best of them, it also boasts the comfort, and just as important, the reliability of a GT car.

The culmination of Horacio Pagani's dream is now a supercar that can hold its own when put up against the established names like Porsche, Lamborghini and Ferrari. And that is one hell of an achievement.

BE 543DC

The Zonda was always going to cause a fuss. With those alien looks, it simply couldn't fail not to.

Exclusivity Guaranteed

The Roadster is regarded as the most desirable of the Zonda range, so interested customers are recommended to put their money down quickly – after all, the Roadster's production will be capped at only 40.

What's In A Name?

What's a supercar without a suitably evocative name? The word Zonda actually comes from a warm wind that blows west across the Andes Mountains in South America.

In Good Company

The Zonda's creator Horacio Pagani had expert help from the now-deceased Grand Prix racing legend, Juan Manuel Fangio. He is credited with aiding Horacio with all aspects of the supercar's creation – from its styling to its world-class handling.

Bespoke Heaven

The interior of the Zonda is as unique as its exterior with its mix of aluminium, leather and carbon fibre. Of course, for that special supercar touch, the company also provides owners with bespoke leather luggage and a pair of driving shoes with every car.

Leap Of Faith

Talk about conviction – Horacio Pagani was so sure that the Zonda would be a hit with the public once they'd seen it at the 1999 Geneva Motor Show, that he'd already had the car crash tested and ramped up ready for production. His instincts proved correct – only months after its unveiling, he had enough orders to take up two years' worth of the car's production.

Pagani Zonda S 7.3: The Specifications

Engine	V12
Valvetrain	DOHC 4 valves / cyl
Displacement	7291cc
Maximum Power	555bhp at 5,900rpm
Maximum Torque	553lb ft at 4,050rpm
Transmission	Six-speed manual
0–60mph	3.6secs
0–100mph	Sub 8secs
Maximum Speed	220mph
Steering	Rack and pinion with power assist
Brakes Front	Ventilated with four-piston callipers, ABS/355mm/14in
Brakes Rear	Ventilated with four-piston callipers, ABS/355mm/14in
Suspension Front	Double wishbones with helical springs, hydraulic dampers & anti-roll bar
Suspension Rear	Double wishbones with helical springs, hydraulic dampers & anti-roll bar
Kerb Weight	1350kg/2976lbs
Length	4395mm/173in
Width	2055mm/81in
Height	1151mm/45in
Wheels Front	9 x 18in
Wheel Rear	13 x 18in
Price	£350,000 US$457,000 estimated

Porsche Carrera GT

Sports car maker Porsche had been out of the supercar game for nearly two decades. Trust them to come storming back onto the scene with a road racer that makes all the right noises...

It's been a long while coming – the last time Porsche unleashed anything resembling a true supercar on to the world stage was with the magnificent 959 back in 1987. Perhaps we would have had to wait even longer if Porsche hadn't abandoned its Le Mans race car project at the end of the 1990s, which subsequently gave birth to this road-going car.

The GT's racing heritage is apparent throughout the car – it's got Formula One-style all-wishbone pushrod suspension, a brand new V10 engine (that was initially bound for Le Mans), and a small ceramic clutch that's mated to a six-speed manual transmission. Thanks to that diminutive clutch, it means the engine can be mounted lower in the car; the end result being better weight distribution and aerodynamics.

Unlike the normally rear-engined Porsches, theV10 is mounted in the middle and produces 612bhp. The low weight carbon fibre monocoque chassis coupled with such power means that the GT can do the 0–60 sprint in 3.8secs and 0–100 in a mere 6.9secs. Porsche also decided that any driver's aids should be thrown out of the window at their factory in Leipzig, Germany-only traction and anti-spin control are included so that the all-important GT driving experience is undiluted.

And the driving experience is what has shaken and stirred supercar aficionados – while in a straight line, the likes of the Ferrari Enzo may just have the Porsche licked, on the twisty stuff though, the GT comes into its own offering a benign drive that is all about feel and communication, coupled with huge grip.

City driving needn't be a handful either with the car willing to idle along before you decide to floor the accelerator and be pushed back into the seat with its startling but ultimately progressive grunt – there are no nasty surprises awaiting the keen, experienced driver.

The interior of the GT is your typical masterclass in Porsche efficiency – you can forget over-indulgent supercar flamboyance distracting you from the road – but looking up, you'll find a removable two-piece hard top that stows under the front bonnet.

No one should be surprised that Porsche have managed to pull off a masterstroke with their supercar entry – the GT shows just what we've all been missing out on while Porsche has been in supercar hibernation. It's just a shame it took them so long to rejoin the party. Welcome back Porsche – we've missed you.

Carrera GT
S GO 448

'...on the twisty stuff, the GT comes into its own offering a benign drive that is all about feel and communication coupled with huge grip.'

S GO 612

S GO 612

Touching Wood

A Porsche with a wood gear knob? It may seem out of place in a car that uses the latest composite materials, but that gear knob is a nod to the 1970–1971 Le Mans champ, the Porsche 917. So, why wood in the 917? Because it was the lightest material of that time – and it stopped the driver from scalding his hand when shifting gears.

Suited And Booted

There is space under the front bonnet for luggage in the GT but don't expect to be able to pack any kind of suitcase in there – after all, there are three radiators up front. In the meantime, Porsche provides a specially tailored travel bag to fit into the limited space.

Wheely, Wheely Good

To make a supercar, you have to be weight-obsessed – and Porsche is the 'supermodel' of supercars. For example, unlike most supercars that use aluminium alloy for their wheels, Porsche has used lighter forged magnesium. And those wheels need to be as light as possible – after all, they measure 19in at the front and a whopping 20in at the rear.

VIP: Very Important Porsche

As should be the case when collecting a hugely expensive supercar, you can opt for the factory delivery program where you can pick the car up from the factory based in Leipzig, Germany, and head out on to their test track.

Perfect Service

Potential owners could be forgiven for thinking that a supercar will need constant attention every couple of thousands of miles. Porsche claim that the GT requires the engine oil and air filter to be changed only every 12,000 miles; and the oil filter every 24,000 miles; and the spark plugs every four years or 24,000 miles.

Porsche Carrera GT: The Specifications

Engine	Aluminium V10
Valvetrain	DOHC 4 valves / cyl with VarioCam
Displacement	5733cc
Maximum Power	612bhp at 8,000rpm
Maximum Torque	435lb ft at 5,750rpm
Transmission	Six-speed manual with two-plate ceramic dry clutch
0–60mph	3.8secs
0–100mph	6.9secs
Maximum Speed	205mph
Steering	Rack and pinion with power assist
Brakes Front	Porsche Ceramic Composite Brake (PCCB). Ventilated and cross drilled with six-piston callipers, ABS/ 380mm/15in
Brakes Rear	Porsche Ceramic Composite Brake (PCCB). Ventilated and cross-drilled with six-piston callipers, ABS/ 380mm/15in
Suspension Front	Double wishbones with inboard springs inc. dampers units
Suspension Rear	Double wishbones with inboard springs inc. dampers units
Kerb Weight	1380kg/3042lbs
Length	4,613mm/182in
Width	1,921mm/76in
Height	1,166mm/46in
Wheels Front	9.5 x 19in
Wheel Rear	12.5 x 20in
Price	£323,000/US$440,000

It's loud; it's rude; it's not one for small talk, and it doesn't want to be everyone's friend... it's a TVR then...

The seaside town of Blackpool, in the northwest of England, is not your typical setting for a supercar maker, but amongst the tourist attractions and arcade venues (and donkey rides) is one of the true greats – TVR. Never mind the sticks of rock that can be bought from any Blackpool tourist shop – it's the sticks of automotive dynamite created by TVR that grab the attention of any discerning car fan. And the new Sagaris is no different...

TVR Sagaris

Visually, TVR doesn't do subtle, and the Sagaris is like being poked in the eye with an electric cattle prod – it's that shocking; it makes supercars such as the Ferrari F430 look everyday and hum-drum. Even the eccentric Pagani Zonda might have a tough time in the "what the hell is that?" stakes as passers-by gawp at the spectacle that is the Sagaris. Look over the composite GRP bodywork of the TVR and your senses are assaulted from every angle – those dragon-esque headlamps, the mass of bonnet vents; and on the car's rump, well, have you ever seen a transparent rear spoiler? No, we thought not.

On looks alone then, the Sagaris is on another level – and underneath, there's typical TVR firepower on offer for the brave-hearted driver. The Sagaris was intended to be a trackday car born out of the pretty TVR T350 that would also be suitable for road use; and with the finished car now bedazzling drivers, TVR has delivered on that promise.

With its 0-60 time of 3.7secs and 0-100 in 8.1secs, the 400bhp 4-litre engine mounted on the Sagaris's tubular steel chassis is easy to exploit with its five-speed gearbox. But for all its obvious drama, the Sagaris is day-to-day useable. While threading in and out of traffic, the car is not trying to scrabble to get away from you; however, show it the right road, and the Sagaris demonstrates its true TVR roots. Of course it's very quick with huge grip but, unlike previous razor-sharp TVRs, it won't grow impatient with your bad driving and suddenly decide that a ditch is preferable to the road. The Sagaris gives the driver plenty of warning if things are about to go wrong. That said, you're behind the wheel of a TVR–so don't expect it to generously forgive your every mistake.

Inside the Sagaris is equally special – two white dials peer out at the driver from the dashboard while the rest of the cabin is smothered in leather. Everything on view is bespoke – apart from the three-spoke steering wheel. You'll also notice the roll cage, there to 'reassure' anyone that while the car lacks electronic safety devices, you'll be well looked after if the worst does happen.

The Sagaris is one of two TVRs to come out of the Blackpool company since it was taken over in 2004 (see p.128), and judging by this and the Tuscan 2 featured in the next chapter, the marque shows every sign of going from strength to strength under its new leadership. With its unmatched 'butch' charisma, no BS approach and obscene performance, the low volume British TVR range is something to be cherished; God bless the (melodrama) Queen.

TVR

'Visually, TVR doesn't do subtle, and the Sagaris is like being poked in the eye with an electric cattle prod. It's that shocking; it makes supercars such as the Ferrari F430 look everyday and hum-drum.'

PN05 OUL

Name Dropping

The marque's lack of pretension is perfectly illustrated by the origins of the company's name – TVR. It's not some acronym for a fancy design philosophy but is actually based on the founder's first name, TreVoR Wilkinson.

A Brief (Recent) History Of TVR

TVR was founded in 1947 – but in2004, the company was sold to a 24-year-old entrepreneur, Nikolai Smolenski, who, at the last count, was worth nearly £55 million/US$105 million. His initial moves to take TVR into the 21st century have been to address the build quality issues that have plagued the handmade TVRs of the past; because customers have been put off by reliability issues, the Russian delayed the release of the Sagaris and the Tuscan 2 to ensure that build quality was improved.

Bound For The USA?

While TVR has amassed a cult following in the USA thanks to games such as PlayStation 2's *Gran Turismo* series and movies like *Swordfish*, the car isn't available to the US public. Only time will tell if the new owner of TVR has plans to unleash the brand in America.

"I'm A TV-R Star"

The Sagaris prototype unveiled to thrilled audiences in 2003 went on to become one of the stars of British reality TV show *The Heist* where ex-criminals were charged with the task of stealing it. They succeeded.

Keeping It Close

The factory in Blackpool, England, makes practically everything you see inside and outside of a TVR, and the company's straight-six engines are the stuff of motoring legend. TVR is obsessed with doing as much of the cars as possible by using local talent and skills.

TVR Sagaris: The Specifications

Engine	All-aluminium TVR Speed Six straight-six
Displacement	3996cc
Maximum power	406bhp at 7,000-7,500bhp
Maximum torque	349lb ft at 5,000rpm
Transmission	Five-speed manual
0-60mph	3.7secs
0-100mph	8.1secs
Maximum speed	175mph
Steering	Rack and pinion with power assist
Brakes front	Ventilated discs with 4-piston alloy callipers/322mm/13in
Brakes rear	Ventilated discs with single sliding piston calipers/ 298mm/12in
Suspension front	Independent double wishbones with coils over gas hydraulic dampers & anti-roll bar
Suspension rear	Independent double wishbones with coils over gas hydraulic dampers & anti-roll bar
Kerb weight	1078kg/2376lbs
Length	4057mm/160in
Width	1850mm/73in
Height	1175mm/46in
Price	£49,995 US price not available

Now in its second generation, the Tuscan has 'grown up' to become a more civilized supercar than the hooligan-like original. But the beast still lurks beneath those strikingly beautiful looks...

The shape of the Tuscan is a classic – it's sensual; it's individual; indeed, psychologists could probably argue for hours about how Freudian the Tuscan is. But all you need to know is that it's an update of the utterly seductive design that was first featured on the original Tuscan – it screams out brute force from every curve.

Featuring TVR's incredible straight-six engine that produces a whopping 350bhp, the Tuscan 2 is blindingly fast – 0-60 takes 4.2secs, and the supercar will happily see 175mph and beyond. But TVR's engineers aren't known for sitting back and slapping themselves on the back for a job well down; they've been busy 'tinkering' and have produced the top of the range Tuscan 2 S that features 400bhp on tap and can hit 0-60 in 3.8secs – goodbye Gallardo. All that power is kept on the road at high speed thanks to a splitter under the front grille and a gurney above the boot lid which ensures downforce over both the front and rear axles.

TVR Tuscan 2

But be under no illusion, the Tuscan 2 S (and the 2 for that matter) isn't a supercar that likes to cosset its drivers – while the Tuscan 2 has been designed to be more 'soft' around the edges than the original, this is still a hugely aggressive car that, compared to its competitors, is as hardcore as they come. The Tuscan 2 will still intimidate

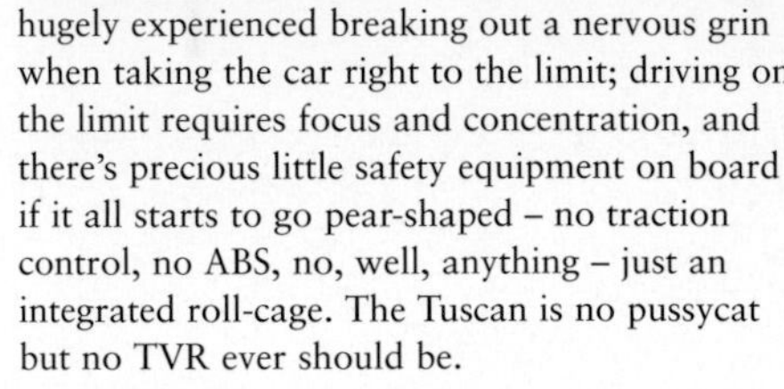

the inexperienced driver – it will even have the hugely experienced breaking out a nervous grin when taking the car right to the limit; driving on the limit requires focus and concentration, and there's precious little safety equipment on board if it all starts to go pear-shaped – no traction control, no ABS, no, well, anything – just an integrated roll-cage. The Tuscan is no pussycat but no TVR ever should be.

Climb inside the TVR and the sight of a fully bespoke interior will greet you; all the vital readouts such as speed and revs are digital; the leather upholstery is made by TVR in-house, and the alloy switchgear is tactile and satisfying to use. There is an issue though for anyone familiar with the TVR brand – build quality. Some have said that a TVR is best to use as a weekend car because you sure wouldn't want to rely on it getting you to work day-in, day-out.

The development of the TVR Tuscan 2 and the Sagaris though saw them being put through punishing conditions in Bahrain, South Africa, Saudi Arabia and Russia for the first time to ensure that the car could take high speeds in gruelling environments. Whether all the 'gremlins' have been wiped out remains to be seen though – only time will tell but with its three year/36,000 mile warranty, TVR is backing up its new found commitment to build quality with its bank balance.

So the TVR Tuscan 2 is something special – its looks, coupled with its outrageous performance, mean that this a true old school supercar. It might have softened up but still treat it with the respect it deserves and you are guaranteed to have the drive of your life. Treat it with contempt, and it will bite back. A true British bulldog then.

PJ54 WNH

'Driving a TVR on the limit requires focus and concentration, and there's precious little safety equipment on board if it all starts to go pear-shaped – no traction control, no ABS, no, well, anything – just an integrated roll-cage. The Tuscan's no pussycat but no TVR ever should be.'

PJ54 WNH

Doing It Differently

TVR is known for not playing by the rules with any element of its cars. They even have to do their doors differently – don't go looking for a traditional handle by the way; pushing a button underneath the wing mirror makes the window slip down, the door gently springing open. Now how's that for 'bespoke'?

Bark Worse Than Its Bite?

The TVR's straight-six engine sounds incredible – the deep roar that bellows every time you floor the car is a marvel – but the original Tuscan could bite in the handling department. The Tuscan 2 features a revised geometry, improved bump stops plus re-rated springs and dampers so that the car can be manhandled more easily when pushing the Tuscan 2 to its limits. But still, it's advised that the TVR is handled with care.

Practical As Well As Powerful

Many supercars require you to shoe-horn any luggage into them using either bespoke bags... or a crowbar. The Tuscan 2 however can happily take two golf bags, which means the car's actually practical as well as sensational.

Lighten Up

The key to the Tuscan 2's searing performance is the fact that it weighs so little – with a kerb weight of only 1,100kg/2425lbs to cart around, that 4-litre straight-six engine can offer supercar performance without the need for added extras like turbo chargers.

TVR Tuscan 2: The Specifications

Engine	All-aluminium TVR Speed Six straight-six
Displacement	3605cc
Maximum power	350bhp at 7,200rpm
Maximum torque	290lb ft at 5,500rpm
Transmission	Five-speed manual
0-60mph	4.2secs
0-100mph	9.5secs
Maximum speed	175mph
Steering	Rack & pinion with power assist
Brakes front	Ventilated discs with 4-piston alloy callipers/ 304mm/12in
Brakes rear	Ventilated discs with single sliding piston calipers/ 282mm/11in
Suspension front	Independent double wish bones with coils over gas hydraulic dampers & anti-roll bar
Suspension rear	Independent double wish bones with coils over gas hydraulic dampers & anti-roll bar
Kerb weight	1100kg/2425lbs
Length	4235mm/167in
Width	1810mm/71in
Height	1200mm/47in
Wheels Front	8 x 16in
Wheel Rear	8 x 16in
Price	£39,850 US price not available

Fact or fiction? The latest legend to bear the Bugatti name could finally be with us after a very long development period...

It shouldn't really be featured in this book – after all, the Bugatti Veyron has been on the verge of hitting the road for what seems like years. Hounded by delays and slips in production, it's become something of a running joke in the auto industry that it will never actually see the light of day.

The trouble is that the industry also happens to be head over heels in love with the Veyron, and who can blame them? First of all, the Veyron is the latest creation from a brand that has fans all over the world – Bugatti was created back at the beginning of the 20th century by Ettore Bugatti; its limos and sports cars from the 1920s and 1930s are now the stuff of motoring legend. And so is the company's history.

Bugatti Veyron

Death in the Bugatti family; a failed revival; and a rebirth followed by a humiliating bankruptcy when the world sank into recession in the 1990s – reading Bugatti's history, you could be forgiven for thinking that the company is cursed. Even in the hands of Volkswagen, the development of the latest car to bear the Bugatti name – the Veyron – was at one point halted. But now VW has the car back on track with delivery of the first Veyron to one lucky (and rich) customer at the end of 2005. Any supercar fan knows why it's essential that the Veyron does finally touch down – after all, it could potentially rip asunder every supercar that's gone before it. Here are the figures – it's got nearly 1,000bhp on tap; it's got not one, but 4 turbos; it's expected to weigh in at just under 2 tonnes; it can go from 0–60 in an estimated 3secs; it has a potentially record-breaking top speed of over 250mph; it features the biggest rear tyres ever fitted on a production car; it has four wheel drive of course; oh, and it's going to cost in excess of 1,000,000 Euros/US$1,000,000 to get your hands on one. In fact, everything about this supercar is big – the DSG gearbox even has 7 gears to make the most of (and more importantly, tame) the Veyron's amazing W16, 64v quad-turbo 8-litre engine.

VW are adamant that they also want the Veyron to be utterly driveable and not simply a car that sees the bare minimum of miles before being locked up in a high security garage with 24-hour surveillance (though the latter is recommended). And VW want the Veyron to be reliable – just under a dozen of them have already been put through the punishing testing that all VWs, from Lupos upwards, have to go through before they head out to the showroom.

If the word supercar ever seemed too underwhelming to describe something as monumental as the Bugatti Veyron, then hypercar would probably do it justice. But only just, mind you.

BUGATTI

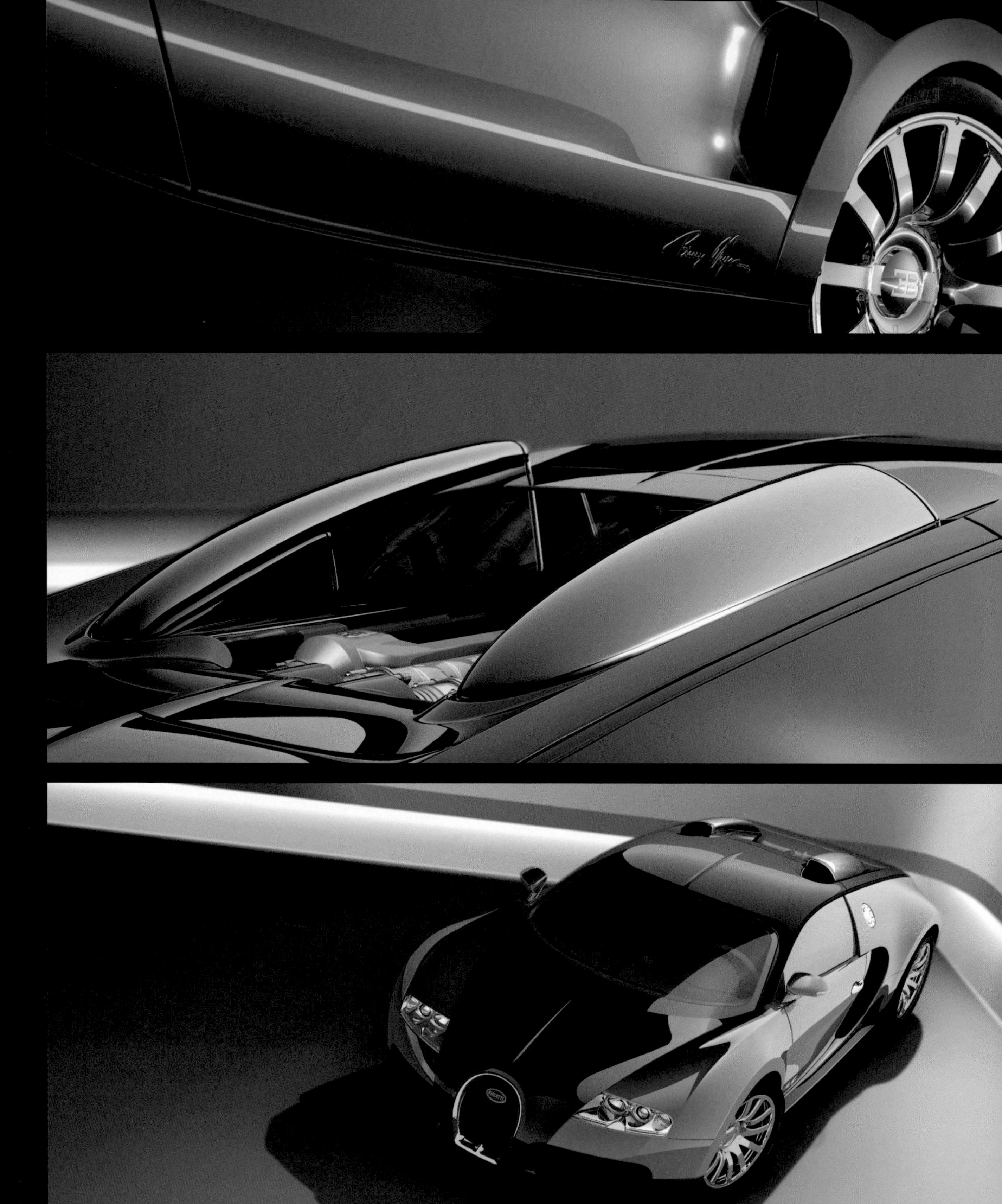

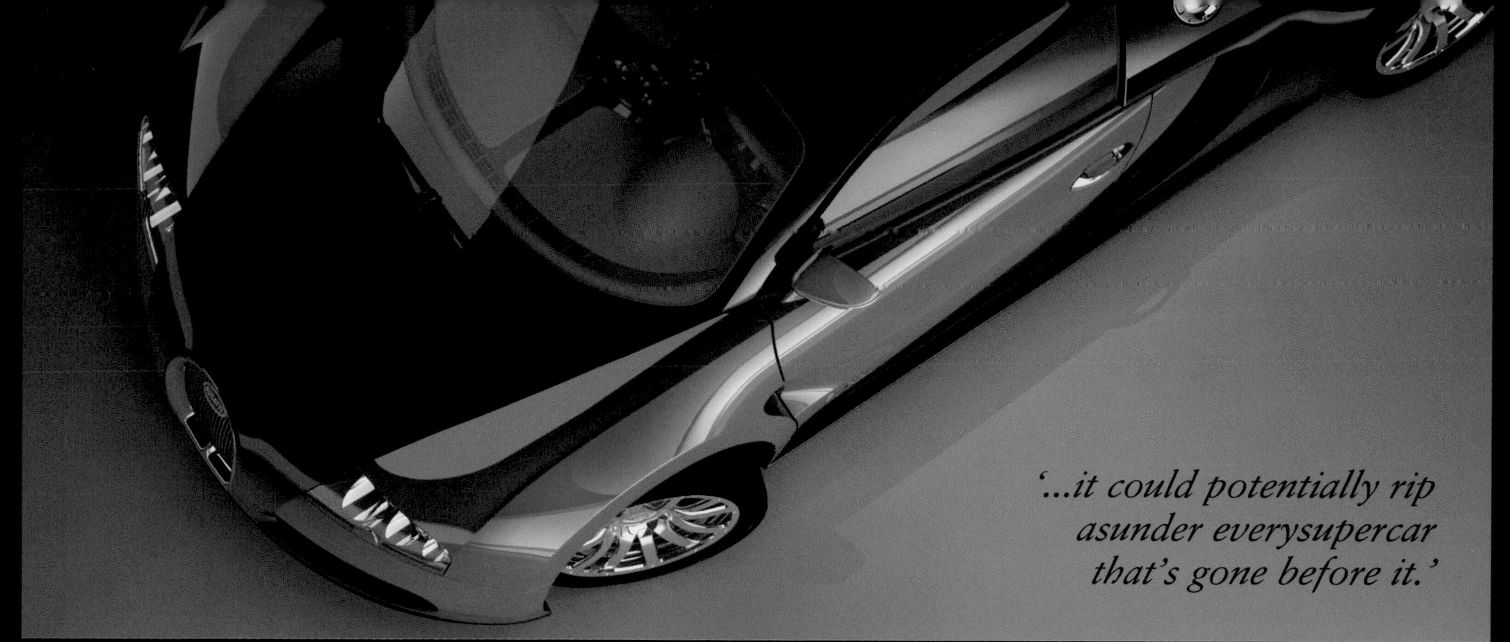

'...it could potentially rip asunder everysupercar that's gone before it.'

Tall Order?

Volkswagen intends to make between 30 to 50 Veyrons a year depending on the demand from customers. And if you're wondering if Volkswagen is actually up to the job of selling supercars, bear in mind that they own Audi – the company that oversaw the creation of the next generation of Lamborghinis.

Back To Its Roots

The Veyron is being assembled at a workshop right next to Chateau St Jean near Mosheim in France – which is the region where the company's founder, Ettore Bugatti, began making his dream cars nearly 100 years ago.

Brake Neck Speeds

With nearly 1,000bhp to propel the driver towards the horizon, it's fairly important that the Veyron can stop as quickly as it can start.

To aid in avoiding near disaster when a car pulls out in front of you while you're doing 200mph + on a German autobahn, the Veyron is fitted with specialist carbon-ceramic brakes and a rear wing that can be deployed as an air brake. It is claimed that slamming on the anchors at 248mph will bring the Veyron to a complete standstill in less than 10secs.

Egg-Face Interface

The car's difficult 'gestation period' has been tough for Bugatti – first, a mule version of the car managed to crash at over 200mph. Then the Veyron made an appearance at California's Laguna race track, USA, last year, only to spin off the track and come to a rest in a gravel trap, missing a concrete wall by inches. Much media mirth ensued, but with the progress Bugatti have made, they seem on course to have the last laugh.

Bugatti Veyron (specifications subject to change)

Engine	64v quad turbo W16	**Maximum Torque**	922lb ft at 2,200-5,500rpm	**Kerb Weight**	1950kg/4299lbs approx.	**Wheels Front**	9.5 x 20in
Valvetrain	DOHC 4 Valves / Cyl	**Transmission**	Seven-speed DSG	**Length**	4380mm/172in	**Wheel Rear**	13 x 21in
Displacement	7993cc	**0–60mph**	3.0secs	**Width**	1994mm/78in	**Price**	1,000,000 Euros approx US$1,000,000 approx.
Maximum Power	987bhp at 6,000rpm	**Maximum Speed**	252mph	**Height**	1206mm/47in		

No, it's not your typical looking supercar but hey, the British aren't known for settling for the same old, same old...

No windshield, no doors, no headlamps – if you're looking for a luxurious GT capable of crushing continents in a single afternoon, while seating the driver in the lap of luxury, then really the Atom isn't for you. But if you want to bag yourself a sports car that can outrun most supercars on the track and the road when it comes to performance and handling, then the Atom is as good as it gets.

Ariel Atom 2

Perhaps the Atom is the antithesis to the supercar scene's sometimes po-facedness. With no swish bodywork covering up its ultra-lightweight chassis, everything is out on display. Perhaps this is a road-going car that can truly be said to be a perfect example of form following function. And the great thing about the Atom is that its function is so simple – to make you remember why you fell in love with driving in the first place.

And it would be hard not to fall head over heels all over again with the Atom's chassis constantly offering up reams of communication, and the suspension based on one-seater racing cars that can easily be tweaked for track or road use; the Atom can be thrown around corners with abandon. The car's unique composite twin seat unit means that you won't find yourself (or your passenger) being thrown all over the cockpit. Well, it's hardly even a cockpit – there are no frills here, merely the basics required to get started.

As for the Atom's performance on the straight stuff, you can see why the car has gone down a storm – the Ariel Atom 2 released in 2003 offers up the perfect performance to help induce that feel-good factor – after all, it features one of world's finest budget engines (and six-speed gearboxes) whipped straight out of a Japanese-spec Honda Civic Type R, which produces 220bhp. But bear in mind that the Atom weighs only 456kg/1005lbs – with such a lean kerb weight, it makes the likes of Zonda and Enzo look in need of a two-week stint on a 'fat farm'. And just to rub the salt into those supercar wounds, Ariel offers the Atom in an 'enhanced' supercharged version boasting an insane 300bhp.

This piece of motoring magic is assembled at Ariel's headquarters in Norfolk, UK – 'headquarters' being seven people led by Simon Saunders, a former designer at Aston Martin and GM.
It's clear that the Ariel Atom is a labour of love hand-assembled by a group of dedicated enthusiasts. Helmet recommended.

WILLANS
WILLANS

'The Ariel Atom 2 features one of the world's finest budget engines whipped straight out of a Japanese-spec Honda Civic Type R'

Ariel Atom 2: The Specifications

Engine	Honda iVTEC / 4 Cyl	**Maximum torque**	145lb ft at 6,100rpm	**Maximum speed**	135mph	**Price**	£26,000 US price not available
Displacement	1998cc	**Transmission**	Six-speed manual	**Kerb weight**	456kg		
Maximum power	220bhp at 8,200rpm	**0-60 mph**	3.5secs				

Offering outstanding performance on the track, and the ability to be an everyday runabout, the Exige is also packed with racing pedigree...

The miracle makers based in Norfolk, UK, first launched the Lotus Exige in 2000; the mid-engine coupé was actually based on the Mk I Lotus Elise, the firm's critically acclaimed two-seater roadster. In 2004 though, the Exige was relaunched this time featuring a Toyota 1.8-litre VVT-i engine instead of the original's Rover K-series. The reason? So Lotus could start selling the Exige in the USA – after all, that Toyota engine passes all the US's strict emissions regulations whereas the K-series never did. The bullet-proof Toyota engine generates 189bhp which makes the Exige zip from 0–60 in 4.9secs.

Lotus Exige

The key as to why the Exige can deliver quite such neck-snapping acceleration from this un-supercar-like lump is thanks to the car's light weight. The Exige's underpinnings are now based on the Elise Mk II – in fact, the extruded and bonded aluminium tub, with a steel rear subframe, is used in the Elise 111R. Lotus though have used stiffer springs and dampers on the Exige to ensure that the driver can make the most of the car's performance and to ensure that body roll is kept to a minimum.

The Exige with its roof scoop, fast back roof and rear wing certainly fulfils Lotus's desire to produce a race car for the road – and it delivers on all its visual drama. Renowned for its communicative chassis, body control and non-power assisted tactile steering, the Exige wasn't born to scare the hell out of you but just to offer the driver an adrenaline rush every time they pressed down on the accelerator.

And with its supreme aerodynamic package, the race car feels nailed to the road with enough downforce being provided no matter how fast you're going. Couple that with its specially designed tyres and no corner is too sharp or scary for the Exige. The question isn't whether the car can take it; the real question is – can you?

The car highlighted on these pages is the specially commissioned Lotus Exige Sport that features carbon fibre bodywork and front splitter, a rear diffuser, and an adjustable rear wing for added downforce. Instead of the Toyota engine, there's a 400bhp 3-litre V6 lump paired with a sequential six-speed gearbox. Unfortunately, the car that took only six months to develop is a one-off that was ordered by a client who is expected to use the Exige Sport in Asian racing.

Customers wanting a more extreme version of the standard Exige will have to make do with Exige Sport 240R which features 240hp and a supercar-crushing 0–60 in 3.9secs – do bear in mind though that only 50 will ever see the light of day. So best to get that order in now.

'...no corner is too sharp or scary for the Exige. The question isn't whether the car can take it; the real question is can you?'

Lotus Exige: The Specifications

Engine	Aluminium Inline-4
Displacement	1796cc
Maximum power	189bhp at 7,800rpm
Maximum torque	133.5lb ft at 6,800rpm
Transmission	Six-speed manual
0-60 mph	4.9secs
0-100 mph	13.2secs
Maximum speed	147mph
Kerb weight	875kg/1929lbs
Price	£29,995 US$50–55,000 estimated

Mercedes-Benz SLK350

'Luxury and performance' all wrapped up in mini-supercar looks. The SLK350 is one very special car...

The original SLK was a great car – for posers. Its main party trick was the ability to turn from a coupé into an open-top roadster in seconds thanks to its smart metal retractable roof. The trouble was, for all its sporty pretensions, it could never match the might of the sublime Porsche Boxster. Enter the SLK MkII; everything about the roadster is infinitely better – this is no poser's car that is destined to be parked outside fancy wine bars or driven by hair stylists. The SLK is actually now a proper sports car that the diehard enthusiast wouldn't be embarrassed to be seen in.

It's those looks – the original SLK may have been a smart if slightly effeminate design, but the SLK MkII is far more like a muscular roadster thanks to its F1-style nose 'inspired' by its (very) big brother, the SLR. The folding metal roof remains and is now more of an elegant design – and more importantly, it goes up quickly in case rain interrupts play.

The entry model SLK200 powered by a supercharged 1.8-litre is best suited to those who want more show than go. It provides adequate performance for a droptop – 0-60 in 8.3secs – but hardly the kind of acceleration that will trouble a sporty family sedan, never mind a full-blooded supercar with a V12. No, the model to aim for is the rather fine SLK350.

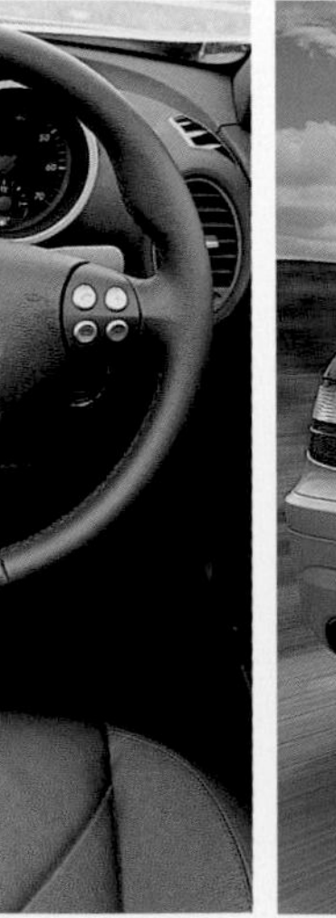

Featuring a warbling 3.5-litre V6, the torque-happy engine offers plenty of power for the thrillseeker. On the road, the little Benz feels planted, tackling corners with the kind of hunger that the original sorely lacked. You also feel safe; perhaps too safe for some – the ESP has been criticized for taking the fun out of the SLK even when switched off (it isn't really ever 'off' – it's always there in the background monitoring). But for the everyday driver, there's more than enough entertainment on offer to make that grin creep higher towards their ears.

Thankfully, the SLK also now has a quality six-speed gearbox as standard for the driver who likes to feel absolutely in control of that V6 in front of him – while the SLK MkI eventually did have a manual option, it was quite frankly naff. For those who want a more leisurely life, the SLK features Mercedes' unique seven-speed auto – in manual mode, it's accessible through the buttons mounted on the steering wheel. Mercedes claims that the auto shaves 0.1secs off the 0-60 time. Whether it shaves some of the fun off too is open to debate.

For those supercar aficionados who are still not convinced, there is the option of upping the budget and splashing out on the £47,730/$60,500 (approx) SLK55 AMG that features a 5.5-litre V8 engine producing a very healthy 360bhp and a 0–60 time of 4.9secs. Surely that's enough power for those who can't stretch to a supercar three times the price?

Most of us though will be happy with the SLK350. It's a near-perfect blend – a bruiser when you're in the mood and an extremely comfortable cruiser when you're not.

KS04 BXJ

'The SLK350 is a near-perfect blend; a bruiser when you're in the mood and an extremely comfortable cruiser when you're not.'

Mercedes-Benz SLK350: The Specifications

Engine	V6
Displacement	3498cc
Maximum power	272bhp at 6,000rpm
Maximum torque	258lb ft at 2,400rpm
Transmission	Six-speed manual/Seven-speed auto
0-60 mph	5.6secs
Maximum speed	155mph
Kerb weight	1465kg/3231lbs
Price	£34,270/US$46,220

KS04 BXJ

Supercar performance, but at a fraction of the price. Discover the small car guaranteed to deliver big grins...

Vauxhall VX220 Turbo

Picture the scene – you've just spent a fortune on an Italian supercar; the cost doesn't matter because you're know you're in something special – that pedigree, those looks... and the bespoke leather luggage. Out on the open road, you decide to floor the accelerator for the first time. And as you roar off – your ego swelling to the size of a small African state – a car that costs a tenth of what you paid for yours overtakes you.

'Ouch' is the only word that will suffice because you've just been 'VX'd'. Welcome to the rather brilliant Vauxhall VX220 Turbo. It's all the more remarkable if you consider the car's manufacturer – Vauxhall (owned by General Motors), in the UK, has been perceived for decades as a rather run-of-the-mill car manufacturer. They've made perfectly good family cars, sedans, MPVS and so on, but Vauxhall always seemed like a car maker that lacked a certain spark – they lacked excitement.

So creating excitement became the job of the original VX220 launched in 2000. On the face of it, Vauxhall should have struggled to produce such a fantastic two-seater roadster but they had

help – they went to Lotus. The rear-engined VX220 is actually a 're-skinned' Elise, but Vauxhall insisted that only 141 parts were shared with its equally illustrious brother. The Lotus-built VX is also acknowledged to be more forgiving for the over-eager driver than the Elise – and it is all the better for it.

Featuring an aluminium chassis and plastic body panels, the original VX220 had a 2.2-litre engine that could do 0-60 in 5.6secs. But that wasn't powerful enough for Vauxhall... so they released the VX220 Turbo. Featuring 197bhp from the 2-litre turbo engine, the car can now make the sprint from 0–60 in a mere 4.7secs – that's Vanquish S country – and it has a top speed of 151mph, which is more than enough for a public road. The handling of the VX is superb as well – flat and taut with large dollops of information being fed back to the driver about what is going on under the tyres. This may be a serious driver's car, but treat it with the respect it deserves, and it's also real controllable fun.

In 2004, Vauxhall released an even hotter version of the VX, the VXR220, which could hit 0-60 in only 4.2secs and only ran out of puff at 154mph. Alas, due to its limited production number of 65 cars, they all sold out in six weeks – typical supercar then.

Luxury lovers may find the VX's interiors somewhat spartan – there are precious few toys and those hoping to find mod cons as simple as electric windows have to make do with manual winders. But such omissions are there for one very good reason – to keep the pocket rocket's weight down. The VX also features a canvas roof that can be rolled off and stored in the tiny 'boot' with relative ease. All in all, the little Vauxhall is a car that offers the thrills of supercar ownership without the costs.

VE52 ZGY

'Vauxhall should have struggled to produce such a fantastic two-seater roadster but they had help... they went to Lotus.'

Vauxhall VX220 Turbo: The Specifications

Engine	Iline-4
Displacement	1998cc
Maximum power	197bhp at 5,500rpm
Maximum torque	184lb ft from 1,950rpm
Transmission	Six-speed manual
0-60 mph	4.7secs
0-100 mph	Under 13secs
Maximum speed	151mph
Kerb weight	930kg/2050lbs
Price	£25,495/Not available in US

MUSCLE CARS

AMC AMX

AMC's cut-down Javelin was an oddball, but it was the company's best player in the muscle car era

The AMC AMX of 1968 was a unique proposition. It was the only two-seater American sportscar of the time.

Essentially a cut-down version of AMC's Javelin the AMX (American Motors eXperimental), was a foot shorter than its sibling. Its proportions were rather odd, but the AMX was significantly lighter than the Javelin.

And with the top-flight 315bhp 390 cubic inch V8 installed, the AMX was a lively performer. Zero to sixty came in just 6.9 seconds and the quarter-mile in 15 seconds. There was a four-speed manual tranny, toughened suspension and bucket seats for the two occupants. A 290 and 343 V8 were lesser options.

Land speed racing legend Craig Breedlove set no less than 106 speed records with an AMX in February 1968 and, to celebrate, a special run of 50 Craig Breedlove editions were built. Finished in patriotic red, white and blue, few survive today.

A few minor cosmetic changes were made for 1969 but the year is best remembered for the Big Bad AMX, available in bold orange, green and blue color schemes with matching bumpers.

Also offered was a Go pack to include power disc brakes, uprated suspension for improved handling and redline tires.

A very limited run of SS cars designed for the drag strip were also produced. Modifications to the 390 cubic inch V8 engine resulted in a claimed power output of 340bhp, but as was frequently the case in the muscle car era, this was a very conservative estimate. The SS package almost doubled the AMX's sticker price, so it's unsurprising that only around 50 were sold.

MODEL HISTORY

1968

AMX launched, based on shortened Javelin

1969

Limited-run SS is the most powerful and most expensive AMX

1970

The last two-seater AMX is built

1971

AMX is now the top model in the Javelin range

1974

AMX production run ends

1970 saw the last of the real two-seater AMX models. Little was changed, but a ram air induction scoop was added to make the hood more aggressive.

In 1971 the AMC AMX ceased to be a model in its own right and was the name for the top model Javelin. Under the curiously-bulbous hood was a choice of two 360 cubic inch V8s with 245 or 290bhp.

More power came with the Go package which slotted a 401 330bhp V8 under the hood and upgraded the wheels, tires and brakes as part of the deal.

1972 would be the last year for the AMX as a muscle car. The Go package was still available but the entry-level engine had been reduced to a 304 cubic inch unit with a paltry 150bhp.

The AMX continued to be sold until 1974, but its days as a muscle car were long finished.

Specification

Years built	1966-1974
Most powerful model	1969 SS
Engine type	V8
Displacement	401 cid
Transmission	four-speed manual
Power	340bhp
Top speed	120mph

'The AMX of 1968 was a unique proposition. It was the only two-seater American sportscar of the time.'

Buick Gran Sport

Buick's entry to the muscle car fray may have been late but it was a worthy contender

Pontiac's success with its 1964 GTO was the spur for Buick to produce the GS. Many consider the GTO as the first true muscle car, setting the formula for others to follow: drop a big-block V8 into an intermediate-sized car and sell it at a budget price.

So Buick shoehorned its 401 cubic inch 'nailhead' V8 into its existing Skylark model, bestowing it with 325bhp, to cash in on this new trend. The 1965 Skylark Gran Sport wasn't as big a hit as the GTO, but it started a model line that would develop truly muscular looks and performance. Despite arriving a bit late in the day, the Gran Sport was a strong seller in its first year and Buick was encouraged to hone the car further.

For 1966, the Gran Sport was treated to a new, hotter 340bhp version of the 401 engine, dropping its quarter mile time by a second to 15.4secs. But buying into the Buick brand wasn't cheap and Gran Sport sales were a lot slower than in its introductory year.

The name was abbreviated in 1967, when the GS 400 arrived with a new, higher-revving 400 cid engine also giving 340bhp. A new three-speed auto transmission and the 260bhp 'junior' GS 340 also saw the light of day and its cut price helped sales.

Through '68 and '69 the GS was weighed down by huge chrome fenders, but an interseting option quietly appeared at dealerships. The Stage One Special Package came with a unique 400 cid motor. Although officially rated at 345bhp (just 5bhp more than the regular 400), the reality was more like 390bhp. In 1969 a Stage Two option came with an official 360bhp.

MODEL HISTORY

1965

Buick fits 401 cid 'nailhead' engine into Skylark, producing the Gran Sport

1967

New 400 cid V8 introduced, along with the smaller-engined GS 340

1969

Previously fake hood scoops became a functional part of the induction system

1970

The GS 455 is born. In Stage 1 tune with the GSX style pack, it is the ultimate Buick muscle car

1972

Last true Buick GS produced. After this the name became a pale shadow of its former glory

In 1970, the GS reached its pinnacle. That year's GS 455 had a brand new 455 cubic inch engine to give plenty of go, while the GSX appearance package provided all the show: spoilers, classic body stripes and supersize tires.

The combination made for the ultimate Buick muscle car of all time, when the Stage 1 performance package was specified, giving a hotter cam, bigger valves and a revised carburetor. The company under-rated it at 360bhp, as road testers of the time claimed it was nearer 400bhp!

Along with its high-performance brethren, 1971 signalled the beginning of the end for the GS, with the introduction of low-lead gasoline lowering power and higher insurance premiums turning buyers away. Post-1972, the GS name was shunted from one Buick coupe to another, the glory of the muscle car years long gone, and in 1975 it ceased to exist.

Specification

Years built	1965 to 1975
Most powerful model	1970 GS 455
Engine type	V8
Displacement	455 cu in
Transmission	three-speed automatic
Power	360bhp
Top speed	130mph

The company under-rated it at 360bhp, as road testers of the time claimed it was nearer 400bhp

Buick Wildcat

Buick's first attempt at high-performance never shrugged off its luxury image

Buick was not a company with a reputation for high performance machinery, but that all started to change in 1962 when the Wildcat hit the scene.

Part of the Invicta line, the Wildcat Sport Coupe (as it was officially called) benefited from a beefed-up chassis and suspension, and more dragstrip-oriented transmission ratios to make the most of the 401 cid V8 engine's 325bhp. It also came loaded with luxury, which helped to pump its weight up to a hefty 4,150 pounds.

During its eight-year lifespan, the Wildcat was bestowed with more and more power. The original two-door hardtop body style was also bolstered by a four-door hardtop, a two-door convertible and finally a conventional four-door sedan.

Despite Buick's view of the Wildcat as a sports car, the public thought different and it was the staid-looking sedan that saw the greatest sales success.

In '64, two new optional 425 cid V8s were made available, with 340 and 360bhp, which helped to offset the increased 4,500-pound curb weight.

The turning point in terms of styling was 1965, which saw the Wildcat sharing its sheet metal with its Buick stablemate, the Le Sabre, and losing some of its individuality in the process.

The introduction of the Wildcat Custom, with more luxurious interior trimming, arrived in 1966 along with an optional high performance package. Only 21 owners are known to have signed up for this high-performance 425 cid V8, which was good for 380bhp and 465 lbft of torque thanks to a pair of four-barrel carbs and a dual exhaust making the gas flow freely.

MODEL HISTORY

1962

First Wildcat introduced as part of Buick's Invicta model line-up powered by 325bhp 401 cid V8

1963

Sports coupe body style is augmented by a four-door hardtop and two-door convertible

1964

Optional 340 and 360bhp 425 cid V8s introduced, along with new four-door sedan

1965

All-new styling sees Wildcat sharing bodywork with Buick Le Sabre

1970

Final model has most powerful standard engine at 370bhp

A more efficient domed combustion chamber in the all-new standard 430 cid engine of 1967 raised power to 360bhp, but by '69 the styling was so similar to the Le Sabre that the two were virtually identical. Only the grille, a few body moldings and the steering wheel differentiated between the two, and the Wildcat's lack of identity led to a drop in sales.

The end came in 1970, but the Wilcat went out with a howl, not a whimper. The run-out model featured Buick's all-new 455 cid V8, producing 370bhp and and 510 lbft of torque.

So what was arguably Buick's first performance car ended its days with the most powerful standard engine it ever had.

The flirtation with muscle cars was a short one and Buick reverted to what its buyers loved best; luxury.

Specification

Years built	1962 to 1970
Most powerful model	1970 455
Engine type	V8
Displacement	455 cu in
Transmission	three-speed automatic
Power	370bhp
Top speed	130mph

'The flirtation with muscle cars was a short one and Buick reverted to what its buyers loved best...'

Chevrolet Camaro

Chevrolet's answer to the Ford Mustang came a bit late, but it was worth the wait

The Camaro was General Motors' belated response to the Mustang. Two years after Ford's pony car appeared GM released the Camaro. Those two years hadn't been wasted though, and the 1967 Camaro was an instant success.

It came as a hardtop coupe and convertible and could be tailored to each individual customer's requirements. There were four engines, a choice of three basic trim packages and no less than 80 factory options and a further 40 dealer options. It took longer to browse the brochure than to build the car!

As standard the Camaro came with a 230 cubic inch straight six with 140bhp or a 250 with 155bhp, but of far more interest were the V8s. A 327 came with 295bhp or 275bhp and there was a 350 offered as part of the SS package with

There were no less than 80 factory options and a further 40 dealer options. It took longer to browse the brochure than to build the car.

1967 SS pace car (opposite), '79 cars (above) and '69 on the beach (right)

325bhp and then a 396 with 375bhp. The SS also offered unique bumble bee stripes, air intakes on the hood and a blacked out grille. To make your Camaro stand out even further there was the RS pack which included hidden headlights, revised tail lamps and a higher level of interior trim. You could even combine the two packages to get performance with style with an RS/SS. Adding further credibility was the Camaro's role as pace car for the 1967 Indy 500.

By the end of the year there was another option: the Z-28. It's a name that would soon become synonymous with serious street performance, but initially the car wasn't even listed in the brochure or advertised.

The Z-28 was a homologation special, built so that the Camaro could go racing in the Trans Am Series, and although its 302

MODEL HISTORY

1967

Chevrolet launches the Camaro – two years after the Ford Mustang

1969

The most powerful Camaros appear. First the COPO 427 with 450bhp and then the ZL1 with 500bhp

1970

The second generation arrives with European-influenced styling

1971

GM's new regulations strangle power outputs

1980

Power outputs drop throughout the decade, leaving a Z-28 with just 165bhp

cubic inch motor was officially rated at just 290bhp, the truth was that this engine threw out closer to 400bhp. Mated to a four-speed manual Muncie transmission and with power disc front brakes and competition suspension there was no mistaking this car's breeding. But just in case you wanted to drum the message home you could add a set of racing stripes.

With a top speed of 140mph the Z-28 was a spectacular way to celebrate the end of 1967 and ring in the new year.

Revisions for 1968 centred on some minor styling changes and uprating the rear suspension to multi-leaf springs, but 1969 would be a big year for the Camaro.

First came a restyle to give the car a wider and lower stance plus there was a new dashboard and seats.

However, the biggest changes were under the hood. SS customers could opt for one of two ram air systems – one was an aggressive new hood, with a rear-facing air inlet and the other, if you didn't want that power bulge on the bonnet, was a dealer-fit plenum kit.

A new 307 V8 was offered with a modest 200bhp but for extreme performance Chevrolet offered a mighty 427 cub inch unit. First there was a dealer-fit engine that offered up to 450bhp. Ordered through Chevrolet's Central Office Production Order System these COPO were installed by well-known dealers including Yenko Sports Cars of Pennsylvania. Yenko also added rallye wheels and upgraded suspension to create their ultimate Camaro.

But even these COPO cars were put in the shade by Chevrolet's own ZL1. This aluminium block engine was rated at 430bhp but was really closer to 500bhp. Designed to compete in NHRA Super Stock

'For extreme performance Chevrolet offered a mighty 427 cubic inch engine.'

1982

The third incarnation is launched with an embarrassing 90bhp engine as standard

1985

IROC-Z is unveiled and boosts power to 215bhp

1993

The final generation appears. Z28 offers 275bhp

1997

30th anniversary celebrated with a 330bhp SS LT1

2003

Camaro production ends

THE ULTIMATE CAMARO

1969 was undoubtedly the best year to buy a Camaro if you really felt the need for speed. COPO cars modified at big Chevy dealers such as Yenko in Pennsylvania, Nickey in Chicago, Dana in California and Baldwin-Motion in New York produced up to 450bhp.But the factory went further. To compete in the NHRA Super Stock drag class they needed to produce 50 road cars. Fitted with an aluminium block ZL1 engine officially rated at 430bhp, the truth was that this car had more like 500bhp. Even on street tyres and a standard exhaust it could run the standard quarter-mile in 13 seconds. In full race trim it was two seconds faster. But it was expensive. At $4,160 just the engine cost more than a standard SS model and only 69 were made.

drag racing, only a handful were sold as the cost of the engine alone nearly doubled the price of the car.

1970 saw the birth of the second generation. It had a more rounded European look and was notably much more refined than the first Camaros.

Engines were carried over, although the 396 actually now displaced 402 cubic inches, and the Z-28 received a 350 LT1 engine with 360bhp.

1971 was a bad year for GM muscle cars and the Camaro's horsepower was slashed thanks to emissions regulations. Even the Z-28 was down to 330bhp.

Throughout the 1970s the Camaro's styling was revised to incorporate new Federal bumpers and power steadily declined. By the end of the mark two's production run a California-spec Z-28 had a paltry 165bhp.

In 1982 the third incarnation appeared. More angular styling and an all-new chassis with new suspension were the highlights.

Under the bonnet it was a bit of a disappointment. The entry-level engine was a 2.5-liter (153 cubic inch) four-cylinder unit with a pathetic 90bhp, then there was a 2.8-liter (171 cid) V6 with 112bhp and

1996 coupe (below) and 35th anniversary specials from 1992 (opposite)

even the highest rated five-liter (305 cid) V8 had just 165bhp. It was the lowest point in the Camaro's production history.

Over its ten-year life power did gradually pick up, though. In '85 came the IROC-Z with a more respectable 215bhp. And by 1992 this was boosted to 245bhp bringing some credibility back to the Camaro brand.

For its final generation the 1993 Camaro relaimed even more street cred. With its aerodynamic new design, revised suspension for improved handling and power levels that once again approached those of the 1970s it was the most accomplished Camaro ever. Engines were a 3.4-liter (207 cid) 160bhp V6 or a 5.7-liter (348 cid) 275bhp V8 in the Z-28.

A convertible joined the coupe a year later and in 1996 the SS model returned with a bang, offering 305bhp. Then to celebrate the Camaro's 30th anniversary in 1997 it received the superb LS1 engine from the Corvette offering 330bhp and making it the most powerful model in over 20 years.

The Camaro carried on long enough to celebrate its 35th anniversary with another special edition but 2002 would mark the end for this once great muscle car.

Specification

Years built	1967 to 2002
Most powerful model	1967 COPO ZL1
Engine type	V8
Displacement	427 cu in
Transmission	four speed manual, rear-wheel drive
Power	500bhp
Top speed	150mph

1969 coupe (above) and 1977 Z28 (right)

1988 T-Top (above) and 1981 Z28 (left)

2001 convertible (above) and1993 T-Top (right),

1994 Z28 (above) and the 1987 collection (right)

Chevrolet Chevelle SS

Chevy's response to the Pontiac GTO soon overshadowed its rival

Initially outgunned by its rivals, the Chevrolet Chevelle SS actually went on to become one of the all time most powerful muscle cars.

Launched in 1964, the Chevelle SS was a fairly plain-looking sedan and , although a 283 cubic inch and 327 V8 were both offered and the maximum output was a sizeable 300bhp, it still fell a long way short of Pontiac's GTO.

Chevrolet reacted quickly and by 1965 the Z-16 Chevelle SS packed 375bhp from its 396 cubic inch V8. Now fiercely fast, it could accelerate from 0-60mph in six seconds flat and do the standing quarter mile in less than 15 seconds.

Such was the pace of muscle car development that the Chevelle was redesigned a year later with a more rounded look and two bonnet scoops that would be a hallmark of the SS.

By 1968 the Chevelle had been redrawn again, with a more aggressive fastback body, although power remained at 375bhp from the highest-rated L78 V8.

MODEL HISTORY

1964

Chevelle SS launched, but lacks punch

1965

Problem solved thanks to the 375bhp Z-16

1968

Major restyle brings a fastback body

1970

Chevelle becomes the most powerful muscle car ever with 450bhp

1973

Chevelle production run ends

But even that wasn't enough in the Muscle Car Wars, so in '69 Chevrolet released a limited number of very special Chevelles. Known as the COPO (Central Office Production Order) cars they packed even more punch from a special order engine that was catalogued as the L72.

1970 was the Chevelle's finest hour, though. In went a 402 or 454 cubic inch motor, with the LS6 454 unit producing an epic 450bhp. It was the fastest SS ever and could do the standing quarter-mile in less than 14 seconds.

But sadly it wasn't to last. Having to run on unleaded fuel and meet tough new emissions standards set by GM management meant that the great V8s were strangled and even the highest output engine was down almost 100bhp on the previous year.

It was a big come down for a once great car and sales dropped by almost two thirds. By 1973 the Chevelle SS was gone.

Specification

Years built	1964 to 1973
Most powerful model	1970 SS
Engine type	V8
Displacement	454 cu in
Transmission	four-speed manual
Power	450bhp
Top speed	130mph

'1970 was the Chevelle's finest hour. In went a 454 cubic inch motor producing an epic 450bhp.'

Chevrolet Corvette

The Chevrolet Corvette has been America's Sports Car for more than 50 years

Now in its sixth generation the Chevrolet Corvette has been America's Sports Car for more than 50 years.

Unlike many of the machines on these pages, the 'Vette was designed as a sports car from the word go. Over the years it has become ever more sophisticated but, like a WWF wrestler in a hand-cut suit, there's never been any mistaking its true purpose.

Originally shown as a concept car at the General Motors Motorama at New York's Waldorf Astoria hotel in January of 1953, it was launched to the public barely six months later.

Penned by legendary GM stylist Harley Earl, the Corvette was undoubtedly a thing of beauty. It was compact and cute and featured some of Earl's best known party pieces including 'twin pod' rear fenders and 'rocket ship' tail lights as well as a snarling

'Originally shown as a concept car, it was launched to the public barely six months later.'

1972 Stingray (opposite page) 1953 original (top) and 1960 convertible (right)

toothy grille. Initially only available in Polo White with a red interior, the Corvette was drop dead georgeous.

It also marked a radical departure in production methods. All Corvettes were hand built, based on a shortened Chevrolet passenger car chassis of 102 inches and with those beautiful curves created not from beaten metal, but moulded fiberglass. The 'Vette boasted coil sprung wishbone suspension at the front and four-leaf semi-elliptical springs at the rear end.

Under the hood was an off-the-shelf 235 cubic inch straight six engine, tricked up with a higher lift cam to produce 150bhp. Chevy's Powerglide two-speed auto transmission was fitted as standard.

The 'Vette is one of the biggest success stories in American automobile history, but it actually got off to a very rocky start.

MODEL HISTORY

1953

Corvette launched. Highlights include Harley Earl-designed fibreglass body, but a very high sticker price

1958

Production almost cancelled. Corvette saved by Zora Arkus-Duntov who fits the first V8

1963

C2 Sting Ray launched – for many the most beautiful Corvette ever

1968

C3 launched, based on Mako Shark II concept car. T-top introduced

1984

C4 goes on sale. The hardest working Corvette lasts 12 years

The hand-built Corvette commanded a hand-built price. In fact it cost more than a Cadillac or even an imported Jaguar.

For '54 Chevrolet offered a wider choice of colors (black, blue and red) and offered a beige interior option, but mechanically and visually the Corvette was unchanged. Sales picked up to more than 3,000, though.

But 1955 nearly saw the death of the Corvette. Sales plummeted to just 700 and the money men within GM wanted to axe the car. Salvation came in the form of a man named Zora Arkus-Duntov. As a former racing driver he believed what the car really needed was more power and better handling. So in went a 265 cubic inch V8 with 195bhp and an optional three-speed manual transmission. At Daytona Duntov ran the measured mile at 150mph and a legend was born.

Over the next two years the 'Vette really came into its own, A '56 restyle gave birth to the famous scalloped sides. In 1957 came a 283 cubic inch V8 offering 220bhp as standard, but with the 'Fuelie' motor a hefty 283bhp. Enough for the Corvette to crack the quarter mile in 14 seconds. Now the 'Vette was a major performance player.

Between '58 and '62 the styling evolved gradually and so did the speed. By the time the end of the line came for the mark one 'Vette a 327 cubic inch V8 was now standard and horsepower had shot up to 360bhp with the 'Fuelie' motor.

1963 brought the Sting Ray body in convertible or split window coupe styles. For many people this is the ultimate Corvette, and in Z06 race trim it was a major player. Over the four years of the second generation Corvette, handling was uprated, brakes became all-wheel discs and the engine choice was widened to include a number of 327 V8s and a mighty 427. Officially rated at 430bhp, true figures of up to 600bhp were widely talked about.

'1963 brought the new Sting Ray body. For many people this is the ultimate Corvette...'

1990

The ZR-1 is unveiled with 375bp – the most powerful Corvette since the 1970s

1996

C5 hits the road and the T-top returns

2001

Z06 offers 385bhp

2004

C6 arrives with 400bhp as standard

2005

Z06 is the fastest, most powerful Corvette ever, with 500bhp

THE ULTIMATE CORVETTE

Born out of tremendous success in the American Le Mans race series the 2006 Z06 is the ultimate Corvette. Its 427 cubic inch V8 packs 500bhp which means this amazing car can hit zero to sixty in four seconds, hack the quarter mile in less than 12 seconds and top out at more than 190mph.

But there's more to it than just horsepower. The hardtop body is super rigid, the brakes feature 14-inch cross-drilled discs and there are 18-inch front and 19-inch wheels. The suspension is stiffer and lower than standard and the whole car is wider than a normal C6.

Based closely on GM's Mako Shark II concept the C3 'Vette made its debut in 1968. New features included a removable T-top for the Stingray coupe and a three-speed automatic gearbox to replace the old two-speed unit.

By 1970 the engine choice was a 350 V8 or a 450 although with 'only' 390bhp offered on the top flight LS5. A year later came the LS6 and power was back up to 430bhp again.

Throughout the Seventies the Corvette was progressively modernised, most notably with the introduction of Federal bumpers in 1974. And in a nod to the oil crisis, the big block V8 disappeared, with only the 350 remaining for the rest of this model's life. The Stingray name also disappeared.

The C4 (below) was the longest-lived 'Vette. The 2003 C5 celebrated 50 glorious years

The fourth generation 'Vette had the longest lifespan. Launched in 1984 (no 'Vettes were sold at all in 1983) it soldiered on for 12 years. The styling was all-new and, although a significant change from the C3, it was perhaps the least visually exciting model. The 350 V8 was carried

over and a four-speed manual or four-speed automatic was offered. Probably the most significant moment in the C4's life came in 1990 with the introduction of a six-speed manual gearbox and the launch of the ZR-1 with its mighty 375bhp. Three years later the ZR-1 was packing 405bhp, although it was only on sale for three years.

The C5 Corvette came along in '97 with a more compact and purposeful look, plus a new small block LS1 engine packing 345bhp. A convertible followed in '98 and a hard top in 1999. 2001 saw the return of the Z06 name with a 385bhp engine and uprated suspension, brakes, wheels and tyres. A year later it was given another 20bhp to match the mighty ZR-1.

2003 marked the 50th anniversary of the 'Vette and to celebrate a limited run of cars was produced.

In 2004 the sixth generation Corvette hit the streets. Widely regarded as the most sophisticated and best-driving of the bunch, it comes with a six-litre (366 cubic inch) V8 offering 400bhp. Included were such high tech offerings as a Head Up Display, ABS brakes and Active Handling. In 2005 the Z06 returned with 500bp. America's Sports Car is now every bit the world player and able to rival the best of European exotica.

Specification

Years built	1953 to date
Most powerful model	2005 Z06
Engine type	V8
Displacement	427 cu in
Transmission	six-speed manual, rear-wheel drive
Power	500bhp
Top speed	190mph+

Sting Rays from 1963 (above) and 1965(right)

1984 C4 (above) and 1968 T-top Stingray (left)

1996 C4 convertible (above) and 1973 Stingray hardtop,

2002 C5 (above) and 2005 C6 (left)

Chevrolet El Camino

The crazy El Camino brought muscle car madness to the pickup market

Chevrolet first introduced its oddball car/truck hybrid in 1959. Based on the Impala, it hardly set any sales records and only lasted two years.

It didn't take long for the name to reappear, though. In 1964 the El Camino was back. Now based on the Chevrolet Chevelle, the El Camino, meant business. Uner the hood came a choice of 283 or 327 cubic inch V8s. Power outputs were respectable, if not awe-inspiring, with the base car offering 195bhp and the top of the line packing 250bhp.

For real muscle El Camino fans would have to wait until 1968 for the arrival of the SS. By now the El Camino looked less truck-like than ever. It was long, low and lean, with its bonnet scoops emphasizing its performance potential.

Like its sister car the Chevelle SS this was a seriously powerful machine, driven by a 396 cubic inch V8 and available in three states of tune. There was 325bhp from the standard SS396, 350bhp from the L34 version and a heavyweight 375bhp from the L78. Given that this machine was essentially designed for the brick yard and not the Brickyard that was pretty impressive.

1970 saw the El Camino receive the same facelift as the Chevelle, and that brought even more power. Gone was the 396 engine to be replaced by a 300bhp 350 for the standard unit with a new 402 offering 350 or 375bhp. Not bad. Until you consider the 454 LS6 option that took the El Camino up to an astonishing 450bhp.

Now here was a pickup that could run the quarter mile in less than 14 seconds. Muscle

MODEL HISTORY

1959

El Camino first appears, based on the Impala

1964

After a short break it's back and now based on the Chevelle

1968

El Camino SS unveiled with 396 power

1970

The Ultimate El Camino arrives with an astonishing 450bhp.

1983

The final El Camino is built

car madness was at its height and the El Camino is probably the most bizarre example of the extreme lenths that car makers went to.

But just as the impending oil crisis and strict new emission rules hit the Chevelle SS, so they hit the El Camino and in 1971 it was massively detuned. Even the LS6 was down to just 365bhp; less than the L78 of 1969. It marked the beginning of the end.

A year later and the most powerful El Camino produced just 270bhp and by the time the final incarnation came along – based now on the Chevy Malibu – there was a maximum of just 245bhp on offer.

The El Camino continued in production until 1983, but never again reached the great heights of 1970.

Its glory days may have been quite short but the Chevrolet El Camino will always be remembered as one of the most unique machines of the muscle era.

Specification

Years built	1959 to 1973
Most powerful model	1970 SS
Engine type	V8
Displacement	454 cu in
Transmission	Turbo-Hydramatic
Power	450bhp
Top speed	130mph

'This was a pickup that could run the quarter-mile in 14 secs. Muscle car madness was at its height...'

Chevrolet Impala SS

The Impala could just be the car that started muscle car mania

Several cars claim credit for spawning the muscle car craze and Chevrolet's Impala is no exception. Born in 1958 as the highest specification Bel Air, the Impala was Chevrolet's most expensive model. It came as a hardtop or convertible with no less than seven engine options varying from just 145bhp to 315bhp.

A year later the Impala was a standalone model. It was longer, wider and only a Cadillac offered more outrageous Batmobile styling. Over the next two years the styling was tamed, but 1961 would be a memorable year thanks to the introduction of the Impala Super Sport or SS. By now the Impala was available with a choice of three 348 cid V8s with 305, 340 or 350bhp plus a mighty 409 offering 360bhp.

In 1962 a pair of four-barrel carbs was added to the huge 409 engine, giving the Impala one horsepower for every cubic inch. By 1963 they had raised the ante again and the Impala packed 430bhp with a special Z-11 427 cubic inch lump.

MODEL HISTORY

1958
Impala introduced as top of the line Bel Air

1961
Super Sport option goes on sale. Epic 409 engine is most powerful

1969
Impala reaches the end of the road

1994
Impala returns for two years as a rebadged Chevy Caprice

2004
Impala returns again – with front wheel drive!

1965 saw a total overhaul of the design, with a more streamlined look. Out went the 409 engine and in came a new 396. A year later the Impala was no longer King of the Hill at Chevrolet due to the arrival of the Caprice and both sales and the car's prestige gradually went into to decline. The last Impala of this generation rolled off the production line in 1969.

Chevrolet briefly revived the Impala SS name from 1994 to 1996 when it wanted to add some spice to the Caprice range. A 350 V8 offered 260bhp, but it was a large and staid-looking machine, and despite a reasonable turn of speed, it wasn't really worthy of the badge.

The Impala reappeared once more in 2000, but now with front-wheel drive and even the latest 2005 SS with its 240bhp supercharged V6 engine can hardly be mentioned in the same breath as the original. The Impala's muscle car days are long gone.

'...1961 would be a memorable year thanks to the introduction of the Impala Super Sport...'

Specification

Years built	1958 to date
Most powerful model	1963 SS
Engine type	V8
Displacement	409 cu in
Transmission	four-speed manual
Power	430bhp
Top speed	130mph

Chrysler 300

Chrysler's luxury 300 started Detroit's horsepower race in 1955 and launched the epic Hemi engine

If one car can take responsibility for the start of Detroit's horsepower race, it's the Chrysler 300. This luxurious coupe, launched in 1955 came with a 331 cubic inch V8 engine as standard. And it was no ordinary V8, either. It was the first Hemi.

Named after the hemispherical shape of the combustion chambers it produced 300bhp. Mated to a PowerFlite transmission, the C-300 burnt its special Blue Streak racing tyres when it ran the flying mile at 127.58mph. This first Chrysler 'letter car' was not cheap, though. And only 1,725 were built.

A year later the 300B was released. Power now came from a 354 cid Hemi with 340bhp as standard or 355bhp in high output form. Once again the 300 set the world alight by achieving close to 140mph in the flying mile.

'At Bonneville Salt Flats a 300D set a new speed record of 156.387mph.'

1955 original (opposite page), 1958 (above) and 2005 (right)

In 1957 the Hemi packed even more power. With a 392 cid capacity it had 375bhp as standard, but if that wasn't enough then a high output version came with 390bhp thanks to a more extreme cam and bigger exhausts. Mated to a four-speed manual transmission the 300B could run the quarter-mile in 17 seconds and crack zero to sixty in just 7.7 seconds. Available as a two-door hardtop or convertible the 300 was establishing a reputation as a real high performance machine.

For '58 the car was renamed 300D and once more Hemi power was raised. Now 380bhp was standard and 390bhp came with the optional addition of electronic fuel injection. Unfortunately the innovative system wasn't very reliable and few buyers opted for it. At Bonneville Salt Flats a 300D set a new speed record of 156.387mph.

'In 2004 Chrysler unveiled a new 300. And, just like the original, it packs a Hemi...'

In '59 the Hemi was replaced by a new Golden Lion 413 cid V8 with 380bhp and a year later a 400bhbp version of the same engine was offered.

1961's 300G was completely restyled and the number of luxury options increased to include a six-way power seat and power door locks amongst a multitude of gadgets.

By the close of 1963 the Chrysler 300 was no more, but the final incarnation, the 300J was the fastest of them all (in standard production form). A new, more aerodynamic body helped it to 142mph.

And that was it for 40 years. But in 2004 Chrysler unveiled a new 300. And, just like the original, it packs Hemi power. Voted 2005 Car of the Year by Motor Trend, the new 300 comes only as a four-door. But its low roofline and ground-hugging stance give it the look of a coupe.

There's a 3.5-liter (213 cid) V6 as standard, but it's the two Hemi engines that have got enthusiasts raving about the 300 again. As standard the 5.7-liter (348 cid) Hemi offers 340bhp, and in 6.1-liter (372 cid) SRT-8 trim there's 425bhp – more even than the greatest 300 of the 1960s muscle car heyday.

The 300 is rear-drive and comes with a five-speed Autostick transmission giving a choice of fully automated or manual shifts. Loaded with electronic driver aids and a taut chassis the 300 handles corners just as well as the straights. And it's every bit as luxurious as a 300 should be.

The name Chrysler 300 name evokes some emotive memories, and it looks set to create some new ones, too.

Specification

Years built	1955 to 1963, 2003 to date
Most powerful model	2005 SRT-8
Engine type	V8
Displacement	372 cu in
Transmission	five-speed automatic
Power	425bhp
Top speed	150mph

MODEL HISTORY

1955
Chrysler launches 300 with a 300bhp Hemi engine and starts the horsepower war

1956
300 achieves 140mph in the flying mile

1958
Electronic fuel injection offered as an option

1958
300D enters the record books with 156mph run at Bonneville Salt flats

1959
Hemi engine dropped in favour of Golden Lion V8

1960

Golden Lion engine now offers 400bhp

1961

Restyled 300 is more luxurious than ever with power seats optional

1963

The last 300J is sold

2004

300 reappears as a four door but still has Hemi power

2005

SRT-8 is the most powerful Chrysler 300 ever

1955300 (above) and meeting 2005 SRT-8 (right)

2005 SRT-8 (above) and 1955 300-C (left)

Dodge Challenger

It was a late challenge by Dodge but this car certainly made a big impact

The Challenger joined the muscle car market pretty late, but despite a lifespan of only five years, it really made its mark on the scene.

What was so impressive about this Plymouth Barracuda-based model when it first went on sale in 1970 was the wide range of engines available.

Performance versions, badged R/T (Road/Track) came as standard with a 335bhp 383 cid engine, with two optional 440 cid V8s available: the four-barrel Magnum with 375bhp and the triple-carburated Six Pack with 390. Top dog was the awesome 426 Hemi with an outrageous 425bhp.

The 440s and Hemi came with TorqueFlite automatic transmission as standard , with a four-speed stick shift and limited slip differential both optional. Just to give you even more choice, the Charger came in hardtop two-door or convertible body styles. It was some line-up.

Dodge even built a street version of its Trans Am racecar, the Challenger T/A, but when the company's lack of success on the race track caused them to pull out after the 1970 series, they pulled the plug on the road car as well.

The Challenger's late start meant that it hit 1971's new, stricter US emissions laws in only its second year, and sales dropped off along with the power output of the engines. The Hemi retained its 425bhp rating and was still offered, but the 440 Six Pack was now reduced to 385bhp.

MODEL HISTORY

1970

Challenger is launched with an impressive engine line-up including jaw-dropping 426 Hemi

1971

A Challenger pace car crashes into a press box at the Indy 500. The press are not impressed

1972

New grille fails to hid the fact that the Challenger is losing its muscle, with top power only 240bhp

1973

New 360 V8 only makes 5bhp more than the 340 that it replaces

1974

The Challenger bites the dust

The Challenger's reputation was tarnished even further when a bright orange convertible, acting as pace car for the Indy 500, crashed very publicly into the press box. Talk about bad publicity.

In 1972, the R/T performance version was discontinued and the convertible version that caused so much embarassment at Indianapolis in 1971 was also dropped. Coincidence?

By now a 340 cid V8 with just 240bhp was the biggest engine on offer. Symbolic of the Challenger's emasculation was the R/T's replacement, the new Rallye edition, which packed only a 318 cubic inch V8 with just 150bhp.

When even that was dropped in '73, the only option for those looking for any kind of performance became the new, 245bhp 360 engine – and it remained so until Dodge admitted that the Challenger had been defeated in 1974.

The Challenger didn't stay long, but when a car quite literally makes such a big impact, it will never be forgotten.

Specification

Years built	1970 to 1975
Most powerful model	426 Hemi
Engine type	V8
Displacement	426 cu in
Transmission	TorqueFlite automatic
Power	425bhp
Top speed	140mph

'The Challenger's reputation was further tarnished when a convertible crashed at the Indy 500...'

Dodge Charger

Dodge's Mustang rival was late to the party, but Hemi power made it a legend that lives on today

Dodge was caught short by the arrival of the Ford Mustang and the Plymouth Barracuda, but the car that it did finally bring to the muscle car party would be one of the most memorable of this great era.

The Dodge Charger was first shown to the public during the auto show season of 1965 as the Charger II concept car. It had a sleek two-door fastback body, hidden headlamps and full-width tail lamps. Inside were four bucket seats that further emphasized this car's performance potential. Within a year the production Charger was on sale, based on the Coronet, but looking almost identical to the show car, right down to those bucket seats.

Backing up that need for speed styling was a choice of V8 engines. Standard issue was a 318 cubic incher with 230bhp and next up was a 361 with 265bhp but the most

'The Charger had the ability to run from zero to sixty in 6.4 seconds and do the quarter-mile in 14...'

1966 Original (opposite page) and concepts from 1965 (above)and 1999(right)

popular choice would prove to be the 383 with its 335bhp giving owners plenty of bangs per buck.

The most spectacular, however, was the 426 Street Hemi. Race-bred, but tuned for the road, this legendary engine had an official rating of 425bhp, but it was a lie. The truth is that this amazing motor had closer to 500bhp. And that gave the Charger the ability to run from zero to sixty in 6.4 seconds and do the standing quarter-mile in just 14 seconds. But the Hemi was expensive, adding $1,000 to the price tag and although Chargers were leaving Dodge dealerships faster than they could build them, few were Hemis.

For 1967 Dodge found a cheaper alternative for those demanding serious horsepower. In went the 440 Magnum engine as part of the Charger's R/T pack.

MODEL HISTORY

1965

Charger II concept car unveiled

1966

Charger hits the streets with awesome Hemi engine as an option

1967

440 Magnum engine offered

1968

First major restyle

1969

Charger 500 and Daytona launched. The year of the General Lee

This was Chrysler's biggest engine and weighed in with 375bhp. It ran the Hemi close in performance, but real hardcore performance fans could still choose the 426.

1968 saw the Charger's first major restyle with a new grille hiding the headlights, and a tweaked tail. The so-called Scat Pack added bumble bee stripes.

The big news for '69 came from the racing scene, with the NASCAR-derived Charger 500 and Daytona hitting the road and track. The regular Charger was pretty much unchanged from '68. It's probably the most famous, though – thanks to a starring role as The General Lee in the hit TV show The Dukes of Hazzard. The General Lee not only charged, it frequently flew as well and during filming some 309 cars were used and most were wrecked, making any surviving '69 Chargers the most desirable.

1970 brought a second facelift that included a bold chrome loop front bumper and new tail lights. A new range of colours included Plum Crazy and Go-Mango, and the four-speed shifter now boasted a very cool pistol grip. In the engine bay there was a new option; the 440 Six Pack which ditched the standard four-barrel caburator in favour of three Holley two-barrel carbs. The result was rise from 375bhp to 390bhp.

The early '70s brought doom and gloom. The restyled 1971 Charger now shared its body with the Dodge Super Bee and power outputs dropped, although not as much as rival muscle cars. However, Chrysler couldn't hold out for long and 1971 saw the end of the Hemi.

1973 arrived with another restyle. Hidden headlights vanished from the options list and the styling was softened. The suspension was, too, meaning the Charger was no longer a real street racer.

For true fans the Charger died in 1974, the car that wore the Charger badge from 1975

The 1969 Charger is probably the most famous thanks to the Dukes of Hazzard.

1970

Second restyle and the 400 six pack is introduced

1971

Legendary Hemi engine is retired

1978

Charger reaches the end of the line

1999

Charger show car unveiled to mixed reaction

2005

Dodge reveals all-new Charger for the 21st century

THE ULTIMATE CHARGER

Many will argue that a '68 Street Hemi should be king of the Chargers, but the fact is the latest 2006 SRT-8 would nail it in a straight line and around every corner. With its 425bhp Hemi engine it's got less raw power than a '68 but it weighs less too and is able to run from zero to sixty in five seconds and do the quarter-mile in 13 seconds. More impressively it can go from 0-100mph-0 in 16 seconds and stop from 60mph in just 110 feet. Special tuned SRT suspension is fitted alongside Brembo brakes and Goodyear F1 Supercar tires on 20-inch alloy wheels.

to 1978 was little more than a renamed Chrysler Cordoba and was certainly no muscle car.

But for 2006 Chrysler is reviving the Charger name and the car's true spirit. It's been a long time coming, with a sleek aerodynamic four-door concept car first being unveiled in 1999. Its teardop shape was wind-tunnel sculpted but somehow didn't seem aggressive enough to wear the legendary Charger badge.

2006's Charger is more muscular, with a blunt snout and kicked up flanks. The high sides and low glass area give the Charger an almost coupe-like look, despite it actually having four doors. Charger purists have bemoaned this decision and the fact that beneath the styling, the new Charger is essentially the same as the Chrysler 300C. But remember, the original Charger was based on the Coronet, so platform sharing has a long history within the Chrysler group.

No enthusiast will have any gripes about the Charger's powerplant. Budget buyers can opt for a 3.5-liter (214 cid) High Output V6 engine with 250 horsepower, but it's the revived Hemi that will get Charger fans going.

The 5.7-liter (347 cid) Hemi packs a 340bhp punch and empowers the Charger with a zero to sixty time of just six seconds.

1999 concept car with ancestors (right), 2006 Charger Police spec (below)

Drive goes to the rear thanks to a five-speed automatic transmission with Chrysler's Autostick manual override system.

And as if that wasn't enough the SRT-8 version has an enlarged 6.1-liter (372 cid) Hemi with 425bhp – that's a power output right back to the good old days of the late 1960s.

But where the new Charger differs substantially is in its all-round performance ability. The original Charger would charge all right, but cornering and stopping weren't its favourite tasks. The 2006 Charger runs on 18-inch performance tires and tuned dampers and there's a Performance Handling Group option to give more steering feedback, better grip and enhanced roadholding. The SRT-8 also gets special Brembo brakes for added stopping power.

Maybe a '69 Hemi could just match the 2006 car in a straight line, but there's no way it could keep up in the corners.

The 2006 Charger may not be quite the same beast as the original, but times change, and the new Charger is every bit the 21st century muscle car.

Specification

Years built	1966 to 1978, 2005 to date
Most powerful model	2005 SRT-8
Engine type	V8
Displacement	372 cu in
Transmission	five-speed
Autostick	
Power	425bhp
Top speed	160mph

1969 Charger (above) and 1968 Charger III concept (right)

1968 model (above) and 1965 Charger II concept (left)

2006 SRT-8 (above) and 1999 Charger concept

2006 R/T Chargers (above) and 2006 SRT-8 (left)

Dodge Coronet

Packing a full race 426 Hemi V8, the Coronet was a mid-size with major muscle

Dodge had used, and then dropped, the Coronet name back in the Fifties, but it returned to grace its new midsize muscle car in 1965.

This car meant business right from the start, being available with the awe-inspiring full race 426 Hemi. This race-bred V8, seriously under-rated at 425bhp, was a little too uncivilised for most folks, though, and the following year saw the arrival of the Street Hemi. Made more manageable by the fitting of a hydraulic lifter cam and a lower compression ratio, it still made the Coronet a fearsomely high performance car.

New for 1967 was the Coronet R/T, marketed as the model equally at home on road or track. It came with heavy-duty suspension and the standard power unit was a new Magnum 440 cid V8, giving 375bhp when fitted with a four-barrel

MODEL HISTORY

1965

Coronet instantly stamps its mark on the muscle car scene, with full race 426 Hemi

1966

The Street Hemi is introduced – same engine but a slightly less raw state of tune

1967

Coronet R/T arrives, with standard Magnum 440, and the range is facelifted

1968

Full restyle introduces more rounded lines, but Charger and Super Bee steal Coronet's thunder

1970

Another facelift, but this is the final year of the high performance Coronets

carburator and working through automatic or four-speed manual transmission. The Coronet range also received a facelift which added such performance pointers as dummy air vents, racing stripes and deep front bucket seats.

A full restyle in 1968 resulted in more flowing, Coke-bottle-inspired lines, but internal competition from other Dodge performance models was looming. The R/T badging was now shared with the more expensive, more alluring Charger and midway through the year the company's new Super Bee undercut the Coronet on price.

The next year saw a new optional engine, the 440 Six Pack, created by fitting three two-barrel carbs to the existing 440 cid V8 and endowing it with 390bhp. The Hemi was still available, along with the original 440, but sales of the Coronet overall were on a definite downward trend.

A restyled front end in 1970 failed to attract further buyers and the R/T and convertible models were discontinued. From 1971 on, the Coronet was only available as a four-door sedan or station wagon and its days as a muscle car were over.

Specification

Years built	1965 to 1970
Most powerful model	1965 426 Hemi
Engine type	V8
Displacement	426 cu in
Transmission	four-speed manual
Power	425bhp
Top speed	130mph

'This car meant business right from the start, being available with the awe-inspiring full race 426 Hemi.'

Dodge Daytona

Dodge's monster racecar for the road was the talk of 1969

Outrageous. That's the only way to describe the Dodge Daytona. Its eye-popping looks and jaw-dropping performance were borne of the company's desire to win races in the hotly-contested NASCAR series.

In 1969, the science of aerodynamics was at the cutting edge of race development, with the slippery shapes of Ford's Torino Talladega and Mercury Cyclone Spoiler gaining supremacy. But Dodge's engineers knew they could do better – and created a wild, 18-foot long supercar in the process.

They took the existing Charger 500 into surgery, adding a wedged nosecone and a massive spoiler at the rear. The Daytona emerged from the wind tunnel with a drag coefficient of just 0.28 (compare that to the modern Dodge Viper's figure of 0.5!).

There would have been even less drag if it weren't for that huge rear wing, which helped to maintain traction on the rear at high speed. And what a high speed! A Daytona racecar hit the headlines with a world closed-course speed record of

MODEL HISTORY

1969

Dodge Charger 500 racecar receives heavy aerodynamic restyle and the Daytona is born

1969

The company has to sell 500 road cars for the racecar to become eligible for NASCAR

1969

The car takes the first four places at Daytona, fulfilling Dodge's racing ambitions

1969

Sales of the street car fail to follow on from the racing success, with only 503 produced

1970

The Daytona doesn't make it into Dodge's road car brochure

201.14mph and another reached 217mph at the Bonneville salt flats.

For the racecar to be eligible for NASCAR, Dodge had to sell 500 Daytonas to the public, so the guy on the street had the chance to buy a hardcore track car that was road legal. The $4,000 price tag was high but not exorbitant, with the standard 440-engined version offering a cheaper option and, with 375bhp, more than enough power for most people. The fearsome 426 Hemi, with its race-bred 425bhp V8, was not for the faint-hearted.

But although the Daytona proved a success on the track, the road car only racked up 503 sales and didn't make it to Dodge's 1970 model roster. The very thing that made it a winner on the track – its aerodynamic add-ons – proved a turn-off for the public. And so did its habit of overheating at speeds below 55mph – a problem that was solved, to greater sales success, by the next year's Plymouth Superbird.

Specification

Years built	1969
Most powerful model	1969 426 Hemi
Engine type	V8
Displacement	426 cu in
Transmission	four-speed manual
Power	425bhp
Top speed	160mph

'A Daytona racecar hit the headlines with a world closed-course speed record of 201.14mph...'

Dodge Super Bee

Dodge's answer to the Plymouth Road Runner never quite took off

The late Sixties saw the height of performance mania in the USA, and with the effects of prosperity filtering down to the country's youth, virtually every 20-year-old with a job could afford an automobile.

This was an emerging market that astute car manufacturers were keen to tap into, with Plymouth launching its budget-priced performance car, the Road Runner, in 1968. That spurred Dodge, Plymouth's fellow Chrysler brand, to bring out its own vehicle for giving the kids cheap thrills – the Super Bee.

Released to the public later that same year, the Dodge also shared the same basic chassis, had a virtually identical curb weight, and was offered with the same range of engines as the Plymouth. But the Road Runner undercut the Super Bee's $3,027 base price by $131, putting the Dodge at a disadvantage from day one.

Still, at least the Super Bee looked the part. Bold bumble bee stripes circled the car's tail and it wore a big Super Bee emblem proudly on its flanks. The grille was a sinister matte black and the hood was adorned with aggressive air scoops.

Based on the redesigned Coronet pillared coupe, the Super Bee was offered with only two engines: the standard 335bhp 383 cubic inch V8 or the Chrysler group's prodigiously powerful 426 Hemi.

It may seem strange today, with original Hemi Super Bees hitting prices near to $100,000, but as this engine option added

MODEL HISTORY

1968

Super Bee introduced as a rival to Plymouth's successful Road Runner

1969

Two-door hardtop model joins the original pillared coupe

1970

A restyle and a $64 drop in price fail to stop sales dropping

1970

Wild colors like Plum Crazy and Go-Mango are offered

1971

Super Bee adopts Dodge Charger platform, but the buzz is over

$1,000 to the price, the car's budget-conscious buyers tended to shy away from it.

The Bee's low purchase price was achieved by minimising equipment. Automatic transmission was an option from the standard four-speed manual shift, but if you wanted disc brakes, air conditioning or cruise control, the 1969 Dodge Super Bee couldn't deliver.

The same year saw the arrival of the Six Pack engine, as offered in the rest of Dodge's muscle car roster, giving buyers an optional 390bhp powerplant topped off with a wild, air-scooped hood. Made of fiber glass it even had NASCAR-style tie-downs to complete the street racer look. Although a capable budget muscle car, the Super Bee was overshadowed by the cooler image and greater sales success of its in-house rival, the Road Runner.

Despite 1970's eye-popping color schemes (such as Plum Crazy and Go-Mango) and a switch to the Dodge Charger platform in 1971, the model didn't make it into the 1972 sales season.

Specification

Years built	1968 to 1971
Most powerful model	1968 426 Hemi
Engine type	V8
Displacement	426 cu in
Transmission	Four-speed manual
Power	425bhp
Top speed	125mph

'Bumble bee stripes circled the car's tail and it wore a big Super Bee emblem proudly on its flanks.'

Dodge Viper

The Viper was a concept car made real and it turned round Dodge's fortunes in the 1990s

The Dodge Viper exploded onto the scene at the 1989 Detroit Auto Show and moved the muscle car into a whole new era. Big, brash and brawny, this concept car seemed way too extreme for a company like Chrysler to put into production. But, within three years the Viper was in the showrooms and an American dream was realised.

But it was harsh reality that helped create this dream car, which spearheaded an attempt by Chrysler to re-energize itself. The corporation was struggling in the late Eighties and its Vice President, car nut Bob Lutz, was looking to produce a headline-grabbing sports car to put it back on the map. When Carroll Shelby, the famous Texan ex-racer and creator of the legendary AC Cobra of the Sixties, joined the project, he brought with him a burning desire to reproduce his success in building an iconic American performance car.

Big, brash and brawny, this concept car seemed way too extreme for a company like Chrysler.

2003 SRT-10 (left), first gen trio (above), 1989 concept (right)

That was exactly what ended up wowing the crowds at that Detroit Show – the spiritual descendant of the awesome Cobra. A raw, no-frills beast with monstrous power from a huge V10 engine, the Viper's vital statistics were: 488 cubic inches displacement, 400 horsepower and 465 lbft of torque, figures to whet the appetite of any red-blooded sports car fan. The bodywork was pure muscle, a strict two-seater layout fleshed out with beefy haunches and a huge hood to cover that aluminum-block V10 which promised 160mph performance. By the time the first Vipers rolled out of the showrooms, it was 1992, and Dodge's first true sports car for years attacked its task of returning the company to its former glories with venom. As celebrity owners such as Jay Leno snapped them up, Chrysler was suddenly cool again.

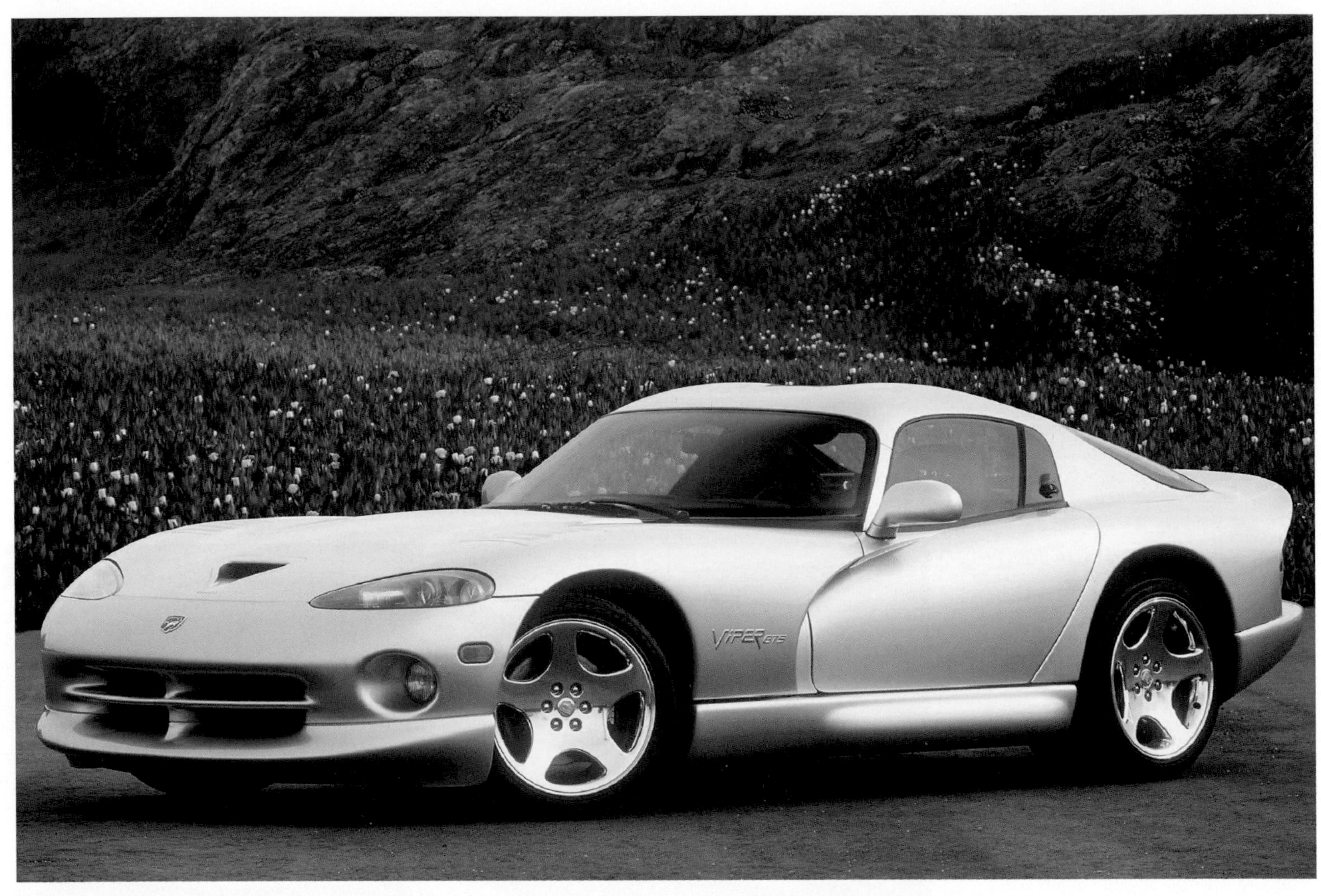

MODEL HISTORY

1989

The Viper concept car makes its first public appearance, wowing the Detroit Auto Show

1989

A wave of positive feedback convinces Chrysler bosses to put it into production

1992

First R/T model cars are delivered to buyers. Only 285 are made – all in red

1996

GTS fixed-head coupe version launched with an uprated 450bhp engine

1996

RT/10 upped to 415bhp when side-exit exhausts are replaced by a rear-exit system

Nothing could challenge the Viper's reign as the supreme expression of American automobile performance, and it remained basically unrivalled for nearly a decade. The introduction of the GTS coupe in 1996 provided a hardtop alternative to the R/T model's removable roof and featured an uprated 450bhp engine, but changed little else. The Viper was continuing to prove a popular image-booster but it needed an overhaul to maintain its profile.

When Dodge engineers literally tried to change the car's profile by adding a few inches to the wheelbase, they discovered that they would also need to rework most of the body panels and suspension. So they decided they may as well create an entirely new car: a true convertible with a revised chassis and shell... and an even bigger, more powerful engine!

Dodge realised the passion that the Viper stirred in its owners, so what better way to gauge what the next-generation car should be like than to ask them? The feedback from current owners of the car was resounding: they wanted more power, less weight, bigger brakes and no unnecessary add-ons like cruise control or cupholders. In a true power-to-the-people gesture, Dodge set to its task...

When the new 2003 Viper SRT-10 emerged, it performed pretty much to the brief these owners had given. For starters, it was 100 pounds lighter than the outgoing model. The car still packed a V10 under the hood, but the new engine displaced 505 cubic inches, producing 500 horsepower and a massive 525 lbft of torque. The previous model's six-speed manual transmission was beefed up to take the extra punishment. A stiffer chassis held everything together, with revised suspension devised to tame some of the Viper's unpredictable behaviour when driven in anger – this new snake would be less willing to bite its driver.

'Nothing could challenge the Viper's reign as the supreme expression of American performance...'

1997

RT/10 receives the uprated 450bhp engine

1998

GT2 produced in limited number of 100 to celebrate success in GT racing

2002

GTS Final Edition is the final Viper coupe, 360 are made with a red and white striped paintscheme

2003

The all-new 500bhp SRT-10 convertible arrives in showrooms

2005

Dodge announces a new Viper SRT-10 Coupe to be released in 2006

THE ULTIMATE VIPER

The snake car continues to evolve, and the next expression of the Viper's extreme performance philosophy is the 2006 SRT-10 Coupe. The ultimate Viper, this car is based on the SRT-10 convertible, but with a fixed metal roof featuring 'double bubble' bulges to give more headroom for driver and passenger. That's to allow the wearing of crash helmets – so there's absolutely no doubt about this car's sporting intent!

The 2006 Coupe's engine and drivetrain are shared with the convertible, so there's still 505 cubic inches of displacement, 500 horsepower and 525 lb-ft of torque driving through a six-speed manual transmission. But as the coupe is more aerodynamic than the convertible, it will beat the latter's 190mph top speed.

The new suspension also improved ride quality and the brakes received the prescribed attention too, with improved Brembo calipers which Dodge claimed would haul the car to a stop from 60mph in an impressive 100 feet. And the remainder of the SRT-10's performance statisics are equally staggering: 0-60mph in less than four seconds, a top speed of 190mph and 0-100-0mph in less than 13 seconds. The Viper re-established its reputation as the wildest beast in the American auto world with a vengeance.

And the story didn't end there. The SRT-10's colossal rear wheels were the widest available on a stock US production car, at 19x13 inches – and the fronts were no slouches at 18x10. The huge contact area of the tires combined with the car's longer wheelbase made the big snake less unpredictable when really pushed.

The general refinements in the Viper's driving experience were echoed with appointments which made living with a Viper a little less rough and ready. The car was now a true convertible, doing away with the R/T's clumsy removable roof and replacing it with an easily-operated bi-fold clamshell top which stowed neatly under the trunk lid. The new model also received a serious cabin makeover, banishing the old

Latest SRT-10 on the road (below and right)

interior, with its creaky plastics and toy-like gauges, to the garbage can. Now the Viper owner could really enjoy a quality cockpit, rather than have to put up with a low-rent effort. And no, there were no cupholders...

Although still recognizably a Viper, the new model's bodywork was sleeker if a little less muscular than its predecessor. The new conventionally-hinged hood was certainly easier to handle than the old front-hinged job, which really required two people to open without a struggle. But you can't please all the people all the time, and some Viper fans mourned the passing of the 'cartoon muscle car' looks of the original.

Now well into its second decade, the Viper continues to provide the glamour that it first injected into the company back in 1992. Its reliability and longevity has been backed up by repeated success in endurance racing when pitched against the best the world can offer.

The Dodge Viper entered the public consciousness as a symbol of American muscle. With the SRT-10, the legend lives on.

Specification

Years built	1992 to date
Most powerful model	2005 SRT-10
Engine type	V10
Displacement	505 cu in
Transmission	six-speed manual, rear-wheel drive
Power	500bhp
Top speed	190mph

1997 R/T-10 (above) and an early '92 (right)

a2003 SRT-10 (above) and early R/T-10 (left)

2003 SRT-10(above) and alongside 2006 Coupe (right)

2006 Coupe (above) and the concept that spawned it (left)

Ford Fairlane & Torino

The Fairlane was a real innovator, but it also had plenty of muscle. And as a Gran Torino it became one of the most popular TV cars ever

Probably one of the few cars to be named after a house – Henry Ford's Fair Lane mansion in Dearborn – the first Fairlanes in 1955 were not a lot faster. But over the next 16 years, this fairly ordinary family sedan evolved into a range of remarkable autos.

The 1957 'Skyliner' had the world's first fully retractable electrically-powered steel roof. The sleek 1960 'Starliner', a pillarless two-door hardtop, set the much-copied 'fastback' look. The 1962 Fairlane 500 Sports Coupe had bucket seats and an innovative lightweight thin-wall cast V8. The 1964 427 cubic inch Fairlane 'Thunderbolt' or 'T-Bolt', built specially for serious drag-strip racing, boasted a highly tuned 427 cubic inch V8 with an astonishing 500 bhp. Fairlane spin-offs, included the mighty Galaxie, the Fairlane GT and GTA, the 500 XL GT hardtop and convertible – and the most famous Fairlane

The most muscular Fairlane ever has to be the Thunderbolt rated at 425bhp but actually producing 500.

1967 Fairlane (opposite page), 1969 Torino (above) and 1969 convertible (right)

of all, 'Zebra Three' the red and white Gran Torino furiously driven by TV cops Starsky and Hutch from 1975 to 1979.

The Fairlane didn't enter the ranks of the muscle cars until the middle of 1962. The Fairlane 500 Sports Coupe was nearly a foot shorter than the previous year's car and boasted a new lightweight 'thin-wall-cast' 221 cubic inch V8. It even had European sports car style bucket seats.

The most muscular Fairlane ever has to be the 1964 Thunderbolt or 'T-Bolt'. Specially built for drag strip racing, the cars' big 427 cubic inch V8s were rated at 425 horsepower, but actually produced 500. In the 1964 NHRA's World Championship, a T-Bolt driven by Gas Ronda took 1st place, running the quarter-mile in 11.6 seconds with a terminal speed of 124 miles an hour. Just 111 T-Bolts were built.

'The car became so popular it actually attracted its own fan mail...'

In 1966 Ford added the Fairlane GT and GTA 500 XL cars. These were fitted with Ford's big-block FE V8 and had special badges, body stripes, heavy duty suspension, disc brakes, bucket seats, and sports steering wheel. The XL featured a 390 cubic inch 335 horsepower V8 with a high-lift cam, performance manifolds and a four-barrel carb. To improve its muscle-car image Ford also made around 60 Fairlanes fitted with the famous 'side-oiler' 427 wedge engines that were raced in NASCAR. Two versions were offered with either 410 or 425bhp. The 425bhp car got to 60 miles an hour in six seconds and ran the quarter-mile in a respectable 14.5 seconds.

1968 saw the introduction of what would become the most famous Fairlane of all, the Torino. The most powerful version of that year boasted a 390bhp 427 cubic inch V8. In 1969 the Torino Cobra was added. With lowered and toughened suspension, wide wheels, black grille and hood air-scoop it looked the business and its 428 cubic inch Cobra Jet V8 was rated at 335bhp, but it really cranked out 400.

1975 was the year of the Torino, for the fall of 1975 saw the screening of the TV cop series Starsky and Hutch. Stars David Soul and Paul Michael Glaser thundered around in a red and white Gran Torino call-signed 'Zebra Three'. The car became so popular it actually attracted fan-mail, and Ford reacted by making 1,000 look-alikes. The TV car had a 400 cid V8, but the look-alike autos had a 351 cid V8, and with just 138bhp could hardly be called muscle cars.

Specification

Years built	1955 to 1971
Most powerful model	1969 Fairlane Cobra
Engine type	V8
Displacement	428 cu in
Transmission	four-speed manual
Power	335bhp
Top speed	125mph

MODEL HISTORY

1955

Ford Fairlane launched as a top of the line full-size Ford in six different body styles

1957

Fairlane 500 Skyliner is the first in the world with an electric retractable hardtop

1960

The Fairlane 'Starliner', a pillarless two-door hardtop, set the much-copied 'fastback' look

1962

First of the Fairlane muscle-cars. Fairlane 500 Sports Coupe

1964

Thunderbolt drag-strip racer is most powerful version of the Fairlane with up to 500bhp

1966

60 Fairlane 500s and 500XLs built with NASCAR 427 410 or 425 horsepower 'wedge' engines

1968

Fairlane Torino launched with 390 horsepower 427 cubic inch V8

1969

Fairlane Torino Cobra added to range. Aggressive looks teamed with 400 horsepower

1970

Just one muscle-car left in the range – the lightweight Falcon offered with the Boss 375 horsepower 429 V8

1975

Gran Torino stars in 92 episode cop series Starsky and Hutch. Ford builds 1,000 look-alike red and white 'Zebra Threes'.

Ford Galaxie

It was the most powerful muscle car ever made, but the Galaxie's performance didn't translate into sales

The Galaxie has the distinction of having the most powerful engine of the muscle-car era. The Cammer 427 engine was developed for the 1965 car and in its dual-four-barrel carb form was rated at a colossal 675bhp. It was, and probably still is, the most powerful production engine ever made in Detroit. However, it made the Galaxie almost impossible to drive on the street. Too few cars were fitted with it for NASCAR to accept the Cammer as a production engine and Ford reluctantly stopped production. But its reputation stands.

The first Galaxie was launched in 1959. It was big. It was heavy. It was wide. It also came with Ford's first production muscle-car engine, the 352 Interceptor Special V8. Rated at 360bhp, it had a four-barrel carb, 10.6:1 compression, a solid-lifter cam and a dual-point distributor. In 1960 Ford withdrew from the Auto

'Rated at a colossal 675bhp it was, and probably still is, the most powerful engine ever made in Detroit.'

1969 convertible (above) and 1969 XL (opposite page and right)

Manufacturers Association's four year ban on stock car racing and almost immediately turned up at the Daytona Speedway with a 360bhp Galaxie Starliner that did 40 laps at an average speed of 142mph. The 1961 Starliner was smaller in size but much bigger-engined. In the middle of the year the 390 cubic inch V8 was available with a triple two-barrel carb rated at a massive 401 horsepower. It pushed the heavy Galaxie to 60 miles an hour in just seven seconds.

Cubic inches counted in the early 60s and Ford came up with the 406 cubic inch V8. With a single four-barrel Holly carb it was rated at 385bhp, and with three Holley dual-barrel carbs it put out 405bhp. Even then it was down four horses on Chevrolet's 409bhp 409 cubic inch V8. The 406 engine was a must to get the big and heavy Galaxies moving in a respectable fashion.

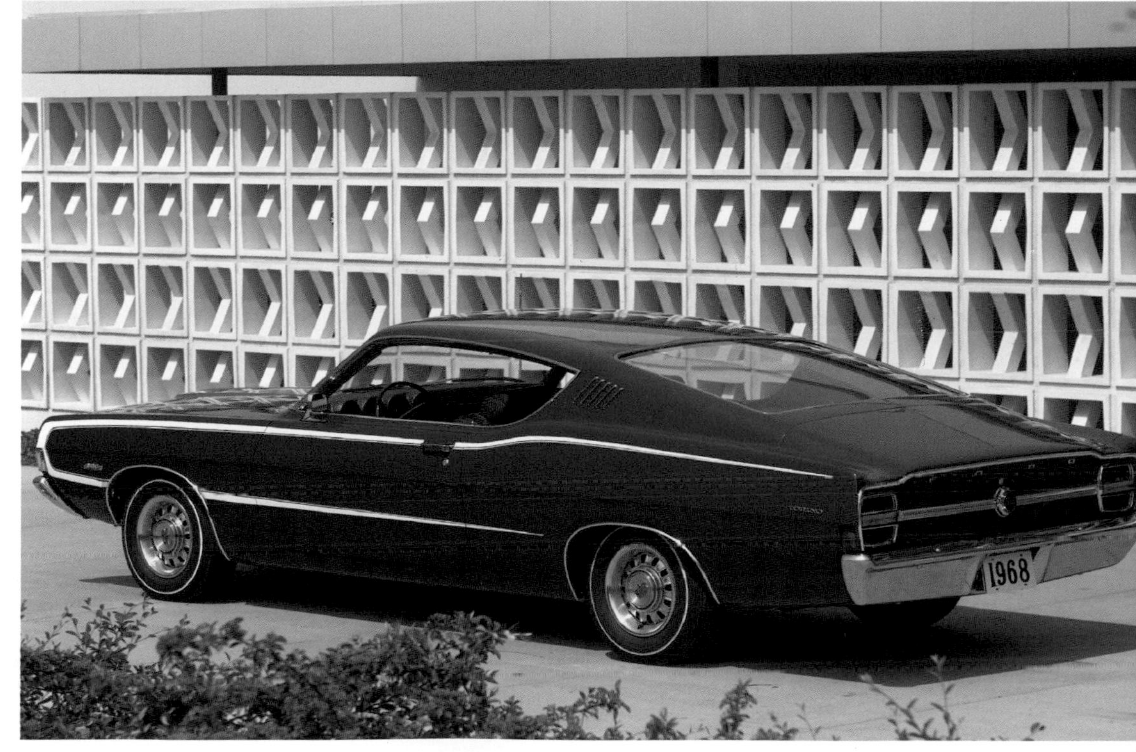

'It won no less than 23 Grand National NASCAR races...'

In 1962 the 406 engine was made available in the lighter Galaxie 500 and 500 XL. The XL had bucket seats and a center console. Both of these 'sportier' Galaxies came with floor-stick four-speed manual transmission, 15-inch instead of 14-inch wheels and heavy-duty suspension.

1963 turned out to be a good year for the Galaxie. The two-door hardtop was re-styled and lowered to improve aerodynamics, and with the new 427 cubic inch 425bhp motor, it won no less than 23 Grand National NASCAR races – including the top five places at Daytona.

Ford also built 50 lightweight Sports Roof Galaxies specially for competition. And with the 425bhp 427 engine the lightweights could manage the quarter-mile in a respectable 12.07 seconds.

1965 saw the sensational Cammer 427, the most powerful production engine ever made in Detroit. With a single barrel carb, this twin-overhead camshaft was rated at a colossal 616bhp. With dual four-barrel carbs the power output was a hardly believable 675bhp. The 'cammer' Galaxie was impossible to drive on the street and NASCAR didn't accept it as too few were built. Neverless it did wonders for the Galaxie's reputation.

Unfortunately reputation didn't result in additional Galaxie sales and only 237 427-engined cars were sold in 1966. This signalled the end of the Galaxie's heydays as a muscle car. From 1967 until its demise in 1972, the Galaxie was developed and promoted as a large and luxurious limo.

Specification

Years built	1969 to 1972
Most powerful model	1965 Cammer
Engine type	V8
Displacement	427 cu in
Transmission	four-speed manual
Power	675bhp
Top speed	130mph

MODEL HISTORY

1959

Galaxie launched with Ford's first production muscle-car engine, the 352 Interceptor Special

1960

Galaxie Starliner does 40 laps at Daytona at an average speed of 142mph

1961

406 cubic inch V8 introduced. With three Holley dual-barrel carbs it puts out 405bhp

1962

Galaxie 500 and 500 XL introduced. Both come with floor-stick four-speed manual transmission

1963

Galaxie wins 23 Grand National NASCAR races – including the top five places at Daytona

1964

Lightweight Sports Roof Galaxies run the quarter-mile in 12.07 seconds

1965

Introduction of Detroit's most powerful production engine ever – the 675bhp Cammer

1966

427-engined Galaxie sales drop away with just 237 cars sold

1967

Galaxie muscle car image dropped as car is promoted as luxury limousine

1972

Galaxie production ends. Top of the line limo is the spacious LTD Brougham

Ford GT

To celebrate its 100th anniversary Ford recreated a racing legend with the glorious GT

The tale of Ford's amazing GT40 has passed into automobile mythology. It's the story of an American company's burning desire to win the world's toughest endurance race against all the odds – a true story of guts and glory. This is a saga of such evocative power that its reprise, four decades after the original events, has led to the rebirth of a legend in the form of the awesome Ford GT.

The story begins back in the early Sixties, when Ford set itself the task of wining the prestigious Le Mans 24 Hour race. By taking the honours in this ultimate test of stamina the corporation hoped to increase sales of its road cars.

In an attempt to fast-track his company to sporting glory, Ford boss Henry Ford II tried to buy Ferrari, the Italian company which had made Le Mans its own with six

'The tale of Ford's amazing GT40 has passed into automobile mythology.'

Le Mans 1,2,3 of 1966 (above) and 2004's tire fryer (right)

consecutive victories. Rebuffed by the firm's owner, Enzo Ferrari, Ford determined to produce, from scratch, a sportscar to crush the Italians on the track.

The schedule was insanely tight. Work started in 1963, with the first prototype produced early in '64. After two failed attempts, the 1966 Le Mans 24 Hours ended in a fairy-tale finish for Ford, with GT40s coming first, second and third. In three short years, the company had made Henry Ford II's impossible dream come true – and the GT40 went on to an unbroken string of Le Mans wins from 1966-69.

With its place in sportscar history sealed, it seemed that the GT40's influence would be limited to being one of the most popular shapes on the kit car scene. A detuned roadgoing version of the car had been

MODEL HISTORY

1963

Work starts on Ford's attempt to win the Le Mans 24 Hour race

1964

The first prototype is produced. The car, dubbed the GT40, races at Le Mans unsuccessfully

1966

GT40s make a clean sweep at Le Mans, taking first, second and third positions

1967

A road-legal GT40 is offered to the public with a detuned 306bhp engine. Not many are sold

1969

A GT40 wins the Le Mans 24-hour race for the fourth year running

offered by Ford from 1967, but few were sold and the rarity of these automobiles added to the model's mystique.

The rebirth of Ford's legend was heralded by a modern interpretation of the GT40, a concept car shown at the Detroit Auto Show of 2003. The show car proved a massive hit and precipitated the decision to produce a road-legal production model. Symbolic of Ford's greatest achievement, it would provide the perfect centrepiece to the company's 100th birthday celebrations planned for the next year.

Just like its spiritual successor, the new car, dubbed the GT, was set an impossibly tight timescale to achieve its objective. This automobile would need to be ready in a mere 16 months. Considering that it was to be a ground-up re-interpretation of a classic racecar, that was a tall order.

The GT40 formula – a hugely powerful American V8, mid-mounted just behind the driver, clothed in low-slung racecar bodywork – was given a 21st century treatment. But this was to be a road car, so the original's 40-inch roof height (which famously helped to coin its name) would have to be stretched. In fact, the cabin's overall dimensions were enlarged, allowing taller drivers to enjoy the GT experience.

Using the latest computerized design technology, Ford designers and engineers labored to create a modern supercar to evoke the spirit of the Sixties legend. The machine they produced managed to reflect its heritage perfectly, its sleek silouhette echoing the GT40's attitude despite completely different dimensions.

At the heart of the GT is that mid-mounted 330 cubic-inch V8 which sends 550 horsepower and 500lbft to the rear wheels. This high-tech, supercharged example of

'Just like its spritual predecessor the new car was set an impossibly tight timetable...'

2003

Ford's 'GT40 Concept' is unveiled at the Detroit Auto Show to rave reviews

2003

Overwhelmed by reaction to the show car, Ford bosses decide to put the concept into production

2004

Dubbed the GT, the car is the star of Ford's centennial celebrations

2004

The first production cars are delivered to their owners

2005

The GT continues to roll off the production line, a true living legend

THE ULTIMATE FORD GT

The most successful GT40 ever is the car which won Le Mans in 1968 and '69 – chassis number GT40P/1075. Built in '68, this was one of the Gulf Racing cars finished in the team's famous powder blue and orangeracing colours. With a super-light and incredibly strong aluminium-honeycomb shell, this ultimate development of the race car was capable of a 220mph top speed. When it comes to who's the daddy of all GTs, it's easy – they all are. Ford only offers this modern-day supercar in one version. Guess they think that just owning one of these cars is the ultimate in itself!

the engine-builder's art drives through a six-speed manual transmission, putting an indomitable surge of urge at the driver's disposal.

The GT is breathtakingly fast – as a test driver for the American automobile magazine Car and Driver revealed in 2004. He managed a 0-60mph blast in a stupendous 3.3 seconds and recorded a scorching quarter-mile time of 11.6 seconds at 128mph. Pitted against Ferrari's Challenge Stradale and Porsche's 911 GT3, the Ford wiped the floor with its opponents, the Ferrari only managing four seconds to 60mph and being 0.8secs and 13mph slower through the quarter mile. A Ford GT showed the Italians the way once more!

Despite the monstrous power, you do not need to be a hairy-chested macho man to enjoy this automobile because the GT is actually an easy car to drive. The power-assisted steering, clutch pedal and stick shift are light to operate, with the brake pedal giving access to the astounding decelerative effects of huge Brembo rotors. This is a car that can be as laid-back as a pussy cat, happy to rumble around with a few thousand rpms on the clock, but just as

2004 trio (below), and GT at 205mph (right)

keen to curl its lip and go wild. Fans of great American car chases from TV and the movies will love the tyre-squealing wheelspin which is available on demand, and all enthusiastic drivers will enjoy the supreme levels of grip and balance.

With an aluminum spaceframe and body panels, a fiberglass hood and with carbon-fiber used in the underbody aerodynamic system and the seats, modern weight-saving methods are much in evidence. And the modern attitude to comfort is also displayed in this car's interior – with standard air conditioning, adjustable seats and plenty of space, it is a million miles from the GT40's cramped cockpit. The GT's doors are deep cut into the roof, echoing the originals, and another cool feature is that, after hitting the red starter button, you can see the supercharger doing its thing as you sit in the driver's seat.

The end of this story has yet to be written, because nobody knows how long the Ford GT will stay in production. The intention was always that this "Pace car for a whole company" would be produced in limited numbers, with Ford aiming to build around 1,500 a year until demand tailed off. This is one exclusive vehicle, with a selling price of $140,000.

The Ford GT is an incredible feat of engineering built to celebrate a famous sporting achievement.

It is a true living legend.

Specification

Years built	2004 to date
Most powerful model	2004 GT
Engine type	supercharged V8
Displacement	330 cu in
Transmission	six-speed manual, rear-wheel drive
Power	550bhp
Top speed	205mph

Ford GTs on track in 2004 (above) and 1966 (right)

2004 GT opens up in the garage (above) and on the road (left)

2004 GT glamor (above and right)

2004 GTs (above) and in wind tunnel (left)

Ford Mustang

The original Pony Car has also proved the most successful over the last forty years

Now into its fifth decade and fifth generation, the Ford Mustang was the original Pony Car. In 1964 it created a whole new muscle car class and it's the only true survivor today.

It was April 1964, mid-size muscle cars were hot, but Ford boss Lee Iacocca thought the public was ready for something else; a small, light and inexpensive sports car. That car was the Ford Mustang.

Originally conceived as a two-seater, Iacocca realized that selling the car in big numbers meant it needed to be more practical. So the Mustang that made its debut at the 1964 World's Fair in New York was shown as a four-seater convertible and hardtop. It was a huge hit, with 22,000 orders received on the first day and one million Mustangs sold within the first two years. The Mustang was a phenomenon.

'It was a huge hit, with 22,000 orders recieved on the first day and one million Mustangs sold within the first two years.'

1964 convertible (opposite page), 1967 GT 500 (above) and 1973 Mach 1 (right)

And that's despite not offering anything like the power of true muscle cars. At launch the Mustang came with a 170 cubic inch straight-six with just 101bhp. Ford quickly realised that this wasn't enough and by the middle of 1964 a 289 K-code V8 was offered with a much more appetising 271bhp as standard as well as a 165bhp 260.

A fastback also arrived and with it a tie-up with racing legend Carroll Shelby. The Shelby GT 350 came with 306bhp in street specification, but the race-ready 350R weighed in with 360bhp. Stripped of any excess weight, including the back seat, the Shelby Mustang would become a legend in its own right.

To make the Mustang affordable Ford had based it on the Falcon, and by 1966 it was decided to hide its roots with an all-new

MODEL HISTORY

1964

Mustang launched at World's Fair. 22,000 orders on the first day

1964

The first Shelby Mustang GT350 appears

1967

Mustang restyled, Shelby GT500 introduced

1968

Cobra Jet engine fitted, with up to 410bhp

1969

Mustang Mach 1 fastback goes on sale

instrument pack. The 260 was dropped and two versions of the 289 offered instead. The Shelby GT-350 could now be specified with an automatic transmission and Hertz rent-a-car even bought a number to rent to weekend racers.

1967 brought the Mustang's first major restyle. It was a heavier look, but more muscular, to compete with the likes of the Chevrolet Camaro SS. A 390 big block V8 was dropped in, although the GT350 still used the 289. Shelby raised his game with the GT500, powered by a race-bred 427 packing 355bhp.

In 1968 the Mustang received the legendary 428 Cobra Jet engine. With ram air induction it produced 335bhp although everyone knew that it was really more like 410bhp. Top of the heap was the GT500KR – King of the Road – with its Cobra Jet engine and Shelby's magic worked on it.

1969's second restyle introduced the Mach 1 fastback body and saw the first Boss cars. With race-ready V8s in 302 or 429 cubic inch capacity the Boss cars were basically NASCAR racers for the road and the 429 offered a mighty 375bhp.

Sadly, 1970 saw the demise of the Shelby Cobra and by 1971 the Mustang's days as a muscle car were numbered. By the time the last of the first generation Mustangs was produced in 1973, the maximum power was just 156bhp. 1974's second generation was supposed to retrace the car's original roots as a small lightweight sports car. It didn't. The Mustang II was underpowered, too heavy and the performance was pitiful. The top flight 2.8-litre V6 took nearly 14 seconds to reach 60mph. It could hardly have been less muscular.

A year later a V8 was back with more power but compared to the previous generation it was still a slouch. Even the King Cobra of 1978 took 11 seconds from zero to sixty.

'Hertz even bought a number of Shelby GT350s to rent to weekend racers.'

1974

Mustang II unveiled, but is a slow performer and a slow seller

1974

Third generation Mustang starts to claw back lost ground

1994

30 years old and the Mustang's fourth generation arrives

2004

40th anniversary and the fifth generation Mustang arrives to celebrate

2005

Most powerful Mustang ever is launched. The Shelby Cobra GT500 has 450bhp

THE ULTIMATE MUSTANG

The 2005 Shelby Cobra GT500 is the most powerful Ford Mustang ever. With 450bhp from its 5.4-liter (305 cid) supercharged V8 engine it offers spectacular tire frying performance. Ford's Special Vehicle Team was employed to fine-tune the all-round independent suspension to give this car track-ready handling. 14-inch crossed drilled disc brakes provide awesome stopping power and the car is finished off with Shelby's trademark white racing stripes. It really is the ultimate Mustang.

The all-new Mustang of 1979 started to regain a little ground. The car was lighter and the most powerful turbocharged four-cylinder engine (still only 143bhp) gave a reasonable turn of speed. In 1983 a convertible was added again after a long absence and in '84 the Mustang celebrated 20 years with a 2.3-liter (140 cid) 174 bhp turbo engine or a five-liter V8 (305 cid) with a little less go. By the end of the Eighties the V8 had its power upped to over 200bhp.

The fourth generation pony car came in 1994 with 3.8-liter (232 cid) V6 or five-liter (305 cid) V8 power. The restyle was softer than before but performance was gradually hardened up over its lifetime. It reached its peak in 2000 with the limited edition SVT Cobra R. Just

The latest Mustang arrived to celebrate the model's 40th anniversary and it's the most muscular and best-performing pony car for three decades.

The styling is unmistakably retro, harking back to the first cars of 1964. Power is as plentiful as it was in the Sixties as well. The entry-level four-liter (245 cid) V6 offers 210bhp and there's a 300bhp 4.6-liter (281 cid) V8 as well.

2005 convertible (right) and 1996 Mustang GT (below)

A five-speed manual transmission is standard, with a five-speed automatic on the options list. There's independent suspension all-round, making this the finest handling Mustang ever. Powerful all-wheel disc brakes with ABS come as standard and there's a long list of electronic driver aids as well.

Newly introduced in 2005 was a convertible version, which, unlike previous rag-top Mustangs isn't simply a chopped hardtop, but was designed as an open car from the word go. With a rigid structure its performance and handling aren't compromised like so many rag top cars.

Finally, to bring this great legend up to date Ford announced the return of the Shelby GT500 in 2005. The Ford Shelby Cobra GT500 adds a supercharger to its 5.4-liter (329 cid)V8 engine to pump out more than 450bhp.

There's a six-speed manual gearbox and suspension tuned by Ford's Special Vehicle Team. Shelby's famous white racing stripes add the final touch to this thoroughly modern muscle car.

With millions of models sold during its 40 year life, the Mustang is the ultimate muscle car success story.

Specification

Years built	1964 to date
Most powerful model	2005 Shelby Cobra
Engine type	V8
Displacement	329 cu in
Transmission	six-speed manual, rear-wheel drive
Power	450bhp
Top speed	160mph

1968 Shelby GT 500 convertible (above) and 1969 Shelby GT350 (right)

1982 Mustang 5.0 (above) and 1993 convertible (left)

2000 SVT Cobra (above) and 2005 convertible (right),

2005 Shelby Cobra GT500 (above) and with original (left)

Ford Thunderbird

Now celebrating 50 glorious years, the Ford Thunderbird has been a muscle car and a luxury car, but it's always been special

The name was inspired, the look low, long and stylish, and it was a hit from the word go in 1955.

Named after the great Thunderbird of Native American legend, Ford's first two-seater sports car was intended to compete with Chevrolet's Corvette, but its eye-candy looks and high equipment levels created an entirely new market segment – the luxury personal sports car. There were 3,500 orders in the first ten days. And in keeping with the new concept the majority of the early Thunderbirds left the dealers equipped with auto transmission and the 212 horsepower version of the 292 cubic inch V8.

The 1956 design changes included flip-out side vents for better ventilation, porthole windows in the removable hardtop, improved rear quarter vision and an outside tire carrier added trunk space.

'The name was inspired, the look low, long and stylish and it was a hit from the word go in 1955.'

2005 convertible (opposite page), 1957 (above) and 1962 (right)

Ford also introduced its new safety idea of "packaging the passengers". Standard safety equipment included energy-absorbing instrument panel padding, a concave safety steering wheel and a shatter-resistant mirror. Safety belts were optional.

Last-minute improvements, including the addition of the optional 312 cid V8 215 horsepower engine, gave the second edition of the Thunderbird better handling and increased performance.

The '57 facelift and performance and handling improvements produced one of the most stylish and sought-after muscle cars of the '50s. New versions of the 312 Y-block V8 were offered that provided serious performance.

The E-code 312 V8 featured two four-barrel carbs and was rated at 270 bhp. The F-code

'In 1999 a two-seater concept Thunderbird was revealed at Detroit...'

312 V8 featured a single four-barrel carb force fed by a Paxton-built McCulloch centrifugal supercharger. The F-code engine was rated at 300 bhp, or at 340 bhp with the optional NASCAR "racing kit." It would be the last of the two-seaters.

From 1958 until 1983, Ford built a heavier, more luxurious sporty-looking but hardly sporty four-seater. The four-seat Thunderbird continued to be produced through the 80s and 90s, but the public taste for the car slowly declined, and Ford announced that the 1997 model would be the last in the line.

But the Thunderbird story doesn't end there. In 1999 a two-seater concept Thunderbird was revealed at the Detroit Auto Show.

The sun-mist-yellow roadster included key styling cues from its classic 1955-1957 forebears. The concept car was a design exercise intended to gauge consumer reaction. It worked. The car proved to be wildly popular with show-goers. Two years later, Ford announced Thunderbird's return.

The 2002 Thunderbird came to market in the summer of 2001 as a limited production model aimed at 20-25,000 units of annual production. It won critical acclaim for its modern interpretation of the classic original roadster styling and was named Motor Trend's "Car of the Year."

A year on and the Thunderbird received improvements including an upgraded 280-horsepower V8. And in 2005, Ford marked the 50th anniversary of the Thunderbird with a special edition. It may not quite be the muscle car it once was, but the Thunderbird is as distinctive now as it was five decades ago.

Specification

Years built	1955 to date
Most powerful model	1957 F-code
Engine type	V8
Displacement	312 cu in
Transmission	three-speed automatic
Power	340bhp
Top speed	125mph

MODEL HISTORY

1955

Launch of Thunderbird, Ford's first two-seater sports car

1956

First restyle also brings option of 312 cubic inch V8 rated at 215 horsepower

1957

Last but most muscular and stylish of the two-seater Thunderbirds is built

1962

Sports Roadster launched with fiberglass tonneau that converts four-seater back into a two-seater

1971

Nieman-Marcus offer 'His and Her' Thunderbirds equipped with telephones and tape players

1975

Thunderbird weighs 5,000 pounds and sold as 'the epitome of luxury'

1983

Introduction of the 'aero-style' Thunderbird

1999

Thunderbird show car wows the crowds at Detroit Auto Show

2001

New two-seat Thunderbird is Motor Trend Magazine's Car of the Year

2005

Thunderbird celebrates 50 glorious years

1965 Thunderbird (above) and 1972 (right)

2005 Thunderbird celebrates 50 years (above and left)

Mercury Cougar

The Mustang-based Cougar came in with a roar but went out with a whimper

It may have the name of a wildcat but the Motor Trend 1967 Car of the Year Mercury Cougar was still classed as a pony car. It had the look of all the Mustang derivatives with a long front end and short rear deck, but the two-door hardtop Cougar looked a bit more balanced than the Mustang as it was three inches longer.

Its equipment also took it upmarket. The XR-7 and GT came with a wood-rimmed steering wheel and bucket seats, and the GT took the Cougar into the muscle car league with its 390 cubic inch 335bhp V8. The GT included firmer suspension, with stiffer springs and shocks, and power front disc brakes. The 390 engine had hydraulic valve lifters and a four-barrel Holley carb.

The Cougar GT-E was new for 1968 and signalled an increase in performance with a 390bhp 427 cubic inch V8. But this engine

'The GT took the Cougar into the muscle car league with its 390 cubic inch 335bhp V8.'

1969 Eliminator (opposite page and right) and 1968 hardtop (above)

made the car nose-heavy and it suffered from a distinct lack of grip off the line. Insurance company complaints led to this engine being replaced with the new and lighter Ford 428 cubic inch engine rated at a low 335bhp. But, according to many experts at the time, the actual output was closer to the 390 horses of the 427. The 428 had a longer piston stroke than the 427 which made it easier to meet increasingly stringent exhaust emission regulations.

1968 also saw the introduction of the Cougar XR-7G. The 'G' stood for Gurney – stock car race ace Dan Gurney who drove a Mercury briefly in 1968. In spite of its go-faster looks, in reality the car was no faster than the GT-E. Curiously the 'G' package was available with any Cougar.

The add-ons included a fiberglass hood scoop, a racing mirror, an optional sunroof,

'Real performance was added to the Cougar with the 1969 Eliminator.'

spoke pattern wheels, four-pipe exhaust and special 'G' emblem badges. Not many 'G' Cougars were made, so very few exist today.

Real performance was added to the Cougar in the middle of 1969 with the addition of the aggressively named Cougar 'Eliminator'. Although the 1969 Cougars were longer, wider and somewhat heavier the availability of the 428 Cobra Jet with Ram Air got the Cougar, with its longer wheelbase, quicker off the line than the Mustang – though the quarter-mile mile times were about the same. With a black grille, front and rear spoilers, side stripes and day-glow blue, orange and yellow body colors, the Eliminators looked the business. The 335bhp 428 also got the Eliminator off the line to 60mph in 5.6 seconds and ran the quarter-mile in 14.1.

Mercury certainly reckoned that bigger was better for the Cougar in 1970. It also had a new look that further reflected its Mustang origins. The Eliminator stayed in the line-up and came with a 429 V8 with Ram-Air and a rated output of 375bhp.

By the beginning of the 1970s the era of the Detroit muscle car was nearing its end. Sales of the performance Cougars declined. In 1971 the Cougars were bigger again and the Eliminator was eliminated from the line-up. Cougar luxury rather than performance was the marketing word. The 429 cubic inch V8 was still on offer, but would be dropped for 1972.

1973 saw the last of the Cougar pony cars. The hottest engine was the mild 351 V8 with 266bhp. So the wildcat Cougar went out with a miaow rather than a roar.

Specification

Years built	1967 to 1973
Most powerful model	1970 Eliminator
Engine type	V8
Displacement	427 cu in
Transmission	three-speed automatic
Power	375bhp
Top speed	127mph

MODEL HISTORY

1967
Cougar is Motor Trend's Car of the Year

1967
Cougar GT has 390 cubic inch 335bhp V8

1968
Cougar GT-E launched with 390 bhp 427 cubic inch V8

1968
Dan Gurney inspired XR7-G fails to inspire many sales

1969
Stringent emission regulations lead to long-stroke 428

1969

Cougar 'Eliminator' launched with 335bhp long-stroke 428 Ram Air Cobra Jet V8

1969

Eliminator runs the quarter-mile in 14.1 seconds

1970

Eliminator scores with 375bhp 429 cubic inch V8 with Ram-Air induction

1971

Luxury pushed instead of performance as sales of Cougar decline

1972

Last of the Cougar pony cars as output drops to 266 bhp

Mercury Cyclone

The warmed up Comet was set up as a rival to the budget-priced Road Runner

The Mercury Cyclone was the hot version of the Mercury Comet. First announced in January 1964, its sporty features included bucket seats, an instrument console, chrome trim bits for the 210bhp 289 cubic inch V8, and chrome wheel trims that gave the impression – from a distance – that the car had chrome wheels. The Cyclone was a budget performer, but it was a performer nonetheless.

For 1966 the Comet was based on the larger Ford Fairlane. The wheelbase was now 116 inches and the front track was wider, making room for Ford's big block engines. Good news.

Both hardtop and convertible body styles were available. There was also a GT option that included Ford's new 335bhp 390 cubic inch V8. Buyers could dress the car up with a fibreglass hood with a fake scoop and GT stripes and badges. The standard transmission was a three-speed manual, with options of a four-speed manual or three-speed automatic.

The Cyclone and Cyclone GT continued in 1967, although for some reason the 390 cubic inch engine was downrated at 320bhp. The 1968 car had a facelift and a new fastback coupe body style was added.

This proved to be a wise move. The fastback outsold the notchback by a factor of 20 to one. The convertible was dropped. The most powerful engine of 1968 was the 390bhp 427 cubic inch V8. This was dropped after just a few months and replaced with Ford's legendary 428 Cobra Jet V8, with 335bhp.

MODEL HISTORY

1964

Mercury Cyclone introduced as sporty derivative of the Comet

1966

Cyclone based on larger Ford Fairlane makes room for big block engines

1967

New fastback body-style outsells notchback by 20 to one

1969

Cyclone CJ introduced – aimed at low-price performance car market

1972

Production of Mercury Comets and Comet Cyclones ends

1969 saw the introduction of the Cyclone CJ (Cobra Jet), aimed directly at the Plymouth Roda Runner in the low-price performance car market. The CJ standard engine was the 335bhp 428 cubic inch. The CJ also came with a four-speed manual transmission, a competition handling pack – and most curiously, a bench seat.

The hottest Cyclone of the year was the Spoiler II with improved aerodynamics aimed at success on the NASCAR circuit. Spoilers came in two levels of trim , named after NASCAR heroes Dan Gurney (blue roof and stripes) and Cale Yarborough (red roof and stripes). Both came with a 351 four-barrell V8 not, as many hoped, the Cobra Jet. Sales of just 519 units hardly seemed worth the effort.

Further hot but re-styled and larger Cyclones continued through 1970, inlcuding a handful of BOSS 429-powered cars, but were dropped in 1971 as the muscle car era slowly came to an end. The last Cyclones were made in 1972.

Specification

Years built	1964 to 1972
Most powerful model	1969 CJ
Engine type	V8
Displacement	427 cid
Transmission	four-speed manual
Power	390bhp
Top speed	127mph

'The hottest Cyclone of 1969 was the Spoiler II with improved aerodynamics aimed at success on the NASCAR circuit.'

Oldsmobile 442

Oldsomobile's answer to the Pontiac GTO may not have been the first or coolest muscle car but it was the real deal

The 442 was originally a performance package rather than an actual model. The numbers signified a four-barrel carburator (4), a four-speed manual transmission (4) and dual exhausts (2), with these sporty ingredients offered on Oldsmobile's Cutlass. The recipe for the 442 was to change over the years, but the name stuck and was to become the byword for Olds' muscle cars.

The Cutlass 442 was launched after the Pontiac GTO had paved the way. Oldsmobile wanted a piece of the action, whacking its biggest-hitting power unit into its midsized chassis. At 330 cubic inches, this V8 came modified with all the performance equipment specified by police departments for pursuit cars. The deal also included heavy duty shocks and springs plus a rear stabilizer bar.

The first model-year of the 442 was a confused affair, with the package being available on the cheaper F-85 as well as the Cutlass. Oldsmobile hadn't got its marketing strategy together, so less than 3,000 442s were sold in 1964. Not a promising start, but better was to follow...

For 1965, Oldsmobile got its act together with its advertising, which gave the 442 a more youthful image and greater sales

'...this V8 came modified with all the performance equipment specified by police departments...'

Awesome Olds/Hurst (opposite page), 442 convertible (above) and coupe (right)

success. The performance package was more attractive too, with a new 400 cid V8 replacing the old unit, bringing power up to 345bhp. The new 442 pack also improved on the class-leading handling, with heavy duty shocks and springs, plus front and rear stabilizer bars along with fat tires.

Clothed in fresh sheet metal, the 1966 model Cutlass 442 emerged with a new option – the first opportunity to have triple carburators fuelling the engine. The set-up was smooth and lifted power output to 360bhp, while suspension upgrades increased handling standards even further.

The tri-carb option didn't last long, with a GM ban on such set-ups forcing Oldsmobile to seek alternative methods to maintain power output in 1967. They did it with the W-30 package, a "forced air induction system" with special air ducting, plus an uprated camshaft and springs.

'The W-30 achieved its highest power output thanks to a balanced, blueprinted 455 V8.'

The 442 of 1968 saw the famous name finally became a model designation in its own right. '68's biggest news was the Hurst/Olds. Originally a one-off marrying of the 442 with the 390 horsepower 455 cid V8 from Oldsmobile's Toronado, a limited run was sanctioned by the company. Capable of 0-60mph in 5.4 seconds, only 515 were made in '68, making them prized collector's items today. The Hurst/Olds returned for 1968, with a new colour scheme and extravagant bonnet scoops, although it was slightly detuned to 380bhp.

In 1970 GM's ban on engines over 400 cubic inches in midsized cars was lifted, allowing Oldsmobile to offer its 455 cid V8 in all 442s as standard. The Hurst/Olds was now dropped, not to reappear until 1972. The W-30 achieved its highest ever power output, thanks to a balanced, blueprinted and generally hotted-up version of the 455 V8. 1970 also saw the arrival of a new option, the Rallye 350 – its 310 horsepower engine wasn't exceptional, but the exterior treatment was, with bright yellow paint – even on the bumpers and wheels!

It was a last joyful fling at outrageous visual effect and hedonistic performance, because from 1971 the 442 faced the same power-capping factors as all muscle cars.

From '72, the 442 merely denoted a handling and appearance package for any Cutlass. The Hurst/Olds was reissued, but with only 300bhp it was a shadow of its former self – and by '73 it was down to a 250. After '73, Olds dropped out of the performance market and although the 442 name later reappeared on many models, none of them could match the originals.

Specification

Years built	1964 to 1973
Most powerful model	1968 Hurst/Olds
Engine type	V8
Displacement	455 cu in
Transmission	four-speed manual, rear-wheel drive
Power	390bhp
Top speed	130mph

MODEL HISTORY

1964

442 option first offered on Oldsmobile's Cutlass model, with 310bhp, 330 cid V8

1965

New 400 cid, engine joins 442 package, generating increased power at 345bhp

1966

Tri-carb option gives 360bhp. 442's reputation for handling enhanced with suspension upgrade

1968

442 becomes a stand-alone model name. Top-dog Hurst/Olds introduced with 390bhp

1970

GM lifts ban on engines over 400 cid

1970

Hurst/Olds dropped as its 455 cid V8 becomes the 442's standard power unit

1971

Power-restricting legislation heralds dwindling performance

1971

Even the W-30is down to 300bhp

1972

442 is now only a hanndling and styling package

1973

The last of the true 442s is built

Oldsmobile Toronado

A front-drive muscle car? Nobody would have believed it until the Toronado

The Toronado was a truly radical machine. Never mind the amazing styling, the Toronado was the first and only true front-wheel drive muscle car.

The story started in 1966 when Oldsmobile launched the largest front-wheel drive car ever made. It received a fantastic reception from press and the public. Motor Trend magazine named the Toronado their Car of the Year.

With a wheelbase of 119 inches this was one big beast, and at 4,366 pounds it was no lightweight, but Olds gave it serious horsepower to compensate for that. Under that long hood was a 425 cid V8 that turned out 385 hp. And that was plenty.

To avoid too much weight over the front end, the torque converter was mounted behind the engine whilst the gearbox sat under the engine's left bank.

It was an ingenious piece of engineering and laid the groundwork for the American automobile industry's switch from rear to front-wheel drive.

The Toronado's styling was no less revolutionary. It was the work of GM design boss William L Mitchell and he really made this Olds stand out from the crowd. Boldly flared wheelarches, fenders that jutted out aggressively from the front, headlamps hidden away and a fastback tail made this one striking car.

The Toronado was a big hit in its first year of production with more than 40,000 models sold.

MODEL HISTORY

1966

Oldsmobile launches the biggest ever front-wheel drive car

1966

Motor Trend names the Toronado Car of the Year

1968

Restyle tames the Toronado a little

1970

But not for long, GT launched with 400bhp

1971

Second generation emphasizes luxury over muscle

A '67 restyle was limited to a new front grille, whilst 1968 saw the Toronado tamed a little. Those stand-out fenders were reigned in and Olds' new split grille was added, whilst under the hood a new 455 cubic inch 375bhp V8 was fitted.

In '69 a longer tail was added and so too was an optional, but ugly and quite unpopular vinyl top.

1970 saw a more significant change, with fixed headlamps replacing the concealed ones and the addition of a 400bhp GT version. With a special cam and torque converter the GT could hit zero to sixty in just seven and a half seconds. You could spot a Toronado GT thanks to its twin exhausts, slotted rear bumper and gold paintwork with black stripes.

During the five-year production run more than 120,000 series one Toronados rolled out of the factory. The series two that followed was a shadow of its former self, emphasizing luxury over performance, so it's the original that is the collectors' item. Just ask Jay Leno, he's a proud Toronado owner.

'With a special cam and torque converter the GT could hit zero to sixty in just seven and a half seconds.'

Specification

Years built	1966-1970
Most powerful model	1970 GT
Engine type	V8
Displacement	455 cid
Transmission	three-speed automatic
Power	400bhp
Top speed	135mph

Plymouth Barracuda

It beat the Mustang to market, but it would be some years before the 'Cuda could be considered a true pony car

A true muscle car it ain't – but the 1964 Plymouth Barracuda did beat the Mustang to market by two weeks. Its other claim to fame was its huge wrap-round rear window, said to be the largest single piece of glass ever used on a production car. Initially the Plymouth sales pitch concentrated on the Barracuda's looks and convenience and the most sporty engine on offer was a 273 cubic inch 235bhp V8.

The Formula S Barracuda, introduced in 1965, was supposed to be a performance car. But it wasn't. The most powerful engine on offer was still the 273 cubic inch 235bhp V8 and it wasn't any faster than standard models. There was a facelift in 1966 and the distinctive 'Fish' badges were added.

Then, in 1967, things began to change. The Barracuda had a redesign and it truly joined

The 1965 Plymouth Barracuda Line . . .
"The fast-moving new fastback at a spectacular low price."
The Barracuda comes in one model: the highly popular and exciting 2-door sports hardtop. It is, beyond doubt, America's best combination yet of sports-car look, all-purpose versatility, and youthful vitality.
It is a boldly different kind of car: a limited edition at present, strong in youth-appeal. Every Barracuda goes with front bucket seats as standard equipment. An optional racing stripe is the crowning "sport" touch on this fast mover. And, of course, the thing that has most people on Barracuda's side is its guys-gals-and-gear capacity. It seats five with the back seat up—two with the back seat down. And putting that back seat down creates a 7-foot-long carpeted cargo space. For power, Barracuda has the 225-cu.-in. engine as its standard "6," and the same standard and optional V-8 engine availabilities as Valiant.

Plymouth Barracuda 2-Door Sports Hardtop

'The 1964 Plymouth Barracuda beat the rival Ford Mustang to market by two weeks.'

1970 'Cuda (opposite page), advert for the '65 (above) and 1970 'Cuda Hemi (right)

the ranks of the pony cars. Notchback and convertible body styles were added to the original fastback. Plymouth even thought about adding their 280bhp 383 cubic inch engine to the options list. The thought didn't make it to production – the engine was too large to fit the power steering pump under the car's hood.

A 383 cubic inch V8 was squeezed into the 1968 car and coincided with an abbreviation of the name. The Formula S Barracuda became the sportier-sounding 'Cuda with no less than 300bhp on tap. The zero to 60mph dash was accomplished in a reasonably rapid 7.5 seconds. But, despite the power upgrade, the quarter mile was managed in the hardly competitive high 15s.

1969 saw more attempts to make the 'Cuda faster and more competitive with its rival muscle cars. On offer were the 383 V8 with

'When the engine shook, which it did a lot, so did the Shaker.'

330bhp and the most powerful engine in the Plymouth stable, the 440 cubic inch, triple carb 390bhp V8 – the largest engine ever offered in a pony car. With a weight distribution of front/rear 57/43 per cent and no room for power-steering the car was a pig to handle. With drum brakes all-round and no power-steering it was also difficult to stop quickly in a straight line. However the engine helped define the 'Cudas sportier image – zero to 60 took 5.6 seconds and the quarter-mile an impressive 14.01 seconds.

The 'Cuda finally made it in 1970. It was given a new platform, the E-body shared with the new Dodge Challenger. The 'Cuda's wheelbase was two inches shorter, though its overall dimensions were the same. No less than five V8s were on offer, the most muscular being the 390bhp 440+6 and the mighty 425bhp 426 Hemi. 'Cudas with these engines had tougher performance suspension and the Hemi had a feature that quickly became a muscle car icon – the 'Shaker' hood scoop – so-called because it was fixed to the engine and protruded through a hole in the hood. When the engine shook, which it did a lot, so did the Shaker.

There was also a special 'Cuda for 1970 – the AAR. It was sparked by 'Cudas raced by Dan Gurney's All-America Racers in the Trans-Am races. But unlike the Boss 302 Mustang and the Camaro Z28, the AAR 'Cuda was built as a street rod. An estimated 1,500 AARs were built.

Then in 1971, tougher emission laws came into force. The Hemi was dropped and the remaining engines were de-tuned. Sales dropped almost as quickly as the engine power and the 'Cuda finally died in 1974.

Specification

Years built	1964 to 1974
Most powerful model	1970 Hemi 'Cuda
Engine type	V8
Displacement	426 cu in
Transmission	three-speed automatic
Power	425bhp
Top speed	130mph

MODEL HISTORY

1964

Plymouth Barracuda beats Mustang to market by two weeks

1966

Barracuda 'fish' emblems introduced. Most powerful engine has just 235bhp

1967

Notchback Barracuda joins ranks of pony cars. Performance Formula S version available

1968

383 cubic inch 300 horsepower V8 Barracuda

1969

440 cubic inch, triple carb 390 horsepower V8 is the largest engine ever offered in a pony car

1969

1969 'Cudas sportier image re-defined – zero to 60 takes 5.6 seconds and the quarter-mile 14.01 seconds

1970

'Cuda makes it as a true pony car as notchback introduced

1970

Hemi gets a feature that quickly becomes a muscle car icon – the 'Shaker' hood scoop

1970

AAR 'Cuda is the first-ever production car with rear tires larger than front tires

1974

Final 'Cuda rolls off the production line

Plymouth Prowler

Plymouth's concept car made real may not have had much muscle, but its hot rod styling made it a hit

The Plymouth Prowler looks like a flight of fantasy, a concept car that has just rolled off a show podium. And basically, that's what it is. The Prowler is one of those rare beasts – a concept car that made it into production.

A modern interpretation of the street hot rods of the Fifties, the Prowler made its debut at the Detroit Auto Show of 1993. Jaws dropped, flashbulbs popped and nobody really thought that Plymouth's parent company, the Chrysler corporation, would ever build it. It was just too wild. But they reckoned without Chrysler president Bob Lutz, whose support for the project was pivotal in getting the Prowler signed off and into production.

It would take until 1997, after four consecutive show-stopping performances at Detroit, for this automobile to finally hit

The Prowler looks like a flight of fancy, a concept car that has just rolled off a show podium.

2001 Prowler (opposite page and above with custom trailer) and 1999 model (right)

the street. But when it did, it remained remarkably true to its original concept. A two-seater roadster with a manually-operated soft top and the sort of radical looks only normally found at hot rod clubs, it was a unique, off-the-peg custom car. For the guy who wanted a street rod but also wanted comfort, reliability and modern automobile attributes, it was a godsend.

The car was the most aluminum-intensive car produced in North America at the time. Most of the bodywork was constructed of this lightweight metal, as was the suspension, helping to reduce weight as much as possible. And it needed to keep itself trim because, unlike its spiritual forebears from the Fifties, it was notpowered by a huge V8.

The power unit was the same 3.5-liter (213 cid) V6 found in Chrysler's sedans,

It remained the same dream machine that inspired so many auto enthusiasts

producing 214bhp. In the (relatively) lightweight Prowler, its performance was brisk rather than roadburning. But who cared when you were at the wheel of something this outrageous and getting all the looks?

The Prowler was given a bit more go to accompany the show when a new aluminum V6 started taking care of business in 1998. Power rose to 253bhp, making this a lively but well-mannered roadster. A four-speed Autostick transmission had manual override, allowing the driver to shift up and down the ratios by tapping a stick shift. The ride quality was firm and performance-oriented, although it would be softened down during its years of production.

Originally only available in purple, a whole slew of retro hot-rod colours gradually became available over the car's five-year lifespan, including yellow, orange and deep candy red. Just to underline the fact that this was a car for extroverts, if you didn't already know.

Luggage space was minimal and there wasn't even room to stow a spare tire. The solutions were to offer a matching trailer to give somewhere to stash the valise (an option which 20 per cent of buyers took up) and fat, run-flat tires.

The Prowler ceased production in 2002, and apart from the original engine being upgraded, few major changes were made to the model during its life cycle.

It remained the same roomy, leather-upholstered, electric-windowed, drop-top dream machine that inspired so many auto enthusiasts to take it to their hearts and onto their driveways.

Specification

Years built	1997 to 2002
Most powerful model	1998 onwards
Engine type	V6
Displacement	213 cu in
Transmission	four-speed Autostick
Power	253bhp
Top speed	125mph

MODEL HISTORY

1993
Prowler is first displayed at Detroit and rocks the show

1994
Prototype is taken to hot rod shows to gauge reaction

1996
Official go-ahead for the model is announced at Detroit

1997
First production Prowlers built alongside the Dodge Viper

1998
All-aluminum 3.5-liter (214 cid) V6 introduced, giving 253bhp

1999

New shock absorbers and springs give a smoother ride

1999

Black and red two-tone Woodward Edition unveiled. Only 150 made

2000

Black Tie silver an black special edition released. Only 163 made

2001

Plymouth brand is discontinued, Prowler is rebadged as a Chrysler

2002

The Prowler cruises off into the sunset as the model is axed

2001(above) and 1999 (right)

1998 model (above) and 1997 (right)

Plymouth Road Runner

The back-to-basics Plymouth Road Runner was one of the most successful muscle cars ever. Beep Beep!

When the Road Runner hit the scene in 1968, it made the biggest impact on the market since Pontiac's GTO back in '64. Four years of muscle car development had resulted in expensive, luxury-laden automobiles, so with the Road Runner, Plymouth decided to get back to base principals. It aimed to create a no-frills road-burner with lots of bang for as few bucks as possible.

For a mere $2,896, the American public could purchase a base-level Road Runner, equipped with a 383 cubic inch V8 pumping out 335bhp. The chassis, based on the Plymouth Belvedere, was beefed up with uprated suspension, while the interior was right back to basics with a simple bench seat and rubber matting replacing carpets.

It was an impressive package for the price, but for an extra $714 you could put a fearsome 426 Hemi under the hood of your

'To go with the decals, there was even a horn that went "beep beep" in cartoon Road Runner style.'

1970 Super Bird (opposite page), 1969 (above) and1974 Road Runner (right)

Road Runner. For just $3,610 you could own an automobile that could do 0-60mph in 5.3 seconds and tear up a quarter-mile in the low 13s.

And what a cool car! Plymouth created the perfect youth-oriented image for its new creation. The company paid Warner Brothers a reported $50,000 to use their famously fast cartoon bird as the car's logo – and adopted its name too. To go with the decals, there was even a horn that went "beep-beep" in cartoon Road Runner style.

Just like its animated namesake, the car was a runaway success. Plymouth expected to sell 2,500 in its first year, but pretty soon it was the car every kid wanted and 45,000 flew out of the dealerships.

Its success prompted Plymouth to expand the range in 1969, bringing in a convertible to bolster the existing hardtop and pillared

'A powered trap door on the hood popped up revealing a shark cartoon...'

coupe. Two new 440 cid V8s included the "440 + 6", a triple-carb job which gave Hemi-like acceleration for almost half the price.

Another feature with hip graphics gave the Road Runner a psychological edge. In 1970, the Air Grabber Hood appeared on the options list. A powered trap door on the hood popped up when operated by a dashboard switch revealing a shark cartoon and the words "Air Grabber". A cool way to demoralize the opposition at the stoplight!

Some say the ultimate Road Runner, the Super Bird, was a cartoonish creation too. Built in 1970 to emulate the racing success of Dodge's Daytona, it featured similarly outlandish aerodynamic bodywork. The wedged nose and huge rear spoiler, even taller than the Daytona's two-foot high affair, guaranteed attention.

NASCAR rules required car makers to build one car per dealer for it to be eligible for the race series and Plymouth ended up making nearly 2,000 Super Birds. But despite success on the track, 1970 remained the only year it was produced.

The next year saw a stripping-down of the Road Runner range. The Hemi was legislated out of existence and the two-door hardtop was the only body style on offer.

The original Road Runner ceased to exist in 1974. The name continued as a trim package on a budget car.

The end came in 1980, with the final Plymouth Road Runner far removed from the 'cheap, fast thrills' philosophy of its original incarnation.

Specification

Years built	1968 to 1980
Most powerful model	1970 Hemi Super Bird
Engine type	V8
Displacement	426 cu in
Transmission	four-speed manual
Power	425bhp
Top speed	160mph

MODEL HISTORY

1968

First Road Runner is a very animated package offering big bangs for low bucks

1969

Range expanded with two new V8s and a convertible added to the line-up

1969

Road Runner sales double

1970

Air grabber hood offered as an option

1970

Ultimate Road Runner, the Super Bird, is created with race-oriented aero styling

1970

2,000 Super Birds sold

1971

Hemi engine legislated out of existence

1974

Original-generation Road Runner discontinued. The name continues as a trim package

1977

Road Runner uses first engine management computer

1980

The Road Runner reaches the end of the road, a shadow of its former self

The star of 1970, Plymouth Road Runner Super Bird

Beep Beep! 1970 Super Bird

Pontiac Firebird

From Smokey and the Bandit to Knight Rider the Pontiac Firebird Trans Am was an American hero for 35 years

The Firebird has a special place in the history of American performance vehicles. It enjoyed continuous production from its inception in the muscle car boom of the Sixties to the modern era, setting a record only the Chevrolet Corvette can equal. When the final car rolled off the line, the Firebird had notched up an amazing 35-year lifespan.

The story started in 1967, when the first Firebird's distinctly beaky hood and GTO-style tail lights successfully established a separate identity to the Chevrolet Camaro that it was based on. Initially available with six different engines, most buyers went for the V8s which included the 400 cubic inch, 325bhp unit from Pontiac's GTO.

As it evolved through four distinct generations of development, the Firebird would go through numerous changes, but a big V8 would always feature as the top performance option. The power peak came in 1970, with the Ram Air V, a special-order 440 cubic-inch motor kicking out 500bhp. The engine formed part of the Firebird's top performance package – called the Trans Am, after the US race series. The name would become an American automobile legend.

The collapse of the muscle car market led GM bosses to consider axing the Firebird,

'When the final car rolled off the line, the Firebird had notched up an amazing 35 year lifespan.'

First (opposite page) and last (above) of the line and 1976 Trans Am (right)

but Pontiac fought to save the 'bird and it won a reprieve. It was a corporate decision that was to provide big rewards.

The early Seventies were tough times for American performance cars, but the Firebird blasted away the clouds with its new Super Duty 455 cubic inch V8. "Super Duty" was the name given to Pontiac's race-ready engines in the Sixties and the Super Duty 455 made the Firebird the only serious performance car on the market. This street-legal, race-prepped engine was rated by the company at 310bhp, although experts agreed it actually produced nearer 370.

When the Firebird Trans Ams which packed these fearsome engines received a new decal, their iconic status was sealed. A huge image of an eagle with its wings outspread took up most of the hood, it screamed a rallying cry to performance car fans throughout the US, giving the Trans Am massive credibility and supercool status.

'It got all the best lines performing as KITT in Knight Rider.'

As the Seventies wore on, however, further power restrictions took their toll, with the Super Duty engine phased out in '75 and the 455 V8 falling by the wayside in '76. Despite the drop in maximum power, the Firebird still managed to score sales of over 100,000 for the first time in 1976. A serious boost for the car's image came the next year, when Burt Reynolds drove a black and gold Special Edition Trans Am in the hit movie Smokey and the Bandit. Pontiac made the most of the car's new-found fame, issuing a flood of Special Edition Trans Ams which helped to almost double the Firebird's overall yearly sales i n 1978.

Another starring role reaffirmed the Firebird's popularity in 1982, when it got all the best lines performing as "KITT", David Hasselhoff's talking techno-car in Knight Rider. The model's top engines had been seeing a steady decrease in power throughout the Seventies and early Eighties, but this third-generation, hatchback-bodied 'bird now saw a gradual increase in output. 1987 saw a new 210bhp 350 cid V8 and in '89 a 250bhp turbocharged V6 powered the special 20th anniversary edition Trans Am.

The fourth and final generation, from 1993-2002, were the fastest and most powerful since the glory days of the muscle car boom. Top dog was a 5.7-litre V8 which developed from 275 to 320bhp during 1993-98. But with customer tastes for performance cars changing, the model didn't live long into the 21st century and its passing into history was ushered by a 35th anniversary Firebird – a specially-painted Trans Am.

Specification

Years built	1967 to 2002
Most powerful model	1970 Ram Air V
Engine type	V8
Displacement	400 cu in
Transmission	three-speed automatic
Power	500bhp
Top speed	130mph

MODEL HISTORY

1967

First Firebird, based on the Camaro chassis from Pontiac's fellow GM brand, Chevrolet

1969

a'Trans Am' first introduced as a performance package. It becomes symbolic of Pontiac muscle

1970

Second-generation 'bird gets the 500bhp Ram Air V engine as an optional power unit

1973

Golden Eagle spreads its wings on the Trans Am's hood

1976

The Firebird ceases to pack 455 V8 power

1976

Not that it stops people buying. Firebird sales hit 100,000 in one year

1977

Burt Reynolds makes the car a star, driving a Trans Am in Smokey and the Bandit

1982

Third-generation Firebird stars as "KITT" in the hit TV show, Knight Rider

1993

The final generation Firebird is unveiled

2002

The Firebird celebrates its 35th anniversary... but then its wings are clipped

Trans Ams from 1967 (above) and 1971 (right)

1999's Firebird (above) and 2003 special (left)

Pontiac Grand Prix

It was the least extrovert of Pontiac's muscle cars, but it still offered plenty of performance

Although tastefully low-key in styling, the Pontiac Grand Prix sported a good few muscle car credentials in its launch year of 1962. Not least was the special build of 16 cars equipped with the 421 cubic inch 370bhp Super Duty V8 that took the Grand Prix to 60 miles an hour in a respectable 6.6 seconds. Just one of these specials is believed to survive. Otherwise muscle car fans made do with the 425-A Trophy V8 engines and a maximum output of 348bhp.

The Grand Prix's interior was fairly sporty with bucket seats, floor shift, and an instrument console with a tachometer. Chequered flag badges front and rear gave a nod to the car's name and race aspirations.

The Grand Prix was given a new look for 1963. Less sculpted lines and a 'Coke-bottle' waist together with a new roof-line and an

'Although tastefully low-key in styling, the Grand Prix sported a good few muscle car credentials.'

1965 in Paris (opposite page), 1971 (above) and 1962 (right)

unusual concave rear window gave the car a very distinctive profile. The rear window was to stay as a Grand Prix feature until the 1968 model year. The high power engines for 1963 were two 421 cubic inch V8s, one with a four-barrel carb that put out 353bhp – the other was a 370bhp version called the HO Tri-Power. The 1963 car proved to be popular with car buyers with a total of nearly 73,000 sold.

Following the Detroit trend, the Grand Prix got bigger and heavier for its next incarnation in 1965 – and it was also moved more towards the luxury market segment. And horror of horrors, a bench seat was on offer to replace the original bucket seats and console. Engine options changed too. Power actually increased with new engine features such as better gas flow through new design manifolds and cylinder heads. The 389 base engine

'The 1969 redesign is reckoned to be its finest incarnation.'

had 256bhp and Tri-Power version increased this to 338. The 421 four-barrel carb also made 338bhp and the two Tri-Power engines put this figure up to 353 and 376bhp respectively.

The beginning of the end for this generation of the Grand Prix came in 1966 as sales of the manual transmission cars fell to under 1,000.

The Grand Prix got even bigger in 1967, and it was the only year a convertible version was on offer. The car now looked massive and to cope with the increased weight the base engine was now a 400 cubic inch V8 with 350bhp – although a low-power 265bhp unit could be substituted. The most powerful V8 was the 421 cubic inch engine which put out 376bhp. 1967 was also the year that exhaust emissions had to meet Federal smog regulations, and the introduction of first-phase safety equipment. The Grand Prix now came with a collapsible steering wheel, dual-circuit hydraulics and optional disc brakes. But the car's size now put off buyers who were looking for smaller cars – and sales continued to fall.

It wasn't until another re-design in 1969 that the buying public took to the Pontiac Grand Prix in reasonable numbers. The car looked sharper and more stylish, almost like a stretched pony car. The wheelbase was three inches shorter. The car handled better and with its new 428 cubic inch 390 horsepower V8 it ran the all-important quarter-mile in 14.1 seconds.

The Pontiac Grand Prix continued in production until 1974, but the 1969 redesign – kept in the main until 1972, is reckoned to be its finest incarnation.

Specification

Years built	1962 to 1974
Most powerful model	1968
Engine type	V8
Displacement	428 cu in
Transmission	three-speed automatic
Power	390bhp
Top speed	129mph

MODEL HISTORY

1962

Pontiac Grand Prix introduced with 425-A Trophy V8 engines and a maximum output of 348bhp

1963

Re-style with lower roofline and concave rear window

1963

Sales of 73,000 prove re-styled car's popularity

1965

The 421 Tri-Power engines put out 353 and 376 bhp respectively

1966

Sales of manual transmission cars fall to under 1,000

1967

Only year with convertible Grand Prix available

1967

All engines have to meet new smog regulations

1967

Collapsible steering wheel and dual-circuit hydraulics to meet new safety regulations

1969

Complete re-design saves Grand Prix bacon as public flock to buy

1974

Production of Grand Prix ends

Pontiac GTO

In many eyes the Pontiac GTO was the first true muscle car with full-size power in its mid-size shell

This is where it all began. In 1964 Pontiac saw a gap in the market. There were plenty of full-size cars packing a serious punch, but the mid-size market was down on performance and prestige as a result of a GM ban on factory-backed racing and a limit of 330 cubic inches on standard engine size.

In a cunning move Pontiac got around these restrictions by offering the LeMans GTO (Gran Turismo Omologato) package as an option on the Tempest model.

It was distinguished from the regular Tempest thanks to air scoops on the hood, special redline tires, heavy duty suspension, three-speed floor-shift tranny, chromed air cleaner and rocker cover and a special 'engine-turned' instrument panel plate.

With a 389 cubic inch V8 from the Bonneville under the hood, the GTO offered 325bhp in standard trim. The Tri-Power kit replaced the standard four barrel carburator with three double-barrel carbs and upped that power to 348bhp.

With a 0-60mph time of 7.5 seconds and able to run the standing quarter-mile in les than 15 seconds the GTO quickly gained legendary status. Sales went through the roof. Pontiac hoped to sell 5,000 in the first year, but in the event more than 32,000 found owners. This car was a sensation.

'Pontiac hoped to sell 5,000 in the first year but more than 32,000 found owners.'

1968 coupe and convertible (opposite), 1965 (above) and 1964 (right) two- doors

For '65 Pontiac capitalised on the astonishing success of the GTO with a major front and rear restyle. The nose now incorporated stacked headlights from Pontiac's full-size models. Engine power was upped with the standard 389 offering 335bhp and the Tri-Power a mighty 360bhp. The bonnet scoops that were just styling ploys on the '64 model could now be used to feed a ram air system that could be bought from dealers.

A year later and the GTO became a model in its own right. There was yetanother restyle to give the car a more sculptured Coke bottle look, but there were no changes under the hood.

By 1967 GM had banned multiple carburators on all models except the Chevrolet Corvette, so Pontiac needed another solution. In went a bored-out 400 cid V8 that came in four states of tune.

'The GTO was reborn in 2004 as a sleek-looking two-door.'

There was Economy with just 255bhp, Standard with 335bhp or HO (High Output) and Ram Air, both with 360bhp.

The GTO was restyled once again for 1968 and sat on a new 112-inch wheelbase. The innovative rubber Endura bumper was now fitted and hidden headlamps were added to the options list. The Economy and Standard engines both gained 10bhp but the HO and Ram Air stayed at 360bhp.

1969 was the year of the Judge. This special edition GTO was named after a phrase on TV's 'Laugh In' this GTO featured wild paint colors and a hefty rear spoiler. Two new Ram Air engines offered 366 and 370bhp. The GTO was getter faster by the year.

1970 saw yet another restyle, with four exposed headlamps and a softer look all over. A new 455 engine was offered that matched the Ram Air's 360bhp, but the coolest trick of 1970 was the VOE option. This Vacuum Operated Exhaust system employed a hot rod technique that opened the exhaust to give more power. The driver pulled a knob on the dash and back pressure in the exhaust was cut, thus giving more go and more noise into the bargain. Sadly GM bosses soon stamped on this option.

Over the next three years the GTO suffered like all GM muscle cars with restrictions on horsepower and emissions. The GTO ceased to be a model in its own right in 1972 and production ended in 1973.

The GTO was reborn in 2004 as a sleek-looking two-door. And with 400bhp from its six-liter (364 cid) LS2 V8 it's a true modern muscle car and not just a namesake.

Specification

Years built	1965 to 1974, 2004 to date
Most powerful model	2005 GTO
Engine type	V8
Displacement	364 cu in
Transmission	six-speed manual
Power	400bhp
Top speed	150mph

MODEL HISTORY

1964

Pontiac fits a Bonneville engine in the Tempest, creating the GTO

1965

First restyle and power increased to 360bhp with the Tri-Power option

1966

GTO becomes a model in its own right

1967

Mutiple carbs banned, new 400 cid V8 installed

1968

Another restyle features indestructible Endura bumpers

1969

The year of the Judge – the wildest-looking GTO yet

1970

Sneaky VOE option makes GTO faster syill, but annoys GM bosses

1971

Horsepower rates reduced to meet tough emissions rules

1974

GTO production ceases

2004

A legend lives on with new 400bhp GTO

1964 convertible (above) and 1970 coupe (right)

1967 convertible (above) and 1974 coupe (left)

Shelby Cobra

When Carroll Shelby teamed American V8 power with a lightweight British sports car he created a legend that still lives on today

Created by one of the most charismatic characters in American sportscar history, the Cobra has attained mythical status amongst automobile fans the world over. Larger-than-life Texan Carroll Shelby was the man who synthesised US muscle and English style so perfectly that the car is still built today – over 40 years after its original inception.

Shelby, a successful sportscar racer and previous winner of prestigious European endurance race, the Le Mans 24 Hours, was forced to retire from the track in 1960 due to ill-health. With a vision of producing a sportscar combining a lightweight European chassis with American V8 power, he set about making his dream a reality. The opportunity came the next year, when English manufacturer AC cars agreed to Shelby's idea of muscling-up its Ace sportscar, and a deal was struck.

The Cobra has attained mythical status amongst automobile fans the world over.

1962 (opposite page), 1964 Le Mans (above) and 1964 road car (right)

Luckily for the Texan, Ford had just developed a new small-block V8 but had no serious performance model to put it in. After successful negotiations, the recipe was written for one of the most spine-tingling sportscars ever made.

During a couple of months in early 1962, the cute little Ace was transformed into a hair-raising beast at Shelby's California workshop. What emerged was a classic expression of muscularity in metal – the original Cobra roadster, the fastest production car ever made at that time. With explosive acceleration from 0-60mph in a breath-taking 3.9 seconds, the car won rave reviews from motoring journalists and its curvaceous lines wowed the crowds at American auto shows. Shelby's visionary concept had struck a major chord in the hearts of sportscar fans.

'The need to conform to race regulations led to the most powerful Cobra becoming available to the public.'

The first Cobra packed a 256 cubic inch engine, but its creator's insatiable desire for power and performance meant that pretty soon a 289 cubic-inch version of the Ford V8 was installed. And it didn't stop there. Shelby campaigned the Cobra successfully in American and European race series – and it was his desire to win that produced the most awesome Cobra of all.

The need to conform to race regulations led to the most powerful road-going Cobra becoming available to the public. Deciding to shoehorn an even bigger Ford V8 under the hood to keep it competitive in production endurance racing, Shelby went for the 427 cubic-inch option. By 1967, 31 competition cars equipped with this engine had been finished – not enough to qualify the model for racing. His only option was to fit windscreens to unsold Cobras that had already been built and offer them for sale to the general public in order to meet the quota.

The 427 Cobra was born – one of the fastest-accelerating production cars of its day, with vital statistics of 0-60mph in 4.5 seconds, a standing quarter-mile in 12.4 and 165mph top speed. That's blisteringly quick, even by today's standards!

The last 427 Cobra was built in 1967, but the model wasn't dead and buried. Shelby reprised his classic sportscar in different guises throughout the Eighties and Nineties – and his company still makes them to order today. It's a testament to the allure of the car which, with its combination of V8 power in a lightweight chassis, many feel started the whole muscle car movement.

Specification

Years built	1962 to date
Most powerful model	1965 427
Engine type	V8
Displacement	427 cu in
Transmission	four-speed manual
Power	410bhp
Top speed	165mph

MODEL HISTORY

1960

Carroll Shelby retires from racing with a dream to build the ultimate sportscar

1962

First Cobra is built from AC Ace chassis and Ford 256 cid V8

1963

The race car wins the United States Road Racing Championship

1964

Hardtop Cobra Daytona Coupe wins GT class at Le Mans 24 Hours

1965

The 427, featuring tube frame and aluminum body, is unveiled

1967

427 available to the public

1967

The last 427 Cobra is built

1989

Shelby begins his 427 Cobra S/C project, finishing "leftover" cars from the Sixties

1995

CSX4000-series 427 Cobra S/C Roadsters are built

2005

Shelby's company continues to build Cobras to order

1965 Cobras for road and track (above and right)

1969 289s (above and left)